CLIL Activities

A resource for subject and language teachers

Liz Dale and Rosie Tanner

Consultant and editor: Scott Thornbury

CAMBRIDGE
UNIVERSITY PRESS

CAMBRIDGE UNIVERSITY PRESS
Cambridge, New York, Melbourne, Madrid, Cape Town,
Singapore, São Paulo, Delhi, Mexico City

Cambridge University Press
The Edinburgh Building, Cambridge CB2 8RU, UK

www.cambridge.org
Information on this title: www.cambridge.org/9780521149846

First published 2012
Reprinted 2013

Printed and bound in the United Kingdom by the MPG Books Group

A catalogue record for this publication is available from the British Library

Library of Congress Cataloging in Publication Data
Dale, Liz.
CLIL activities with CD-ROM : a resource for subject and language teachers / Liz Dale, Rosie Tanner ;
consultant and editor, Scott Thornbury.
    p. cm. -- (Cambridge handbooks for language teachers)
Includes bibliographical references and index.
ISBN 978-0-521-14984-6
1. Language and languages--Study and teaching. 2. Language arts--Correlation with content subjects.
I. Tanner, Rosie. II. Title.

P51.D275 2012
418.007--dc23

                          2011046098

ISBN 978-0-521-14984-6 Paperback and CD-ROM

Contents

Thanks

Profound thanks to Scott Thornbury for his astute, prompt editing and inspirational encouragement across cyberspace, and very special thanks to Wibo van der Es for being a cheerful, caring and cooperative CLIL colleague. Thanks also to Jacque French for her eye for detail and insightful questions at the copy-editing stage.

We would like to offer our warm thanks to the teachers we have worked with on both pre-service and in-service CLIL courses. This book would not exist without them. The following teachers provided inspiration, feedback and ideas for the CLIL snapshots, subject pages and classroom activities: Albert van den Berg, Yvonne Boelman, Jan de Brauwer, Scarlett Hasselt, Matthijs Hekkelman, Mireille ter Horst, Frankje Huisman, Arthur van de Graaf, Vincent Koerse, Heidi Krieger, Dennie Lodders, Annelet Lykles, Nigel Osborne, André van Raalte, Menno Ruppert, Marc van Velden, Hein Woutman, Jeroen Verbiest. A special thank you goes to Sally Hill for her inspiring, sparky ideas on integrating language with biology.

The following learners' work is included in *CLIL Activities*: Eef van Schaik's aboriginal painting and artistic statement; Ren Hui Yang's detailed history posters; the mnemonics and animal posters supplied by pupils in Frankje Huisman's chemistry class and Sally Hill's biology classes.

Tom Morton inspired us, at a conference in Madrid, to use the Escher woodcut print *Sky and Water I* as a brilliant metaphor for CLIL.

Rick de Graaf and Gerrit Jan Koopman from the Centre for Teaching and Learning at Utrecht University in the Netherlands cooperated with us in developing the rubric about collaboration.

We are extremely grateful for the calm, professional support of Noirin Burke, Claire Cole, Roslyn Henderson and Jane Walsh during a tumultuous year.

Liz Dale also wishes to thank Eline van Batenburg, Max Carbaat, Sabine van der Heijden, Vincent Hernot, Tracy Lagas-Gee, Paul Moeyes, Liz Savage and Saskia Sollie-den Bleker at the Amsterdam University of Applied Sciences, School of Education, for their spirited and supportive collegiality. Thanks, too, to Roger and Sylvia Dale and Catherine Lord for being there.

Finally, we would like to dedicate this book to our children: to Sam and Lottie, for their laughter and love (LD), and to Hugo and India, for being tolerant and easy-going about growing up with a writing mum (RT).

Acknowledgements

The authors and publishers acknowledge the following sources of copyright material and are grateful for the permissions granted. While every effort has been made, it has not always been possible to identify the sources of all the material used, or to trace all copyright holders. If any omissions are brought to our notice, we will be happy to include the appropriate acknowledgements on reprinting.

M.C. Escher's "Sky and Water I" on p.3 © 2011 The M.C. Escher Company-Holland. All rights reserved. www.mcescher.com;

Poster on p. 9 reproduced with kind permission of Ren Hui Yang;

Poster on p. 10 by Eef van Schaik;

Extract on p. 50 adapted from *Edexcel GCSE Design and Technology Resistant Materials Student Book* by Barry Lambert. Published by Edexcel, 2010;

Extract on p. 54 adapted from www.onestopclil.com Written by Lilia Ratiskaya and Stuart Cochrane. © Copyright Macmillan Publishers Ltd 2009;

Extract on p. 58 adapted from *Geography for the IB Diploma Patterns and Change* by Paul Guinness. Published by Cambridge University Press, 2010;

Extract on p. 62 adapted from *Contrasts & Connections, Year 7: Discovering the Past* by Mike Corbishley, Alan Large, Richard Tames and Colin Shephard (Editor). Published by John Murray, 1991;

Extract on p. 66 adapted from *GCSE Applied ICT: Student Book* by Maggie Banks, Colin Harber-Stuart and Dave Parry. Published by Oxford University Press, 2003;

Extract on p. 70 adapted from *International GCSE - IGCSE Mathematics for CIE* by Paul Metcalf. Published by Collins Educational, 2006;

Extract on p. 74 adapted from *Music Worldwide (Cambridge Assignments in Music)* by Elizabeth Sharma. Published by Cambridge University Press, 1998;

Extract on p. 78 adapted from http://www.teachpe.com/basketball/shooting/improve_your_shooting.php Copyright © TeachPE;

Extract on p. 82 adapted from *Cambridge Essentials Science Core 7* by Sam Ellis and Jean Martin. Published by Cambridge University Press, 2008;

Extract on p. 114 adapted from www.collaborativelearning.org Reproduced with permission;

CLIL Activities also contains a number of extracts adapted from *CLIL Skills* by Liz Dale, Wibo van der Es and Rosie Tanner, published under Creative Commons Licence by ICLON, Leiden University Graduate School of Teaching, The Netherlands.

The publisher has used its best endeavours to ensure that the URLs for external websites referred to in this book are correct and active at the time of going to press. However, the publisher has no responsibility for the websites and can make no guarantee that a site will remain live or that the content is or will remain appropriate.

Introduction

If you are reading *CLIL Activities*, you may be

- a subject teacher who is teaching your subject through English in a bilingual setting.
- a language teacher working in a bilingual setting.
- a subject or language teacher in training to become a teacher in a bilingual setting.

We have designed *CLIL Activities* to help you in your professional development and to provide practical ideas and background on integrating language and content. We hope this book will also stimulate you to collaborate with colleagues, and to integrate subject and language teaching in your own setting. *CLIL Activities* is a sister volume to *CLIL: Content and Language Learning* (Coyle, Hood and Marsh, 2010), which gives an overview of CLIL theory and some practical applications. This volume provides practical classroom ideas for CLIL teachers, and while it is aimed principally at secondary school teachers of 11- to 19-year-olds, many of the ideas and principles presented are relevant to primary and higher education, too. The ideas in *CLIL Activities* have largely been developed, tried and tested by language and subject teachers at secondary schools across Europe. We hope that they inspire you to experiment.

The book is divided into three parts – Part 1: *Background to CLIL*, Part 2: *Subject pages* and Part 3: *Practical activities*. Part 1 outlines some theoretical principles underpinning the design and content of the book. In Part 2, four pages are dedicated to each of nine subjects or sets of subjects: art, design and technology; economics and business studies; geography; history; information and communication technology (ICT); maths; music and drama; physical education (PE); and science (biology, chemistry and physics). Each set of subject pages includes information about the language of the subject, an annotated sample text used in the subject, and sample language and content aims. Part 3 provides CLIL teachers with classroom activities to support their learners in learning language and content. This final part is divided into six chapters: 1. *Activating*, 2. *Guiding understanding*, 3. *Focus on language*, 4. *Focus on speaking*, 5. *Focus on writing*, 6. *Assessment, review and feedback*.

Part 1: Background to CLIL

What is CLIL?

CLIL is an abbreviation for Content and Language Integrated Learning. It is a way of teaching where subject content – for example, history, science or physical education – is taught in another language (often English). We like the following definition of CLIL by Coyle, Hood and Marsh (2010, p. 1):

> Content and Language Integrated Learning (CLIL) is a dual-focused educational approach in which an additional language is used for the learning and teaching of both content *and* language. That is, in the teaching and learning process, there is a focus not only on content, and not only on language. Each is interwoven, even if the emphasis is greater on one or the other at a given time.

What speaks to us in this definition is the idea of interwovenness. As a CLIL subject teacher, you interweave language into your lessons; and as a CLIL language teacher, you interweave the subject into your language lessons. For us, M. C. Escher's famous woodcut print entitled *Sky and Water I* (1938) offers an excellent pictorial representation of this idea of interwovenness that characterises the CLIL approach. In CLIL, you can imagine the birds to be the subject elements and the fish to be the language elements. Sometimes as a teacher you focus on the birds – the content of your lesson – and sometimes you focus on the fish – the language. But sometimes you are focused on both, and the birds and the fish – the content and the language – are more intertwined and connected.

Sky and Water I (1988) by M.C. Escher

3

[1]

CLIL, content-based language teaching (CBLT) and immersion

There are differences between content-based language teaching (CBLT) and content and language integrated learning (CLIL), the main one being that CBLT deals with teaching content in language lessons, whereas CLIL deals with teaching a subject at the same time as teaching language. CLIL is also different from immersion, where learners learn all their subjects in another language and there is no focus on language in subject lessons, for example in an international school. These ideas can be visualised as a continuum. On the left-hand side of the continuum, content-based language teaching is where language teachers teach another language through content – so the focus is on language and the input for language classes is topics based on subject content. On the right-hand side of the continuum, learners are working all the time in another language. CLIL can be placed somewhere in the middle of the continuum: learners are learning content through another language. Typically, they have a number of lessons in one or more subjects per week in another language (for example, geography, history, science, PE or music) and the rest of their lessons in their first language. We summarise these differences in the table below.

Some differences between teachers of content-based language teaching (CBLT), CLIL and immersion				
More language ◄————————————————————————► More content				
	CBLT	**CLIL**		**Immersion**
Who teaches?	language teachers	CLIL language teachers (in language lessons)	CLIL subject teachers (in subject lessons)	immersion subject teachers
What kind of language work do they do?	work on language through content	work on general language while supporting subject-related topics and language in their language lessons	work on the language of their subject	little or no attention paid to language per se as teaching is done in another language
What is the aim?	to teach language	to teach language	to teach content and some language	to teach content
What do they teach?	non-curricular subject matter (extra topics) in another language	the language curriculum as well as the language of the subjects to support subject teachers	curricular subject matter and subject language	curricular subject matter

Who do they work with?	often work alone in teaching language related to topics OR work with language department colleagues	work with language department colleagues and subject teachers on developing subject and language with learners	work with language teachers on developing subject and language with learners	work with their subject department colleagues
How do they assess?	assess and mark language	assess and mark language	assess and mark content (and sometimes language)	assess and mark content
What do they give feedback on?	give feedback on language	give feedback on language	give feedback on content (and sometimes on language)	give feedback on content but not on language
What kind of knowledge do they refer to?	language knowledge rather than content knowledge	knowledge of the content of the subject teachers' lessons, which is sufficient to be able to work on related ideas and language during language lessons	content knowledge and knowledge about the language of their subject, such as text-types, vocabulary, typical writing or speaking activities, language functions	content knowledge
What assumption do they have about learning?	that language is learned in context, through topics	that language depends on content; content depends on language	that content depends on language; language depends on content	that content is learned without explicit attention to language

Teaching in another language versus teaching through another language

As a CLIL subject teacher, rather than teaching a subject *in* another language – doing the same in another language as you do in your monolingual classes – we suggest teaching your subject *through* another language. By this, we mean that subject teachers pay attention to both language and content in their lessons, to help learners learn both language and content as they learn a school subject.

CLIL snapshots

Many teachers have inspired us to write this book. Below we provide some snapshots of 'CLIL moments'. These classroom scenes show motivated learners and teachers actively engaged in CLIL. They illustrate the wide variety of activities we have seen in our visits to CLIL schools. They also show just how inventive CLIL teachers can be in their daily interactions with learners, and how creative and stimulated learners can be when learning in CLIL lessons. These are some of the practical classroom activities which have informed and inspired us in the writing of this book.

Activating: China (geography)

A geography teacher is starting work on the topic of China with her class of 14- to 15-year-olds. She asks all the learners to bring in any recent quality newspapers and news magazines from home – either in their first language or in the language in which they are learning. She also brings some copies to the class herself. At the start of the lesson, she asks her learners to write down, in the language in which they are learning, at least five things they know about China. She divides the class into pairs and gives each pair one second language and one first language newspaper or magazine. She asks the pairs to find any articles on China and to write down each headline of the articles they find. As the learners work, she hangs up four posters on the walls around the classroom, each one with a different title: 'Economic issues', 'Political issues', 'Historical/social issues' and 'Environmental issues'. She then asks the learners to write the headlines they have found on the most relevant poster. Next, as a class, they discuss two aspects of the headlines written in the second language: firstly, whether they are placed in the most appropriate category, and secondly, whether there are any headlines which don't fit into any of the categories. She asks the learners to refer back to their initial list of five things they know about China to see if any of their points have been missed in the headlines. They have. She asks the learners to say which new category might be added; the class decides to add an extra category: Cultural issues.

Guiding understanding: sources on the Romans (history)

A history teacher wants his class of 12- to 13-year-olds to learn about Roman reactions to the lifestyle and ways of warfare they encountered when they invaded Britain and the Iberian peninsula. He uses photocopies of illustrations and eyewitness accounts by Romans. These include drawings of houses, everyday objects, people dressed for battle and weapons, and short accounts from primary sources by Roman authors. He divides the class into pairs and asks the learners to skim the illustrations and texts and discuss if they were describing lifestyle or ways of warfare. He gives each pair two A3 sheets of card, a blue one headed 'Warfare' and a yellow one headed 'Lifestyle'. He then asks the learners to cut up the texts and illustrations, pasting all those to do with lifestyle on the yellow cards, and all those on the subject of warfare on the blue cards. He then gives the learners a graphic organiser: a table with four columns headed 1. Text/illustration, 2. Lifestyle, 3. Warfare, 4. Objective/subjective. He asks the learners to complete the table, summarising the information from each text or illustration and deciding for each one whether the information in it is objective or subjective. Finally, he asks the learners to note down five key words to describe lifestyle and five key words to describe ways of warfare.

Focus on language: animal poem poster (general science)

At the end of a unit on classification, a biology teacher asks her 12- to 13-year-old learners to create a 'poem poster' on their favourite invertebrate or vertebrate animal. The requirements for the poster include the use of scientifically accurate and relevant information about the animal they choose, illustrations and a poem of twelve lines describing the animal. The scientific information includes the animal's classification, its main body features, its natural habitat, its feeding habits, its way of reproducing, its natural enemies, environmental adaptations and any threats to its survival. On the back of the poster, learners are asked to list their resources. The teacher introduces the poster with an example she has made herself and asks the learners to find all the adjectives she has used in the poem. She then gives the learners a list of words used to describe the features of animals and asks them to find any words which are not adjectives. The learners make colourful, creative posters and original poems about many different animals – a dolphin, a tiger, an elephant, a mole – which illustrate clearly that they have learned valuable biology knowledge and skills about classification. Here are two examples, including the learners' original errors, created by learners at van den Capellen school in Zwolle, the Netherlands.

African elephant

> African elephants are very big
> And they are also a little bit thick
> Tusks, so are called their two teeth
> Fruits, flowers, roots and grasses is what they eat
> The women are pregnant for two years
> And they also have very big ears
> An elephant's tusk is a union of the upper lip and nose
> Elephant's live together very close
> Were they live is the savannah
> You have the Asian and the Africana
> People poach on the ivory of the beast
> And when they are 71 they have mostly been deceased

The Tiger

> Sneaking trough the woods,
> Ready to take their prey,
> Sneaking trough the woods,
> Deadly, yes, they are,
>
> Sneaking trough the woods,
> Very big and strong
> Sneaking trough the woods,
> Two pairs of legs, no wings
>
> Sneaking trough the woods,
> A head, sharp teeths,
> Sneaking trough the woods,
> A fat, long tail,
>
> Sneaking trough the woods,
> Hunters looking for him,
> Sneaking trough the woods,
> It's the tiger!

Focus on speaking: Lego® bricks and horses (biology)

A biology teacher has a practical idea to encourage his 14- to 15-year-old learners to speak. He gives learners Lego bricks and horses to demonstrate their understanding of homeostasis – how the pancreas regulates glucose in the blood. He uses this activity to consolidate what learners have already learned about homeostasis. In groups of four learners get a pile of coloured Lego bricks and horses; the bricks represent food entering the body. The white bricks represent glucose in the food, and the horses represent the messengers the body sends to different organs in order to maintain the sugar balance. Each of the four learners receives a role: digestive system (stomach), transport system (blood), pancreas or liver. The learners then use the Lego bricks to demonstrate and explain to each other how the body maintains its blood-sugar levels. They first practise in groups, and then present the process to the class.

Learner A: (stomach)	I am the digestive system. The food (holds stuck together coloured Lego bricks) enters the stomach, and I break it down into different bits (gives broken up bits of Lego to circulatory system – learner B).
Learner B: (blood)	I am the circulatory system. I transport the different bits, including the sugar (white Lego bricks) around the body (gives white bricks to pancreas – learner C).
Learner C: (pancreas)	I am the pancreas. I notice that there is a lot of sugar (white Lego bricks) in the blood. I send insulin (a brown Lego horse) to the liver to say that there is a lot of sugar in the blood (gives brown horse to liver – learner D).
Learner D: (liver)	I am the liver. The insulin makes me (and the muscles) store the sugar (puts white Lego bricks on brown horse).
Learner C: (pancreas)	I am the pancreas. I notice that there is very little sugar in the blood. I send glucagen (white horse) to the liver (gives white horse to liver – learner D).
Learner D: (liver)	I am the liver. I release some sugar into the blood (takes white Lego bricks from brown horse and gives to circulatory system – learner B).

Focus on writing: Sahara brochure (geography)

At the end of a unit on deserts, a geography teacher asks her 13- to 14-year-old learners to do a mini-project: to produce an illustrated brochure for an expedition through the Sahara desert. In groups of four they gather information from the Internet to create a brochure containing the following information: an introduction to the destination, a map of the route (avoiding conflict zones), a paragraph on landscape, culture and people, a packing list (including reasons why each item is helpful in the desert), a risk assessment chart on hazards and ways of avoiding them, a food web of plants and animals, a sample diary excerpt from a previous participant and a conclusion. Learners produce imaginative brochures. Below is a sample of some original writing – including their errors!

Extract from brochure on the Sahara
We will move through the lands Libya, Egypt and Sudan to reach our end: the city Khartoum. We are travelling east after we all reach Tripoli. At the intersecting point of the Nile right above Cairo, the pyramid Khufu can be seen. When we arrive at Cairo, we will go further south along the river Nile. After a little while we will change our course and head out for the magnificent oasis Ai-Fayyum, where we stay for two days and rest. Then we will move on along the Nile and reach Khartoum.

Assessment, review and feedback: using multiple intelligences (history)

A history teacher is applying multiple intelligence theory to his ways of assessing. He gives his 13- to 14-year-old learners a choice about how to display their knowledge and skills about historical change between 1350 and 1600 and creates assignments for them which aim to appeal to different intelligences. Some write a rap about it (musical and linguistic intelligences); some write an essay (linguistic and logical intelligences); some make drawings (visual-spatial and bodily-physical intelligences); some work together on their assessment (interpersonal intelligence) and others choose to work alone (intrapersonal intelligence). Here is an example of two beautifully drawn comparative posters drawn by a learner who is not very strong, linguistically. He spent many extra hours creating these posters and was extremely motivated by the idea of being able to show his understanding visually. The posters show, in an amazing amount of detail, not only his skill as an artist, but also his depth of understanding of the changes during this historical period.

Posters showing historical change from 1350 to 1600

Team teaching (art, design and technology)

As part of an art project, learners in their first year of CLIL have produced some aboriginal paintings, using aboriginal techniques, colours and symbols to tell their own modern Dreamtime stories. Their art is framed and the paintings and the artistic statements are exhibited at school. For example, one learner's aboriginal painting shows the story of how she fell off her bicycle when she was small; another about driving to a shopping centre; another about a family reunion. To accompany their aboriginal art, learners work in their language lessons on writing an artistic statement to explain their work. During one of the last lessons, both the language teacher and the art teacher are present: the language teacher helps learners work on their artistic statements and the art teacher supports their artwork. Here is an example of a painting and its accompanying artistic statement. (NB This is the learners' original work, including errors!)

Artistic statement

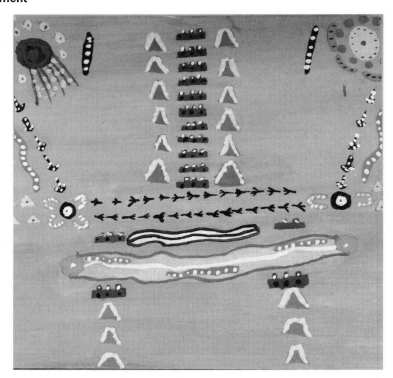

This painting is about a group of aboriginals. This group is divided in women and men. The children of both groups want to play with each other. But the parents believe that if the children don't see each other they will become stronger.

There is only one way which the children can try to see each other; A river with snakes. Everyday the children try to cross the river. Once it was done without being attacked by snakes.

Benefits of CLIL: why is integrating content and language a good thing?

Schools start working with CLIL for several reasons. In some countries, CLIL developed as a grassroots movement and in others, with the aid of government funding in large- or small-scale projects. Elsewhere, CLIL has been implemented in schools as part of a nationwide policy. In many cases, the appeal of CLIL to primary and secondary schools is the way it addresses the need for plenty of practice in a foreign language, without increasing the number of dedicated language classes.

Why embark on CLIL? Why choose CLIL? There are many benefits to integrating content and language. General learning theories as well as language learning theories suggest that CLIL has great educational potential and perhaps help to explain why, by 2004, 80% of the member states of the European Union provided some form of CLIL provision in mainstream education (Eurydice, 2006). What are these possible benefits of CLIL? Which insights into the way that people learn content and language underpin these suggestions? The following section summarises the main ideas about learning which inform CLIL. If you are interested in a more comprehensive description of these theories in relation to CLIL, see Coyle *et al.* (2010).

Benefits for learners

CLIL learners are motivated

Learning a subject through another language can also provide extra motivation for the subject – a subject taught in another language may be more appealing to learners simply because they feel they are developing language skills along with the subject. Learners blossom and feel challenged because they are learning both a subject and a language. They develop a strong sense of achievement as they notice their rapid progress in their other language.

CLIL learners develop cognitively and their brains work harder

Cognitive learning theories suggest that people remember things more effectively if their brains have to work harder to complete a task. For example, it is likely that bilinguals form more connections in the brain, make new connections and expand their memory because they are learning in another language. Learning a subject through another language may broaden and deepen CLIL learners' understanding of subject concepts, their thinking skills and their creativity: their brains have to work harder when they learn through another language. As one CLIL learner put it, 'It is harder to learn like this, especially at the beginning, but if it makes you concentrate more, then you learn it better, and so it is better to do it this way' (Coyle, 2006, p. 7). CLIL learners may, therefore, be more likely to remember what they have learned – both the language and the content.

CLIL learners develop communication skills

The most obvious benefit of CLIL for learners is that their language skills and ability to communicate effectively improve. Through CLIL, learners develop an ability to understand a wide range of spoken and written language in both general and more specialised topics. They also learn to use the target language to achieve their communicative goal in a variety of situations, formal and informal, specialised and general.

CLIL learners make new personal meanings in another language

Constructivist theories of learning suggest learners build up knowledge for themselves and that learning involves making personal meaning of new material and combining it with what is already known. Learning takes place when learners themselves make sense of what they are learning. In CLIL lessons, learners link new information or ideas in another language to previous content or language knowledge in their first language. Relating activities in the classroom to real life helps learners to transfer the personal meanings they have from one language to the other.

CLIL learners' language progresses more

Several second language learning theories suggest that CLIL helps learners to learn another language more efficiently than separate language lessons. These theories imply that CLIL learners will learn the language quickly and achieve a high level of proficiency: they will become fluent and accurate. In order to learn a language, you need to hear and read it, understand it, use it to speak and write in meaningful interactions and notice how the language is used in practice: this all happens in CLIL lessons. Learners who spend time focusing on *how* language is used (form), as well as *what* is being said (meaning) also progress faster in learning a language and have less chance of *fossilisation* (a term referring to a state of learning where progress ceases despite continuing exposure to the language) than learners who simply use language without paying attention to form.

CLIL learners receive a lot of input and work effectively with that input

Language input is the language we read and hear. Input theories of second language acquisition suggest that language input should be meaningful, relevant and realistic, that there should also be plenty of it, and it should be *multimodal*. Multimodal input includes, for instance, 'live' or recorded spoken input, written input, visual input in the form of gestures, objects, videos, DVDs, photographs and pictures. However, input alone is not enough: learners also need to understand it! During CLIL lessons, learners are more likely to learn the second language if they do activities to help them actively process input.

CLIL learners interact meaningfully

Social constructivist theories of learning emphasise that learning is a social, dynamic process, and that learners learn when interacting with one another. Meaningful interaction is also important in CLIL. Learners who focus on communicating about the meaning of what they are learning are likely to be more effective language learners than those who concentrate mainly on grammatical accuracy. CLIL is, therefore, ideal for language acquisition because it provides meaningful interaction about both the content (meaning) needed for language acquisition and the language needed for subject development.

CLIL learners learn to speak and write

Output theory argues that in order to learn a language, learners need to produce language, in other words to speak or write. When they speak and write, they can experiment, be creative and make mistakes, and in CLIL, when teachers encourage their learners to speak and write, this helps learners to become more proficient users of language.

CLIL learners develop intercultural awareness

Through CLIL, teachers help learners to develop intercultural awareness: they learn about ideas and communicate with people from other cultures. Learners can develop and explore different, international perspectives on the subjects they are learning. Materials in the target language may contain cultural information or attitudes which are new to the learners and the teachers. CLIL learners also often have experience of communicating with learners in other cultures – through exchanges or video conferencing or email projects, for example.

CLIL learners learn about the 'culture' of a subject

Sociocultural theories of learning suggest that language, thinking and culture are learned through social interaction, and that all three are intertwined and interdependent. These ideas also show how learning a subject involves learning the language of a subject and how each subject has its own language and 'culture'. Historians, for example, value particular ways of thinking, and history teachers are not only teaching information about history but teaching their learners to think and act like historians, and use language in a way that other historians value. The way historians think and the language they use is different from the way in which scientists think and the language *they* use. So CLIL teachers are not only teaching information about a subject, but also teaching learners to think, write and speak like subject specialists.

CLIL learners are prepared for studying in another language

CLIL learners are often very confident and fluent in their second language at the end of their school careers. An ability to communicate effectively in an additional language prepares learners for studying and working in countries where the language is used. For example, many higher education institutions offer courses completely in English to attract international students; international corporations often use English as their sole language of communication.

CLIL learners learn in different ways

All learners are different and CLIL learners are as diverse as monolingual learners. An important difference is that using another language to learn may make these differences more significant for CLIL learners. The American professor Howard Gardner maintains that there are at least eight different kinds of intelligences and that we are all intelligent – to a greater or lesser extent – in at least eight different ways: linguistic, logical-mathematical, bodily-physical, visual-spatial, musical, naturalistic, interpersonal and intrapersonal (see *Key idea*: *multiple intelligences in a nutshell*). Good CLIL caters for a broad spectrum of multiple 'intelligences'.

When CLIL teachers appeal to a variety of learning styles, using, for example, multiple intelligence theory, they give their learners the opportunity to process and produce information and language in a variety of ways. This can reinforce the learning of both content and language because it offers learners the chance to review content and language several times, in different ways. This helps information and language to be stored in the brain and makes it easier for learners to produce the information and language in new situations.

Key idea: multiple intelligences in a nutshell

Linguistic-verbal: You like working with words, reading and writing.

Logical-mathematical: You like concepts, think logically and like puzzles and problems.

Bodily-physical: You enjoy sports and games. You like to move around and learn by doing. You use body language to communicate.

Visual-spatial: You think in images or pictures, learn by seeing and by using charts or diagrams.

Musical: You enjoy learning and/or making music. You have a sense of rhythm and melody.

Naturalistic: You enjoy the natural world, animals and are interested in the environment.

Interpersonal-social. You like working in groups, and learn well if you study or discuss things with other people.

Intrapersonal: You understand your own feelings and thoughts. You like to daydream and fantasise and to work alone. You like to know why you are doing something.

Benefits for teachers and schools

There are many benefits for CLIL teachers and schools, too. The implementation of CLIL encourages whole school development and innovation: implementing CLIL can be a powerful impulse for renewal and reflection in a school. It can also be an impulse for a school to think about language policy, not only for English but also for other languages taught in school. CLIL teachers often become enthusiastic as they think about and discuss learning, curriculum development and materials. They may reconsider how learners learn both language and content and as a consequence may often develop a completely new curriculum.

Non-native speaker teachers improve their language skills: through attending language development courses, teaching their subject in another language and using their language skills in practice, teachers become more fluent and develop a more sophisticated command of the language. Furthermore, if they go on CLIL methodology courses, teachers are exposed to new ideas about their subject and how their subject is best learned and taught. They also learn about the language aspects of their own subject. These new perspectives lead teachers to broaden their understanding of both the subject and the teaching of the subject. Our work in CLIL schools has shown us that CLIL provides a real impulse – often for other departments in the school – for more active learning.

Subject and language teachers start to collaborate more, for example on how to work on language in lessons or on cross-curricular projects. And with learners and teachers who have high-level communication skills in English, schools are better equipped to participate in and benefit from international educational projects. CLIL also encourages greater collaboration among subject teachers as well as between subject and language teachers.

The CLIL teacher's role

CLIL teachers have an important role in helping all those involved in CLIL to realise these potential benefits. In order to maximise the language learning and subject learning potential of CLIL, they need to develop a range of skills. CLIL subject teachers need to have a clear understanding of how their subject uses language so that they, in turn, can help learners to notice how language is used in their subject and support them in overcoming the specific challenges associated with the language of their subject. They also need to learn how to activate their learners' existing knowledge about the topics they are teaching, to provide appropriate, multimodal input and to guide learners to actively understand and process input. Moreover, they need to encourage learners to interact in their classrooms, to use activities which encourage them to think and speak and write. CLIL teachers also need to know how to assess their learners' progress, in both content and language, and give them feedback which will help them to develop in both areas.

How 'CLIL' are you?

According to Coyle *et al.* (2010, p. 86) 'there is no single CLIL pedagogy'. This is true, but there are certainly characteristics which show that a CLIL classroom is different from a 'standard' classroom. To start you thinking about the extent to which you integrate your subject and language in your teaching, complete the 'How "CLIL" are you?' checklist. There are six statements per CLIL topic in this book, which correspond to the six chapters of practical ideas in Part 3. Tick one box only per statement (*always*, *often*, *sometimes*, *occasionally* or *never*) to see how 'CLIL' you are. You might also like to use the checklist with your team, as a basis for development.

Checklist: How 'CLIL' are you?					
Statements	always	often	sometimes	occasionally	never
ACTIVATING					
1. At the start of a lesson or topic, I find out what learners know about the topic.					
2. At the start of a lesson or topic, I find out what language related to the topic learners already know.					
3. I use visuals (photos, video, drawings, etc.) to introduce new topics.					
4. I use hands-on activities (experiments, objects, etc.) to introduce new topics.					
5. I use graphic organisers (mind maps, tables, charts, diagrams), which learners complete, to find out and organise what learners know about a topic.					
6. I ask learners to talk to each other when I am activating their prior knowledge.					

Statements	always	often	sometimes	occasionally	never
GUIDING UNDERSTANDING					
7. I provide different sorts of input (multimodal input) – texts, pictures, real objects, videos, models – to help my learners understand the topic.					
8. I formulate and use different kinds of questions – some related to LOTS (lower-order thinking skills) and others related to HOTS (higher-order thinking skills) to help learners understand input and process information actively.					
9. I encourage my learners to interact in my classes and use a lot of pair and group work.					
10. I use graphic organisers or other forms of support to help my learners understand input.					
11. I use a number of strategies or activities to help learners improve their reading and listening skills.					
12. I work actively with my learners on developing their thinking skills.					
FOCUS ON LANGUAGE					
13. I use a variety of activities to help my learners to recycle vocabulary related to my subject.					
14. I help learners notice how language is used in my subject, for example we look together at the grammar or we work on the vocabulary of the subject.					
15. I help learners notice the similarities and differences between English and their first language.					
16. In my classes, learners use a personal vocabulary file actively.					
17. I help my learners learn and use subject-specific terminology.					
18. I discuss ways of learning words with my classes.					

FOCUS ON SPEAKING					
19. Learners often speak in English during my classes, i.e. I encourage spoken output.					
20. I use speaking frames or graphic organisers to support learners' speaking.					
21. I use a varied repertoire of speaking activities.					
22. I use a lot of pair and group work.					
23. My learners learn to speak about my subject for different audiences, informally and formally.					
24. I create speaking activities with information gaps so learners need to communicate.					
FOCUS ON WRITING					
25. Learners often write in English for me, i.e. I encourage written output.					
26. My learners learn to write different types of texts in my subject.					
27. I use writing frames or graphic organisers (e.g. diagrams, tables, model texts) to help my learners organise their writing.					
28. I help learners with the different stages in writing (brainstorming, organising ideas, drafting, editing)					
29. When learners write for me, they know what the aim is, who their audience is and the text-type they are writing.					
30. I help learners move from concrete to abstract language in their writing.					

ASSESSMENT, REVIEW AND FEEDBACK					
31. I use a variety of ways to assess my learners on both content and language.					
32. My learners give each other feedback on their spoken/ written language.					
33. I give feedback to my learners on their language.					
34. I give marks for my learners' use of language as well as for my own subject.					
35. I provide clear assessment criteria when learners present or write for me.					
36. I know how to design and use a rubric.					

From *CLIL Activities* © Cambridge University Press 2012   PHOTOCOPIABLE

Scoring: How 'CLIL' are you?

After you have responded to each statement, you add up your scores as follows:

Always	4
Often	3
Sometimes	2
Occasionally	1
Never	0

You should take the following comments on your scores with a pinch of salt of course – just as you would were you to do a quiz in a magazine picked up in a doctor's waiting room. However, your scores may be used as a general pointer to the areas of development you and CLIL colleagues need to work on. If you score low in a particular section, you can turn to the practical activities in Part 3 to see how to develop further.

If you have a score of over 100, you are most likely a well-informed and experienced CLIL teacher who understands why you are teaching CLIL and how to put CLIL into practice. You realise that, as well as being a subject teacher, language learning and teaching is an integral part of your role as a CLIL teacher. You activate both language and content when you start a lesson or topic. You provide multimodal input and know how to select and adapt appropriate materials. You organise speaking and writing activities in your classroom and notice and deal with language errors. You assess your learners' subject knowledge and their language.

A score of between 75 and 100 shows that you are on your way to being an effective CLIL teacher who is applying many aspects of CLIL methodology in your classroom. However, you could think more about the language element of CLIL teaching and how to integrate language learning more with content learning.

If you have scored between 35 and 70, you are a teacher who is starting to integrate language with content. You probably do it on an ad hoc basis. You sometimes think about the language element in your subject lessons, but your lessons are mostly concentrated on subject knowledge and skills.

A score below 35 means you are probably a beginning CLIL teacher who needs to start thinking about how to integrate more language into teaching practice. This book will be a great help to you!

From *CLIL Activities* © Cambridge University Press 2012   PHOTOCOPIABLE

CLIL teachers: new roles

The checklist 'How "CLIL" are you?' shows how teachers take on new roles and responsibilities in CLIL. These affect both subject teachers and language teachers. Subject teachers with non-native-like language proficiency and little formal training in language teaching find themselves in a challenging situation. How can they deal with language issues when they may lack language skills and knowledge themselves? Language teachers with no specialised training in a subject find themselves in a similar situation. How do they support their learners and colleagues with issues related to subject knowledge and subject-specific terminology?

New roles: CLIL subject teachers

CLIL subject teachers may go through a number of phases in their development, which we describe below. How long it actually takes to become a proficient CLIL teacher depends on teachers' own motivation and time constraints: if schools facilitate teacher development (by, for example, encouraging teachers to take internationally recognised language or CLIL methodology examinations, by giving them paid study time, or by sending them to CLIL methodology workshops or courses), teachers will, of course, develop their CLIL skills faster than if schools do not.

Phase 1: developing my own language skills

The initial phase may be one when non-native-speaker teachers feel insecure about their own language skills and language knowledge. These are some of the questions they ask:

- Are my language skills ever going to be good enough to teach my subject in another language?
- How much new vocabulary do I – and my learners – need to learn?
- Where can I find the words I need?
- What if the learners ask me questions about language which I cannot answer on the spot?
- Will I lose credibility if my language skills aren't good enough?
- Will my relationship with the learners be compromised because I cannot express myself as easily in another language?

During this phase, subject teachers tend to interpret their role as a CLIL teacher as one which involves supplying learners with subject-specific vocabulary lists to learn. Their concerns with the development of their own language skills and knowledge may lead them to focus on themselves, and so there is a tendency to teach from the front and put less emphasis on activating learners. During this initial phase, teachers tend to use a lot of the learners' first language: they worry that their ideas about their subject don't come across. However, shifting the focus from the teacher to the learner and encouraging learners to interact with each other can alleviate teachers' anxiety about their own language skills. The realisation that their own language skills are less important than encouraging learners' use of the second language is an important step in CLIL subject teachers' development.

The subject teacher's language is not of course the only source of language input for learners. It may reassure non-native speakers to realise that they can supply their learners with examples of fluent, accurate spoken and written language by making use of audio, video and written material from television, radio, the Internet and published course materials. In addition, learners new to CLIL may find a non-native speaker who uses simple, direct language easier to understand than a native speaker who does not adapt their language use to the level of the learners. Non-native speakers, having experienced similar difficulties themselves, may also be in a better position to understand some of the problems their learners have with another language.

Phase 2: developing learners' vocabulary

Once teachers are reassured about the role that their own language skills play in their learners' learning, they may move into a second phase, where they become more aware that they are language teachers as well as subject teachers. They encourage learners to learn language – still mainly new vocabulary – and organise a variety of activities to help them to acquire new words and phrases. They feel more confident about their own language skills and less concerned about making mistakes. They start to notice aspects of language in their materials which cause learners difficulties and endeavour to build up a repertoire of classroom activities to help learners with these difficulties.

Phase 3: facilitating learners' language

In Phase 3, experienced CLIL teachers become aware that language consists of more than just vocabulary and start looking at their material as language learning material as well as content material. They encourage different kinds of writing and speaking activities, become more aware of the differences between, for example, spoken and written language, or between formal and informal language. They feel more knowledgeable about the language (vocabulary, grammar, functions, text-types) of their own subject and how to support learners in learning that language. During this phase, teachers are less concerned about their own language skills and develop ways to respond flexibly to questions from their learners. They can assess input for appropriateness at different levels and use a range of activities to help learners understand and develop language at different levels. They can teach Basic Interpersonal Communication Skills (BICS) and help learners to develop Cognitive Academic Language Proficiency (CALP) (see *Key idea: BICS and CALP*, page 35). Furthermore, they can activate and encourage learners to communicate in the second language at all stages of the lesson, which means that little or none of the first language is heard during lessons. During this phase, mature CLIL subject teachers have developed a wide variety of ways of giving feedback on language as well as content to their learners.

New roles: CLIL language teachers

The language teachers in a CLIL school or CLIL department may also find themselves taking on new roles. They may start off with a fixed language syllabus and a language textbook, perhaps published in the country where they work and which includes some of the foreign language. As the years go by, language teachers might choose an internationally published textbook, written totally in English and usually at a slightly higher level than the one they use with their monolingual learners in other classes. Their role in the school may also change.

Language teachers are often asked to correct their colleagues' language work on paper – activities or tests – and sometimes to observe colleagues and give them feedback on their language. This corresponds with Phase 1 mentioned above, where the subject teachers remain unsure about their own language skills. Language teachers may have similar concerns about their lack of subject knowledge and subject-specific terminology. They have no specialised training in physics, music or PE, for example, and may not understand subject-specific concepts or terms.

One way to deal with this and to integrate subject and language for the learners is for language teachers and subject teachers to collaborate closely. Some schools develop short projects between two or more subjects and the language department. Others timetable complete project weeks where all learners work around the same topic in both the subject and the language lessons, or where learners work for a complete week on the same topic with a variety of teachers. Teachers first brainstorm a topic together and then create activities related to it; for an example, see the brainstorm on the topic of water on page 22.

Through the years, language teachers gradually become more aware of the possibility of integrating language and different subjects and the need to support subject learning in the language lessons. Some language teachers give up having a coursebook for English, for example, or use it a lot less, since the learners receive so much input in subject lessons. They spend time in the language lessons working on academic language tasks linked to subject material. Some (lucky!) CLIL language and subject teachers are able to plan lessons and team teach classes together.

Collaboration between language and subject teachers

Collaboration between subject and language teachers can take many forms. For example, subject teachers rely on language teachers to correct tasks or tests they have made; language teachers work on subject language in their lessons. Some schools also have the luxury of subject and language teachers team teaching the same learners at the same time. Collaboration can take place before, during or after the lesson as outlined below.

Before the subject lesson
The language teacher can

- work with the subject teacher to prepare an activity by finding appropriate materials, assessing the language level of materials, designing possible tasks or questions.
- edit the subject teacher's language in tasks he or she has made.

Economics
- Economic development related to water: seas, rivers, deserts and jungles
- Global warming and carbon trading
- World Wildlife Fund
- Decline and recovery related to water

Music
- Classical music related to water (e.g. Handel's *Water music* and Ravel's *Jeux d'eau*)
- Composing music related to water
- Making water-related musical instruments (e.g. bottles and jars of water)
- Pop songs about water

Chemistry
- The chemistry of H_2O
- Electricity and water
- Ph levels
- Water chemistry, e.g. aquarium water, swimming pool water

Geography
- Flooding and drought
- How water forms our planet
- Collecting and recycling water
- Rainfall worldwide
- Rivers and oceans

Physics
- Steam engines
- Waves
- Water towers
- Water heaters
- Water slides and the laws of physics

Art and design
- Artists depicting water
- Photographs: reflections in water
- The Impressionists
- Liquid sculptures
- Water symbols in art
- Water colours

Water

English
- Poetry related to water, e.g. 'Not waving but drowning' (Stevie Smith)
- Novels or films related to flooding, drought or the sea, e.g. *The story of Pi* (Yann Martell), *On Chesil Beach* (Ian McEwan), *Jaws, Titanic*

Biology
- Water creatures and plants
- The human body in relation to water (dehydration, diving, hypothermia)
- Coral reefs

History
- Water mills and the Industrial Revolution
- The Great Fire of London and its effects on water management
- Roman water systems

- identify the language used in an activity (e.g. the relevant functions such as explaining, cause and effect, arguing; the grammar used in the activity; the relevant vocabulary or words which are hard to pronounce), and then pre-teach or practise that language with learners.
- identify the text-type that the learners are working on within an activity and work on typical language used in this text-type.
- identify a specific language skill (reading, listening, speaking, writing, dictionary skills) that is used in an activity and practise it.
- identify learning strategies (e.g. reading strategies such as using visuals or subheadings in a text) that are needed for an activity and practise them with learners.
- do a similar activity in the language lessons but with different input.
- introduce and practise with a correction code so the learners know which language points they can pay attention to.
- introduce and use an assessment rubric so the learners understand assessment criteria in advance.

During the subject lesson
The language teacher can

- monitor and support learners' language production.
- give feedback on good examples of learner language.
- give feedback on common language mistakes.
- monitor and note learners' language issues for work in a language class.
- give the class instructions on or remind learners about relevant language learning strategies for the activity.
- help learners to speak by eliciting and encouraging useful language through questioning.
- collect learners' written work or make video/audio recordings of spoken work.

The subject teacher can monitor, support and give feedback on ideas or content.

After the subject lesson
The language teacher can

- give feedback or teach a remedial lesson on a language issue which needs attention.
- provide feedback on language that the learners produced, for example writing learners' mistakes on the board or creating a handout.
- do a follow-up activity on language, for example grammar, vocabulary or pronunciation.
- do a follow-up skill (listening, watching, reading, writing, speaking) activity related to the practical activity done by the subject teacher.
- review written work or audio recordings of spoken work and note common language problems before having a lesson focusing on these problems.
- use subject material as input for language lessons.

The language teacher and the subject teacher can both assess the work done and give a joint mark. In many of the practical activities in Part 3, we provide concrete tips for collaboration between subject and language teachers before, during and after lessons.

Rubric: 'Collaboration in CLIL'

The rubric 'Collaboration in CLIL' below describes the amount of collaboration between subject and language teachers. Its aim is to show CLIL departments the different amount of cooperation there might or might not be at their school. It describes seven collaboration roles which language teachers fulfil in a CLIL stream or school and the role of the school in organising CLIL:

1. Language coach or instructor for colleagues
2. Giver of learner feedback
3. Stimulator of spoken and written language
4. Language methodologist
5. Team worker
6. Assessor
7. International consultant

The final section of the rubric relates to the role that the school plays in facilitating cooperation between the language and subject teachers.

One useful way of using the rubric is to read it and to discuss questions like the following as a team:

- Where can we place ourselves as a CLIL school or department on the rubric?
- Are we happy with our place on the rubric?
- Where would we like to be on the rubric (a) next year and (b) in five years' time?

Rubric: Collaboration in CLIL

Scenario→ Role of language teacher↓	LESS COLLABORATION → 1	2	3	MORE COLLABORATION 4
Language coach or instructor for colleagues	Language teachers do not work with their subject teacher colleagues on their language.	Once subject teachers have reached a recognised level of language proficiency, there is little formal incentive to carry on improving their own language. There is occasional or casual contact about language between a few language and subject teachers.	Language teachers react to queries from subject teachers about their own language and/or tests. Subject teachers are allocated a language teacher to go to with queries.	Language teachers and subject teachers work closely and regularly together. The language teacher observes subject teachers' lessons now and again and gives feedback on language use. Subject teachers keep up their language skills through workshops which they attend. The teachers are formally facilitated with a number of hours per week to do this work.
Giver of learner feedback	The subject and language teachers do not discuss feedback to learners.	The subject teachers occasionally notice spoken and/or written mistakes made by learners and correct them.	Subject teachers sometimes create tasks to help learners with mistakes that they make in spoken or written language.	Subject teachers provide the language teacher with mistakes that their learners make on a regular basis. The language teacher (or language and subject teachers together) creates tasks for the learners to work on these problems.

Scenario→ Role of language teacher↓	LESS COLLABORATION →→→ MORE COLLABORATION			
	1	2	3	4
Stimulator of spoken and written language	The CLIL team works in their original, native language.	The CLIL team speaks English in meetings and with the language teachers, but not at school in general.	The CLIL team aims to speak English together, but discuss sensitive or emotional issues – such as learners' problems – in their native language, to facilitate communication. The language teachers always (try to) speak English to their CLIL colleagues.	The CLIL team speaks English together at all times. Minutes of CLIL meetings or other memos or newsletters are circulated in the language the learners are learning. The language department recommends language books and/or websites to their colleagues.
Language methodologist	Language and subject teachers work separately on their own curricula. Language teachers and subject teachers do not discuss language or language teaching methodology together. It's not really an issue at school.	Subject teachers occasionally ask language teachers for support in how to teach a difficult language point. Methodology is sometimes discussed informally during meetings or in the staff room. Learners make glossaries.	Subject teachers discuss the language problems of their learners with the language teachers, and language teachers work on difficult language points brought up by their subject colleagues in the language lessons. Language assistants are present in school. There is policy about the use of glossaries and some teachers stick to the policy.	Language teachers (or an in-house specialist trainer) give workshops about language to colleagues. Language teachers suggest how subject teachers can add language aims and activities to their lessons. Language assistants help actively in the lessons. There are clear agreements about the use of glossaries. All subject teachers see themselves as subject AND language teachers and understand the role of language in learning their subject.

Team worker	Language teachers teach a curriculum which is unrelated to that of the subject teachers. They have their own programme and separate materials.	There is some informal ad hoc collaboration between language and subject colleagues about curriculum content and materials.	There is some collaboration between subject and language teachers related to curriculum development and materials. This cooperation is encouraged but not formalised.	Language teachers help subject teachers to create or adapt material which relates to language in their subject. Collaboration is planned in the CLIL department. Language and subject teachers design and carry out cross-curricular projects together, which are spread throughout the year or carried out in specific weeks. There is some team teaching between language and subject teachers.
Assessor	Subject teachers and language teachers test their subjects separately.	Learners carry out occasional projects or work in subject lessons where they are assessed on their language. There are some general assessment criteria.	Language teachers sometimes assess work produced in subject lessons with their colleagues. Clear assessment criteria are used by teachers.	Language and subject teachers collaborate together so that tests and projects are marked consistently on both subject and language. Transparent criteria (e.g. in the form of rubrics) are given to learners in advance. Each year, language-level expectations are more demanding for the learners.

| Scenario→ Role of language teacher↓ | LESS COLLABORATION ◄─────────►────── MORE COLLABORATION | | | |
	1	2	3	4
International consultant	Language and subject teachers go on trips abroad with learners and receive foreign guests on exchanges.	Language and subject teachers go abroad and collaborate in travel arrangements. Learners do tasks for language and subjects separately. Learners from abroad do tasks related to their own curriculum in their home country. The school is interested in international projects.	Language and subject teachers cooperate on organising trips and exchanges abroad. Learners do projects or tasks related to language and other subjects. When learners from abroad visit, the school gives guest lessons which combine language and content. The school is working on collaboration in official international projects.	Language and subject teachers cooperate on organising trips and exchanges abroad, where learners work specifically on both their content skills and their language skills. International visits are clearly embedded in the curriculum. Staff from home and abroad collaborate in projects which the learners carry out together on exchanges. The school is involved in formal international projects.

Role of the school

Scenario→ Role of school↓	LESS COLLABORATION		MORE COLLABORATION	
	1	2	3	4
Organisation	The school does not organise any formal collaboration or development for the CLIL team on language or methodology or coaching on the job.	The school facilitates external courses in, for example, the UK. There is some facilitation for collaboration between the teachers in the CLIL team.	The language teachers give language lessons to their colleagues on a voluntary basis. There is a slot in the timetable for occasional CLIL team meetings.	The school has a policy on language and language methodology within the CLIL team and works to help individual teachers and the team on improvements. It facilitates collaboration between language and subject teachers, through organising meetings or workshops, a newsletter and/or giving them time to work together.

PHOTOCOPIABLE

Challenges in CLIL

The potential benefits of CLIL and new roles for teachers present a number of challenges. Below, we discuss these in relation to the six features of CLIL focused on the chapters comprising Part 3: 1. *Activating*, 2. *Guiding understanding*, 3. *Focus on language*, 4. *Focus on speaking*, 5. *Focus on writing* and 6. *Assessment, review and feedback*.

1. Challenges in activating

How can I activate content? How can I activate language?

At the start of the lesson, as a warm-up activity, have a brief discussion on the new topic with learners. Ask questions and use visuals (e.g. photographs, diagrams) to find out what learners already know about the topic. Find out, too, what they know about the language of the topic, by setting tasks such as 'Which group can write down the most nouns related to cells (biology), the Industrial Revolution (history)?' or by creating a mind map on the board with the class, using words related to the new topic and eliciting words to help them.

Key idea: the Zone of Proximal Development (ZPD)

Vygotsky (1978) coined the term *Zone of Proximal Development* (ZPD) to describe a point just beyond what a learner already knows or is able to do on his or her own. He suggested that learning takes place when learners interact in the ZPD with someone who is more expert than they are. Activating helps learners to work in their ZPD. (See also *Key idea: scaffolding* on page 31)

See Part 3, Chapter 1 for practical activities on activating in CLIL.

2. Challenges in guiding understanding

How can I evaluate the level of the materials I am using?

Find out the level of difficulty of a digital text you want to use by cutting and pasting it into an online readability test: to find such a test, search the Internet using 'online readability test' or use one of the sites in the box below. Use a benchmark such as the Common European Framework of Reference for Languages (CEFR; see Appendix) to assess the language level your learners need in order to understand your input (text, video). Estimate how much the visual support (photographs, diagrams, charts and other illustrations) really support the input. Does a diagram in the book, for example, help learners to understand what is described? Look at the vocabulary in a text: as a rule of thumb, learners can understand a text if there are no more than 10 to 15 new words per page in it. Any more and the text is likely to be too difficult.

Online readability tests

Online-utility.org (http://www.online-utility.org/english/readability_test_and_improve.jsp)

Readability index calculator (http://www.standards-schmandards.com/exhibits/rix/)

What sort of input can I provide?

Use 'multimodal' – or very varied – input. Use video input, your own written or spoken stories, and texts with accompanying visuals. If a text is very long, deal with it in chunks. When choosing texts, look for those that are clearly organised and well illustrated. Simplify your own language and repeat information in different ways.

How can I help learners to understand input?

When working with input, formulate clear subject and language aims (see Part 2: *Subject pages* for examples of CLIL aims): what do you want the learners to understand and learn when using this input? Do a short warm-up task to focus learners on the input first (see Chapter 1: *Activating* in Part 3). Always provide a task to guide learners through the input, starting with a general task the first time they read written input or listen to spoken input. Once they have understood the general meaning of the input, provide more specific and challenging tasks using some higher-order thinking skills (HOTS; see *Key idea: questions and tasks for CLIL according to Bloom's new taxonomy*, page 32, and Activity 2.12: *Skinny and fat questions and thinking skills*). Get learners to write their own questions for each other. However, don't ask them to read new material aloud, as reading aloud will not help them to understand difficult written input.

Key idea: scaffolding

The idea of scaffolding is based on work by Wood, Bruner and Ross (1976) and Vygotsky (1978). Builders use temporary scaffolds to support a building during construction, and then – once the building can stand alone – the scaffold is removed. CLIL learners can be helped with teacher scaffolding in the same way. There is an important difference between help and scaffolding. An example of help is when a child asks how to spell a word, and the teacher tells them. If, instead of providing the answer, the teacher asks the child to sound out the word and write down the sounds they hear, the teacher is providing scaffolding, which helps the learner to solve a similar problem themselves next time.

Provide scaffolding for both language and content learning. For guiding understanding, provide reception scaffolds (Dodge, 2009). For example, give learners a Venn diagram to complete if input is comparing two things; when working with a factual text, however, give them a chart to complete about a factual text.

Examples of reception scaffolds can be found in the following activities in Part 3: 1.2: *Graphic organisers for activating (1) – Venn diagram*; 1.3: *Graphic organisers for activating (2) – target practice*; 2.4: *Graphic organisers*; 2.1: *Expert groups*.

Key idea: reception scaffolds

Reception scaffolds help learners to understand and process information from input.

What sorts of questions can I ask?

When learners find the input difficult, firstly use questions which appeal to lower-order thinking skills (LOTS), such as remembering and understanding. However, since analysis of teachers' questioning in the classroom has shown that 70–80% of classroom questioning focuses on these skills of remembering and understanding (Wragg and Brown, 2001), it is important to challenge learners' thinking behaviours too. In this regard, Bloom's new taxonomy (Anderson *et al.*, 2001) is a useful framework for creating tasks or questions that demand the use of higher-order thinking skills (HOTS), such as applying, analysing, evaluating and creating.

Key idea: questions and tasks for CLIL according to Bloom's new taxonomy

Skill	Question	Words	Examples of tasks and questions
Remembering	Can learners remember?	tell, recall, repeat, list	• Tell me what Pythagoras' theorem is. • Identify five characteristics of a living organism.
Understanding	Can learners explain?	describe, explain, paraphrase	• Tell me what you observed during the experiment and explain why that happened. • Describe Mary Queen of Scots' character.
Applying	Can learners use the information in another situation?	demonstrate, dramatise, illustrate	• How can you interpret these graphs about AIDS? What do they mean? • Make a brochure to inform teenagers and give them some advice about sexually transmitted diseases (STDs). Provide illustrations.
Analysing	Can learners break the information into parts and see relationships?	compare, contrast, criticise, test	• Compare plastics with polymers in this Venn diagram. • What is the relationship between oil production and consumption?
Evaluating	Can learners justify a position?	argue, judge, evaluate	• Design a questionnaire for our class to evaluate and assess our work during the project. • Select and explain the most important improvements which you can recommend for this experiment.

Creating	Can learners create new products?	construct, create, design	• Create a lighting circuit for a greenhouse which comes on at sunset and goes off at sunrise. • Compose eight bars of a melody with the same rhythm as the one we are studying.

See Part 3, Chapter 2 for practical activities on guiding understanding in CLIL.

3. Challenges in focusing on language

How do I choose which aspects of language to focus on?

One way of looking at the language in your materials is to use a checklist like the one below. It will help you to assess text difficulty as well as to identify the kind of language that you might focus on in your lessons. Look at some lesson materials with a colleague and note down or discuss your answers to these questions. After you have considered your answers, decide which language aspect(s) of your material it is relevant to pay attention to in your lesson. For more detail about the characteristics of language for your own subject and for an annotated text related to it, refer to Part 2: *Subject pages*.

Checklist: language in lesson materials

1. Which type of text is your material? Does it recount, report, instruct, explain, persuade, discuss, predict or hypothesise?
2. Which level on the CEFR does a learner need to be able to use this material? See Appendix.
3. How do the reading tasks help the learners to make sense of the texts? How might you supplement these?
4. What listening is there involved? If there is none, how might you include some listening work?
5. Which tenses are used (present simple, present continuous, past simple, present perfect, etc.)?
6. What kinds of modal verbs (e.g. *can, could, might*) are there?
7. How long are the sentences? How complex are the sentences?
8. Which linking words are used?
9. Which other language features does the material have (e.g. prepositions, phrasal verbs, dates, *if*-sentences)?
10. Count the number of words you think your (average) learners will NOT understand per page (see section 2. *Challenges in guiding understanding*, pages 30–1).
11. Which important new vocabulary items in the material do your learners need to (a) recognise and (b) use actively? Which can they ignore?
12. Which chunks of language (or phrases) in the text are useful for your learners to learn?
13. How much does the material encourage speaking? If it doesn't, how might you promote it?
14. How much does the material encourage writing? If it doesn't, how might you promote it?
15. What grammar and vocabulary will learners need to carry out the speaking or writing tasks in the material?

Should I explain grammar? I'm a physics (history, music) teacher

If you feel uncertain about your own grammar, work with the language teachers in your school to look at grammar in your material. Ask the language teacher to explain the grammar in your materials in their language lessons. If you notice grammar mistakes that your learners make and can help them with their errors, go ahead! Create activities with the language teacher to practise the content using the grammar in your materials.

How can I deal with new vocabulary?

Don't expect learners to be able to produce new vocabulary after they have come across it once: they need to hear and read it several times before it becomes part of their productive language. Check your input for new vocabulary and pre-teach only the key words which you think learners really need to understand new input. Help them to guess the meaning of new vocabulary by looking at how a word is formed (for example, -*ed* ending means a regular past tense, the ending -*ion* often means the word is a noun) or the context surrounding the word. They will learn more effectively if they do active tasks with the new vocabulary.

How can I help learners remember vocabulary?

Recycle vocabulary, reminding learners about words they learned in previous lessons. Create tasks which use the new vocabulary so that learners see and use it. Use a personal idiom file (PIF) or vocabulary notebook, especially for new vocabulary. Ensure that if learners learn new words, they write them down in the notebook. Learners write down the word, its meaning and a sentence which shows how it is used.

Word	Definition	Examples
Carbon monoxide(CO)	A poisonous gas that has no smell	You can't see or smell the gas carbon monoxide, so it's dangerous.

See Part 3, Chapter 3 for practical activities for working on language in CLIL.

4. Challenges in focusing on speaking

How can I get beginners to speak in English?

Make very easy tasks, where learners have to respond with only one or two words, and gradually build up to sentence level. As learners progress, create questions which involve higher-order thinking skills (HOTS; see 'What sorts of questions can I ask?', page 32). Encourage every effort and praise learners who really try to speak. Allow some learners time before you insist they speak in the language in which they are learning: some learners need this 'silent period'.

How can I keep learners using English?

Use English all the time yourself and 'ignore' learners who don't speak it. Reward and praise learners for trying to speak in English. Discuss with learners why you should all use English all of the time.

Provide useful phrases. Give learners thinking time to prepare for speaking. Formulate speaking aims in advance and tell the learners what those speaking aims are. Use pair and group work often. Set tasks which include information gaps so learners have to communicate (see Activity 4.4: *Information gaps*). Ask some learners to monitor their group during group work, to keep them on track when speaking another language.

Key idea: effective talk

Mercer (2000) has shown that some types of talk are more effective for learning than others. When teachers encouraged learners to explain and justify their ideas using words like *because*, *but* and *so*, their learners developed better understanding. Encouraging learners to speak helps learners understand a subject and it also helps them to write better. When they talk about their ideas before they write, learners also produce better quality writing. They also write better if teachers give them plenty of models of the texts they need to write and if they talk about how texts are organised. Guidelines showing learners how to produce similar texts then help learners to become successful independent writers.

I don't feel confident speaking English. The learners even correct me sometimes!

It is more important that your learners use English. Set up pair- and group-work tasks so they interact with each other. Thank them for correcting your language and make a joke of it. Ask your school if you can go on a course to improve your own language.

My learners can speak English fluently. Why can't they understand or produce more academic language? How can I develop CALP in speaking?

Key idea: BICS and CALP

Cummins distinguishes between two dimensions of language: conversational and academic. To describe these dimensions, he uses the terms *Basic Interpersonal Communication Skills* and *Cognitive Academic Language Proficiency* (Cummins, 2000), often referred to as BICS and CALP. Effective CLIL teachers help learners to bridge the gap between BICS and CALP.

BICS refers to the ability to understand and take part in everyday conversations and carry out daily activities in the target language: basic language skills used in informal communication, for example in school, talking about recent activities at breaks or parties, in classrooms to ask about where things are, or to organise learners into teams when playing sports. BICS involve situations where learners can use visual clues, gestures or facial expression to communicate with each other. Second language learners who are immersed in the target language generally achieve BICS in two to five years.

CALP refers to more formal, academic language learning. CALP requires higher-order thinking skills such as applying, analysing and creating. In CALP, clues to help learners understand are often reduced or absent. Lesson input for CALP is read from a textbook or presented by the teacher, and the concepts are often academically more demanding. Consequently, the spoken and written language that learners need to understand and produce for CALP is more complex than for BICS. It may take five to seven years for second language learners who are immersed in the target language to become proficient in academic language skills (Collier, 1995).

Introduce a variety of higher-level speaking tasks into your teaching, such as an interview on a news programme or a speech. Watch videos of formal speakers and help learners notice how they organise their speaking. Use a benchmark like the CEFR (see Appendix) to help you to develop higher-level speaking tasks. Use production scaffolds or speaking frames to help learners prepare for speaking. For example, ask them to write down their arguments for and against a point of view before they speak about those ideas. Formulate questions which involve higher-order thinking skills (HOTS; see page 32) so that learners produce stretches of language.

Key idea: transformation and production scaffolds

Transformation scaffolds help learners to select, change and organise information into a different form. Production scaffolds help learners to produce or create something new with the information they have collected in order to show their understanding.

See Chapter 4 of Part 3 for practical activities for working on speaking in CLIL.

5. Challenges in focusing on writing

What kind of writing can I do with my CLIL beginners?

Write short model texts with a whole class on the board. Get learners to complete gapped texts (see Activities 3.1: *Academic word list*, 5.1: *Advice column*, 5.6: *Framing writing*). Provide a model paragraph and ask learners to write a similar paragraph on a different topic. Keep writing tasks short (one paragraph), simple and realistic (a paragraph in an email to a friend, a note to a member of the family).

I don't know what kind of writing activities to use. What sort of writing activities are good for CLIL?

When designing writing activities, ensure that they include a purpose (to describe, explain, instruct), a realistic audience (readers of a website or a magazine) and a text-type (a brochure, a webpage, an email). Work with the language teacher: look at your coursebook together and come up with possible writing ideas. Ask learners to write a variety of different types of texts.

Key idea: genres

Different texts have different purposes, for example to recount, report, instruct, explain, persuade or discuss: these are known as different *genres*. Texts which recount retell events in chronological order. Reports describe what things are like. Instructions tell people how to do things. Explanations show how or why things work or happen. Persuasive texts argue one point of view, explaining why the reader should think something, and discussions present arguments from several points of view. Each school subject uses these genres to a greater or lesser extent. History, for example, often recounts events in chronological order, biology often describes what things are like, chemistry lessons often involve instructions on how to do things. Geography often explains how or why things work, art may argue from a particular point of view, and many subjects will ask learners to present arguments from different points of view.

My learners don't know what to write about: how can I help them?

Before learners write individually, brainstorm ideas about content and also possible language with the whole class. Show learners examples and models of what you expect. Provide input on ideas in the form of texts or websites.

My learners write in one long paragraph and can't organise their ideas

As preparation for writing, discuss with learners what information might appear in each paragraph. What appears in an introductory paragraph? What do you need in a final paragraph? What comes in between? Explain as a rule of thumb that they should write about one main idea per paragraph. Talk about linking words (*firstly*, *secondly*, *but*, *furthermore*, *lastly*, etc.) and explain how to use them.

I don't feel confident writing in English.

If you don't feel confident writing in the English language, work with the language teacher. Think of a writing task for your subject and ask the language teacher to spend time on it in the language classes. He or she can help the learners to organise and edit their writing. Give a joint mark: you give a mark for the subject content, the language teacher for the language.

My learners write as if they are speaking and can't write in a more academic or formal style. How can I develop CALP in writing?

Introduce a variety of higher-level writing tasks into your teaching, such as a brochure, a page for a website or a newspaper article. Look at models of writing with different content to help learners to organise their ideas. Use a benchmark like the CEFR (see Appendix) to help you to develop higher-level writing tasks. Use production scaffolds or writing frames to help learners prepare for writing (see Activities 5.5: *Class magazine* and 5.6: *Framing writing* for examples of production scaffolds). For example, give learners a series of questions to help them with ideas for writing. Formulate writing activities which involve HOTS (see page 32). Learn about the academic language related to your own subject (see Part 2: *Subject pages*) so that you are more aware of it.

See Part 3, Chapter 5 for practical activities for working on writing in CLIL.

6. Challenges in assessing, reviewing and giving feedback

How can I assess my learners for CLIL?

CLIL learners perform better when a *range* of assessments is used. This means they can use context or other means to show their understanding in different ways, which do not always involve language. CLIL teachers can thereby reduce the risk of language negatively interfering with learners' performance in assessments. So in addition to written assessments, such as a magazine article or an essay, use spoken assessments, such as oral or dramatic presentations, or drawings to show understanding.

Key idea: assessment of learning versus assessment for learning in CLIL

Assessment of learning

Assessment *of* learning provides a summary of what a learner knows: it uses written or spoken tests, consisting of open or closed questions, presentations, essays or reports, completed under exam conditions and resulting in a mark for the learners. For example, an in-class biology test in which learners answer multiple-choice questions about classification tests how much the learners know about classification and whether they can classify animals accurately. In order to pass the test, they will learn the facts in their biology book about classification and reproduce these in the test.

Assessment for learning

Assessment *for* learning involves using assessment in the classroom to raise the learners' achievement rather than simply measure it. It can include, for example, informal classroom observations (how learners work together) or performance assessments where learners make authentic products (brochure, poster, letter). Assessment for learning is important for CLIL teachers, since they can develop assessments that encourage the development of both subject and language. In order to pass these types of assessments, learners will focus on performing well in group work and creating high-quality authentic products. On the one hand, teachers need to make sure that the integration of subject and language does not get in the way of learners' performance in tests of subject-specific skills and knowledge. On the other hand, they need to ensure that the means of assessment reinforces the learning of the subject *and* the language.

Ten research-based principles of assessment for learning (the Assessment Reform Group 2002)

Assessment For Learning (or AfL) should:

1. be part of effective planning of teaching and learning.
2. focus on how students learn.
3. be recognised as central to classroom practice.
4. be regarded as a key professional skill for teachers.
5. be sensitive and constructive because any assessment has an emotional impact.
6. take account of the importance of (and foster) learner motivation.
7. promote commitment to learning goals and a shared understanding of the criteria by which they are assessed.
8. recognise the full range of achievements of all learners.
9. develop learners' capacity for self-assessment so that they can become reflective and self-managing.
10. provide constructive guidance for learners about how to improve.

How can I give feedback on speaking and writing to my learners?

As learners speak, or when you look at their writing, note errors that they make. Give these to the language teacher to work with, or – if you feel confident enough about your own language – make a handout of the errors and ask learners to correct their mistakes. Using a correction code consistently (see Activity 6.3: *Correction code* in Part 3) can help learners to become more able to self-correct: it is helpful if all the teachers at your school use the same one!

Should I assess content and language separately or together?

It is unfair to mark learners down for language when you are testing content. In this case, ignore language mistakes or pass them on to the language teacher to deal with them. It is beneficial to learners if you can sometimes work with language teachers on projects or other work and provide marks for both content and language.

How can I use rubrics?

Rubrics can be used at three stages of the assessment process: at the start of an assignment to clarify assessment criteria, during an assignment for self-assessment or peer assessment, and at the end of an assignment to award a final grade. For example, if the learners are halfway through an assignment, the teacher can coach the learners with the rubric by asking them to assess their progress so far.

Key idea: using rubrics for assessment, review and feedback

A rubric is an assessment tool in the form of a matrix which is used to evaluate progress based on a range of criteria, rather than one single score. It consists of rows listing characteristics which will be assessed (criteria), and columns indicating the qualities of each characteristic. Each written description in each square in the rubric is called a descriptor. For an example of a rubric and ideas related to rubrics, see Activities 6.2: *Complete a rubric* and 6.7: *Jigsaw rubric: assessing speaking*.

Rubrics and descriptors are constructed using two features:

1. measurable criteria (e.g. accurate biological classification, punctuation, accuracy);
2. descriptors of (usually) four aspects or points to rate the quality of performance (e.g. poor, average, good and excellent; or a scale of 1–4).

Why rubrics?

Rubrics make the assessment of subject and language more transparent to learners, teachers, colleagues and parents. A rubric can be handed out along with the instructions for an assignment to show learners: before they start, how they are going to be judged. Rubrics also support learning by providing feedback to learners: if they know where they are on a rubric, they know in which area(s) to improve. Another advantage of using rubrics is that once they are designed, they reduce the amount of time CLIL teachers need to spend evaluating their learners' assignments.

See Part 3, Chapter 6 for practical activities related to assessment in CLIL.

Who is this book for?

In CLIL schools, both language and subject teachers are searching for a 'CLIL methodology'. Teachers ask questions like 'What does CLIL methodology look like in practice? What can I actually do in my classroom that is CLIL?' We hope that this book answers such questions. In *CLIL Activities* content and language are seen as equal partners, and this book aims to support them both. It supports subject teachers with activities to help learners acquire both the language and the content of their subject. It also makes suggestions about how language teachers might support and cooperate with subject teachers during their language lessons and sometimes in team teaching.

Part 1: *Background to CLIL* has highlighted many benefits of CLIL but also drawn attention to the challenges teachers face in helping their learners realise them. These challenges are reflected in the structure and content of this book. Part 2: *Subject pages* goes into more detail about the language of nine school subjects and illustrates the language used in CLIL materials. Part 3 consists of six chapters of classroom activities covering the main features of the CLIL approach. These are how to activate, guide understanding, focus on language, focus on speaking, focus on writing, assess, review and give feedback to CLIL learners. *CLIL Activities* provides ideas to support teachers in implementing CLIL successfully in the classroom.

Part 2: Subject pages

Introduction

CLIL subject teachers who have been formally trained in their subject, rather than language, may be unfamiliar with the language demands their subject makes of their learners studying in another language. Similarly, teachers who have been formally trained in language may not be aware of how specialised language is used in subject lessons, and of the kinds of linguistic challenges learners face in CLIL subject classrooms.

Part 2: *Subject pages* is a collection of subject-specific pages. They provide examples, encouragement and support to CLIL subject teachers without a language teaching background, and to language teachers with some insight into the demands being made on CLIL learners in nine subject areas. These pages form a foundation for working with both content and language and deal with challenges which relate particularly to school subjects taught in another language. For example, how can PE teachers encourage learners to speak? What sort of writing can learners do in science? What is specific to vocabulary in history? What do language aims for maths look like?

We begin Part 2 with an overview of some of the different challenges CLIL learners face when learning a subject in another language. Following the section on challenges, we explain briefly how to use these subject pages and summarise their features. Four subject pages are then included for each of the following nine subject areas:

Art, design and technology
Economics and business studies
Geography
History
Information and communication technology (ICT)
Maths
Music and drama
Physical education (PE)
Science

Challenges for CLIL learners

CLIL learners face some common challenges when learning a subject in a second language. These challenges may be divided into three different types: (1) affective, (2) linguistic and (3) cultural, and some of these challenges will be more relevant for some subjects and teacher situations than others. We comment on each of these briefly in turn.

1. *Affective challenges*

Affective challenges are the emotional challenges learners face when hearing, reading or using a second language. Learners may feel disempowered, overwhelmed, anxious, inadequate, helpless or even silly, and these feelings can affect how long they can listen and read for, and how much they can read or listen to. These challenges can also affect learners' willingness to take risks when using another language: for example, a lack of confidence may affect their readiness to speak or to attempt to be creative in their writing.

Emotional factors may affect CLIL learners' ability to undertake any of the following:

- to concentrate when reading, listening to or watching input for long periods of time without a focus, such as on a two-hour-long film (drama) or a one-hour-long account of an earthquake on a DVD (geography).
- to dare to speak in another language in front of peers and the teacher.
- to express emotions in another language or to avoid using their first language in emotional situations, such as during a volleyball match when shouting at their fellow learners or complaining about an unfair ruling by the referee (PE), or voicing their own opinions on a piece of art (art).
- to keep talking in another language when working in pairs, in groups or spread out on a field or in a gymnasium, such as when creating artwork (art) or playing hockey (PE).
- to encourage and motivate their peers to use a second language for social talk in the classroom (e.g. *Did you see that programme last night on TV? Are you going to the school disco on Friday?*).

2. *Linguistic challenges*

This section deals with linguistic – or language-related – challenges for CLIL learners, that is challenges associated with the language they read in texts or listen to, or input they watch, or the language they themselves use when they speak or write. They can face challenges on three levels: (1) discourse-level, (2) sentence-level and (3) word-level.

2.1 Discourse-level challenges

Discourse refers to any stretch of spoken or written language longer than one sentence. Discourse-level challenges are challenges which affect learners' ability to understand or produce longer pieces of spoken or written information, for example a newspaper article, a video clip or an explanation.

Reading, listening and watching

When reading, listening and watching, CLIL learners may find it a challenge to, for example:

- process a lot of new or complex, dense or abstract spoken or written information with little or no visual support: a financial newspaper article about inflation in a specialist sector such as the oil industry (economics).

- interpret data from visuals such as tables, diagrams, graphs or charts without any spoken or written explanation: a histogram about rainfall (geography).
- understand how to 'read' an illustration: an old map (history).
- identify the main points in long spoken or written texts: a chapter on the causes and effects of an invasion (history).
- find specific information from spoken or written texts: a brochure from a fitness centre with tips on keeping fit and taking exercise (PE).
- recognise the different purposes of texts (e.g. to argue in defence of a modern work of art (art)).
- understand references in text where words such as *it*, *she* or *they* refer to earlier information.
- jump backwards and forwards to find relevant information when reading (e.g. finding important figures in a word problem (maths); surfing webpages (ICT)).
- follow a teacher or speaker on a DVD who speaks fast or with a strong accent.
- understand information in primary sources: archaic texts or objects (history and art).
- understand lengthy written problems or long spoken instructions (e.g. *Fill in the gap: Joyce is playing in a tennis match. The rules say that the average age of the pair of players on each side must be ten years old or younger. Joyce is eight years old so her partner must be _____ years older or younger* (maths)).
- evaluate bias and the accuracy, reliability or unreliability of sources: a website representing a political party (ICT); the bias in an original source (history).
- distinguish between facts and opinions: *Napoleon was French and he was an effective leader* (history).

Speaking and writing

When speaking and writing, CLIL learners may also find it a challenge to:

- speak spontaneously for any length of time and at the same time develop their thinking about complex issues (e.g. a public debate on reasons why a city should put in a bid for the Olympics (geography).
- organise and use information clearly and systematically from different sources when doing a spoken or written task: writing a brochure for teenagers about safe sex (biology).
- show how conclusions or explanations are logical (e.g. to explain how they arrived at a solution to a problem using concise and appropriate language (maths)).
- organise and structure their ideas to achieve a set task (e.g. to classify causes and effects of global warming (geography)).
- produce appropriate language for the type of text they are producing: a brochure for parents on gaming (ICT).
- use appropriate language for the type of performance or text they are producing: words such as to *recount, describe and inform, instruct, explain, persuade, discuss, predict, hypothesise*).
- use appropriate language for a specific audience – that is, formal language in a presentation, informal language in a conversation: e.g. to classmates: *You swallow the food and the stomach breaks it down*; in a presentation: *When you swallow, food is digested in the stomach* (biology).

- use linking words appropriately to show how ideas are connected (e.g. to explain the causes of erosion using linking words such as *firstly*, *secondly*, *lastly* (geography)).
- use spoken and written language appropriately: spoken: *there was a lot less water in this one than the other*; written: *the sandy soil sample retained much less water than the clay soil sample* (biology).

2.2 Sentence-level challenges

CLIL learners may experience challenges when understanding and using grammatical structures in sentences. For example:

- tenses: *During the 30s the crisis reached its peak. Before that prices had been rising slowly* (economics and business studies).
- word order: *Small cumulus clouds usually have just a light grey shading underneath* (geography).
- question forms: *Where did the term 'holocaust' originate?* (history).
- reporting structures: *By the end of the eighteenth century, most scientists agreed with Darwin that evolution occurred* (science).
- verb patterns: *Rembrandt was admitted to a guild. His maid admitted having an affair with him* (art).
- phrases and clauses: *An entirely new theme emerges in the second movement. As the band warms up, the lighting technicians run through the changes* (music).
- comparisons: *Angle A is smaller than angle B* (maths).
- pronouns: *Different cells have different structures. These reflect their function* (science).
- linking clauses (*First calculate the mean and then the median* (maths)).
- linking sentences: *When you hit the ball, aim high* (PE).

2.3 Word-level challenges

CLIL learners can experience difficulties with the meanings or form of words. They may find it a challenge to understand

- and process a lot of new vocabulary at one time.
- subject-specific, non-standard, archaic or technical vocabulary.
- everyday words with specialised meanings: *cell* (biology); *pitch* (music); *table* (maths); *energy* (physics); *depression* (history/georgraphy); *composition* (art, design and technology); *interest* (economics or business studies); *power* (science).
- words which have different meanings in different subjects: *primary figure* (maths/ history); *solution* (science/maths); *triangle* (music/maths); *cell* (biology/history/ICT); *table* (art, design and technology / chemistry); *interest* (drama/economics); *depression* (geography/ history).
- the difference between terms with similar meanings: *add, combine, sum, and, plus* (maths).
- the use of figurative language – symbols, metaphors and similes: *The Golden Gate Bridge swayed like a deck of cards about to fall over* (geography).

- how linking words (connectives) show the relationships between ideas in speaking and writing: *If T is 567, then what is V?*; *If and only if x is 3.6, then what is y?* (maths).
- the meaning of Greek and Latin-based words: *photosynthesis* (science).
- compound phrases which represent new concepts: *highest common denominator* (maths).
- acronyms: *WYSIWYG* – what you see is what you get (ICT).
- the meaning of common prefixes (*un-, in-, im-*) and suffixes (*-ion, -ment*).

They may also find it a challenge to:

- spell and pronounce Greek and Latin-based words, subject-specific, archaic or technical vocabulary.
- recognise and use words belonging to the same word family: *soluble, solution, solve, dissolve* (chemistry).
- put symbols into words: *a x b* can be said in three different ways: (1) *a times b*, (2) *the product of a and b*, (3) *multiply a and b*; *sixty-four* or *four and sixty* instead of *forty-six* (46); 0.3 is *nought point three recurring* (maths).
- connect the pronunciation of words with their written versions because of inconsistent spelling: *throw, straight, knee, kneel, thumb* (PE).
- move from everyday to academic language: *magnets with the same polls push away* vs. *repel each other* (physics).

3. Cultural challenges

Learners may also face specific challenges related to the differences in their cultural background and the cultures where a second language is used. If teachers use materials designed for native speakers, CLIL learners may find their ability to understand is affected for a number of different reasons. They may find it a challenge to:

- understand culturally specific references: *'guys' are placed on the top of bonfires and set alight on 5 November* (history); *This houseboat feels like the tardis – does it travel through time, too?* (music or drama).
- understand issues from different cultural perspectives: e.g. the use of child labour in developing countries (geography); interpretations of events in a war in books from 'enemy' countries (history).
- interpret the use of visual, historical or cultural images: the use of the colours orange and green in Ireland and Scotland (history).

CLIL in subject teaching

In the next section, we give more information and teaching tips for CLIL related to the nine subject areas focused on in this book: art, design and technology; economics and business studies; geography; history; information and communication technology (ICT); maths; music and drama; physical education (PE); and science (biology, physics and chemistry). Of course, other CLIL subjects are also taught in another language. We recommend that teachers of other subjects take a look at the subjects we have included. For example, teachers of subjects such as citizenship, philosophy, religious education or sociology will find the history and geography pages of particular interest, in combination with music and drama. Domestic science teachers will find art and technology helpful, in combination with science.

How to use the subject pages

The subject pages offer some clear examples of how subject teachers can think about the language of their subject. They offer a condensed overview of the language of each subject, but do not claim to be fully comprehensive. Teachers can use the subject pages in several ways:

- as a reference tool: teachers can use them to learn about the language of their own and their colleagues' subjects
- as a resource for the development of language in the teacher's subject, for example as an aid in identifying language aims for their lessons
- as a basis for discussion and cooperation in planning joint work
- as a source of ideas on cooperating across language and subject lessons. For example, if a science teacher is working on a poster related to classification of animals, the English teacher can identify vocabulary and grammar items which will support the learners in the task. The English teacher could work on adjectives to describe animals in the same week. Or if a history teacher is working on the concept of causes and effects of an historical event, the English teacher can plan work on the language of cause and effect and help the learners better formulate and organise their writing about cause and effect. So, the subject pages can be useful to plan support, progression and learning in both content and English over a few weeks or a term.

Features of the subject pages

Each set of subject pages contains the following similar practical information:

1. *The language of the subject.* We firstly describe how language in that subject is typically used. Secondly, we suggest examples of input (spoken, written and visual information) in that subject. Thirdly, we list some important features of spoken, written and visual information for the subject, illustrated with examples of the type of language involved.
2. *Sample text and comments for the subject.* In this section, teachers can find an annotated page from a coursebook or a webpage related to their subject. Each of these pages illustrates and contextualises some of the main typical language features of the subject.
3. *Sample language and content aims for the subject.* The third section provides some examples of aims for speaking, writing, grammar and vocabulary in each subject. These aims are linked concretely to the Common European Framework of Reference for languages – also known as the CEFR. A copy of the CEFR can be found in the Appendix at the end of the book. For each

suggested speaking and writing aim, we indicate the level at which a learner needs to be on the CEFR in order to achieve that aim.

We provide just one example of an aim per level, but of course it is possible to have many different aims. The examples are there to help teachers to formulate aims that are relevant and useful to their own learners, in whichever form best suits their context.

Art, design and technology

1. The language of art, design and technology

Art, design and technology use language to describe, explain and evaluate objects and techniques from learners' own, as well as from different, cultures. In the art, design and technology classroom, learners develop their knowledge and understanding through visual, tactile and cognitive experiences. These are subjects where learners can work on developing creative and abstract language and the complex language of emotion and expression. Input for art, design and technology lessons is mostly hands-on and informal. This practical work can be an effective catalyst for language work, but the fact that most work is done with materials rather than language means that CLIL art, design and technology teachers need to create opportunities for language work such as developing learners' social talk, and language for thinking skills such as questioning, hypothesising, evaluating, as well as developing their language for thinking about complex issues. Art, design and technology can provide opportunities for the development of written language, too: labelling, describing or evaluating existing objects and techniques as well as learners' own products. As they develop their knowledge and understanding of art, design and technology, CLIL learners can be taught how to think, talk and write like artists, designers and technology specialists.

Examples of input (spoken, written and visual information) in art, design and technology include the following:

- teacher explanations, instructions and demonstrations about objects
- written texts: (auto)biographies, informative websites, commentaries, reviews, letters, reference books
- video or audio input about artists or techniques
- objects and models that learners evaluate or produce (a chair, a painting, a sculpture)
- visuals: paintings, photographs, models, sculptures.

The language of art, design and technology uses a variety of language functions, genres and text-types. For example:

- It recounts – i.e. retells events in chronological order in biographies and descriptions of artistic or design movements: it uses past tenses (*By the time Van Gogh was 30 he had refined his technique*), time clauses (*After moving to France, he worked on creating texture*), phrases to place an event in time (*in 1894*), words for periods of time (*in the 50s*), organising words for time (*eventually*).

- It describes and informs – i.e. describes works of art, design and technology: it uses the simple present (*The* Mona Lisa *shows a woman smiling*), numbering words (*Mondriaan makes use of three colours*), words explaining function (*The bricks form a solid foundation*), the passive voice (*is made of*), comparatives and superlatives (*The colours are brighter in the first painting*), linking words (*in addition*), prepositions (*in the corner*), adjectives to describe line, shape, form, colour, texture, space, light (*wavy, round, red, rough, empty, bright*).

- It instructs – for example, how to use subject materials and techniques: it uses imperatives (*Hold the nail still with one hand*), infinitives (*To cut metal, use a junior hacksaw*), modal verbs for requirements (*you must use a sharp blade*), adjectives (*large, flat, sharp, deep*) and adverbs (*carefully*), question forms in all tenses to check understanding of instructions (*What do you do next?*), questions by learners to clarify understanding (*Do I have to use a hacksaw?*), linking words to number steps (*first, then, finally*).

- It explains – for example, how or why objects and artistic design or technological processes work: it uses present tenses and verbs to show cause (*The clean lines are produced by a sharp cutting blade*) and effect (*Plastic feels warm to the touch*) and causal linking words (*so, therefore*), the passive (*Metal is joined using a soldering iron*), time phrases (*As the watercolour paint dries, it stops spreading*), linking words for processes (*to begin with*), numbering words (*A number of factors influence the choice of materials*).

- It persuades – i.e. attempts to convince someone of a point of view about an object or movement: it uses linking words to support ideas (*This sculpture is more effective because …*), describes mood and emotion with reflexive verbs (*it makes me feel*), uses judgement words (*valuable, appalling*).

- It discusses – i.e. presents reasoned arguments about objects and movements: it evaluates, argues and gives opinions (*This design appeals to teenagers because of the cool, bright colours*); uses conditionals (*If we use this technique, it will improve the end result*), linking words to show logical relationships – contrast (*conversely*), reinforcement (*in addition*), effect (*therefore*), opinion phrases (*in my opinion*), verbs to show value judgements (*would rather*), linking verbs for conclusions or recommendations (*to summarise*).

- It uses symbols, metaphors and similes (*In* The Last Judgement *by Michelangelo, Saint Bartholomew's knife represents his martyrdom*) and culturally specific references (*the meaning and use of the colour red in Chinese art*).

- It uses archaic language in primary sources (Leonardo da Vinci: '*That figure is most praiseworthy which, by its action, best expresses the passions of the soul.*'), specialist nouns for tools and techniques (*flatwash*), Latin and Greek-based words (*geometrical*), everyday words in specialist ways (*grain, mould, tension, bias*).

2. Sample text and comments for art, design and technology

The main purpose of this text is to describe the characteristics of softwoods. The text also explains how trees grow and how wood is produced.

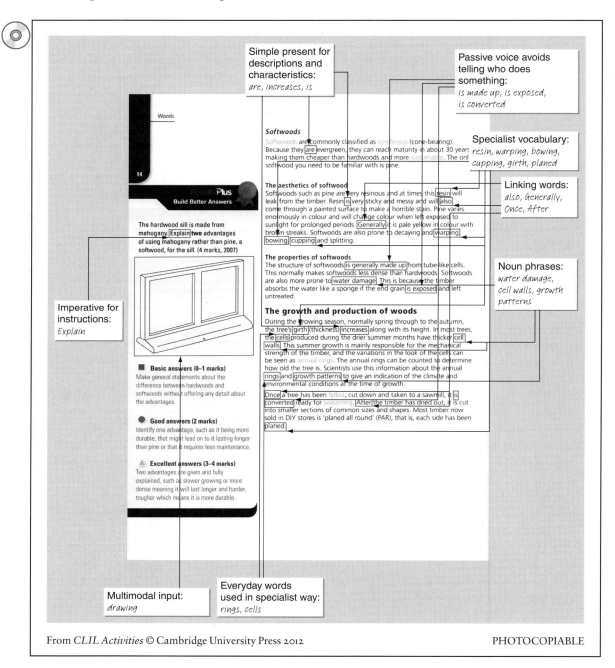

Simple present for descriptions and characteristics:
are, increases, is

Passive voice avoids telling who does something:
is made up, is exposed, is converted

Specialist vocabulary:
resin, warping, bowing, cupping, girth, planed

Linking words:
also, Generally, Once, After

Noun phrases:
water damage, cell walls, growth patterns

Imperative for instructions:
Explain

Multimodal input:
drawing

Everyday words used in specialist way:
rings, cells

Woods

14

Result**Plus**
Build Better Answers

The hardwood sill is made from mahogany. Explain two advantages of using mahogany rather than pine, a softwood, for the sill. (4 marks, 2007)

Basic answers (0–1 marks)
Make general statements about the difference between hardwoods and softwoods without offering any detail about the advantages.

Good answers (2 marks)
Identify one advantage, such as it being more durable, that might lead on to it lasting longer than pine or that it requires less maintenance.

Excellent answers (3–4 marks)
Two advantages are given and fully explained, such as slower growing or more dense meaning it will last longer and harder, tougher which means it is more durable.

Softwoods
Softwoods are commonly classified as coniferous (cone-bearing). Because they are evergreen, they can reach maturity in about 30 years, making them cheaper than hardwoods and more sustainable. The only softwood you need to be familiar with is pine.

The aesthetics of softwood
Softwoods such as pine are very resinous and at times this resin will leak from the timber. Resin is very sticky and messy and will also come through a painted surface to make a horrible stain. Pine varies enormously in colour and will change colour when left exposed to sunlight for prolonged periods. Generally it is pale yellow in colour with brown streaks. Softwoods are also prone to decaying and warping, bowing, cupping and splitting.

The properties of softwoods
The structure of softwoods is generally made up from tube-like cells. This normally makes softwoods less dense than hardwoods. Softwoods are also more prone to water damage. This is because the timber absorbs the water like a sponge if the end grain is exposed and left untreated.

The growth and production of woods
During the growing season, normally spring through to the autumn, the tree's girth (thickness) increases along with its height. In most trees, the cells produced during the drier summer months have thicker cell walls. This summer growth is mainly responsible for the mechanical strength of the timber, and the variations in the look of the cells can be seen as annual rings. The annual rings can be counted to determine how old the tree is. Scientists use this information about the annual rings and growth patterns to give an indication of the climate and environmental conditions at the time of growth.

Once a tree has been felled, cut down and taken to a sawmill, it is converted ready for seasoning. After the timber has dried out, it is cut into smaller sections of common sizes and shapes. Most timber now sold in DIY stores is 'planed all round' (PAR), that is, each side has been planed.

3. Sample language and content aims for art, design and technology

Speaking

Learners' CEFR level	Sample aim
A1	Learners can name the tools used in the art, design or technology classroom in a class quiz on materials.
A2	Learners can give a brief description of an artwork or design for an audio tour in a museum.
B1	Learners can explain their choice of materials to an art critic at an exhibition or to a client who has commissioned a design.
B2	Learners can make a video clip for a TV programme for teenagers in which they compare and contrast two works by an artist or designer.

Writing

Learners' CEFR level	Sample aim
A1	Learners can design a poster for an exhibition at school.
A2	Learners can write labels for an artwork or design for an exhibition.
B1	Learners can write a description of an art, design or technology exhibition for a webpage.
B2	Learners can write a review of an exhibition in a museum for the school newspaper.

Grammar

Learners understand how comparatives are used in a text comparing two paintings.
Learners know how to form comparatives using *-er than* (*brighter than, cooler than, redder than*).
Learners can use superlatives accurately (*most impressive, brightest*) in a written review of an artwork.

Vocabulary

Learners can recognise words used to describe materials (*wood, metal, watercolour, oil*).
Learners can use specialised words when they describe art and design techniques (*flatwash, pigment, brushstroke*).

Economics and business studies

1. The language of economics and business studies

Economics uses language to describe, explain and analyse the production, distribution and consumption of goods and services. Business studies combines the language of accountancy, economics, finance, marketing and organisational behaviour. Both economics and business studies offer CLIL teachers the opportunity to provide a variety of input: texts, but also up-to-date media coverage of recent economic events in modern-day language, along with visuals such as graphs and charts and written texts in textbooks. Through learning about economics and business, learners develop language for thinking skills such as reasoning, questioning, hypothesising and evaluating. As the language and subject matter become more challenging through the years, learners can learn to speak and write about the complex processes of financial and business markets. As they develop their understanding, CLIL learners can be taught how to think, talk and write like economists and business specialists.

Examples of input (spoken, written and visual) in economics and business studies include the following:

- teacher explanations, instructions and demonstrations about economics and business matters
- written texts: online finance games, newspaper articles, financial websites, business reports, marketing plans
- video or audio input: online games, TV programmes about business, podcast of a radio item on business
- performances: online presentation by an economist
- visuals: graphs, diagrams, statistics in charts, photographs.

The language of economics and business studies uses a variety of language functions, genres and text-types. For example:

- It recounts – i.e. retells events in chronological order in news articles and annual reports: it uses past and present perfect tenses to describe past events (*The market figures dropped*), factual, technical and informative language, often without a personal storyline, the passive voice (*businesses were affected by*), organising words for time (*after that*) and dates (*in 1983*).

- It describes and informs – i.e. describes current trends and characteristics of a product or economic phenomena: it uses present tenses to describe current information that is accurate, clear and concise (*Shares are rising rapidly*); compares and contrasts, for instance, products and services, two different currencies, economic growth in different parts of the world (*The more production there is, the more output a business produces*).
- It explains – for example, how or why business services or economic processes work: it uses present tenses to explain flowcharts, linking words to order (*then*) and show effect (*therefore*); uses the language of cause and effect, determining verbs (*The Great Depression in the US resulted in these changes*), passive structures (*The fall in the NASDAQ was caused by the change in share prices*), numbering words (*a number of factors influencing why production falls*).
- It persuades – i.e. attempts to convince someone of a point of view about an issue related to economics and business: it uses value-laden adjectives (*catastrophic situation*), emotive words (*vitality*), the infinitive (*to increase market share, the company needs to*), figures and calculations to support arguments (*95% of the population has a mobile phone*), the third person (*market research shows*), questions to draw in the audience (*How can we …?*).
- It discusses – i.e. presents reasoned argument from different points of view: it uses impersonal language, the third person (*opponents of fair trade disagree, they claim*), tentative verbs (*imply*), abstract nouns (*the exploitation of developing markets*), conditionals (*if these figures are correct, it could be argued that*), linking words to show logical relationships – contrast (*on the other hand*), reinforcement (*furthermore*) and effect (*therefore*).
- It predicts and hypothesises: it uses future tenses to forecast (*Sales will / are going to increase*), modals (*could*), the passive (*markets are expected to*), conditionals (*if … then*) and recommendation (*the company needs to*); it uses modals, verbs and adverbs to show tentativeness or inconclusiveness (*These factors might well bring about a fall in sales*).
- It uses figures with few or no words (spreadsheets).
- It uses vocabulary related to trends (*fluctuated*).
- It uses specialist vocabulary and phrases used only in economics and business (*franchise, deregulation, supply and demand, cash, loan, assets, liability, mortgage, transaction, credit, debit*) and everyday words in specialist ways (*party, interest, raw, value, free, market, fire*).
- It uses compound nouns (*exchange rate, hedge fund, sales forecast*) and nouns made from verbs or adjectives (*analysis – analyse, conversion – convert*).

2. Sample text and comments for economics and business studies

The main purpose of this text is to explain how labour markets work.

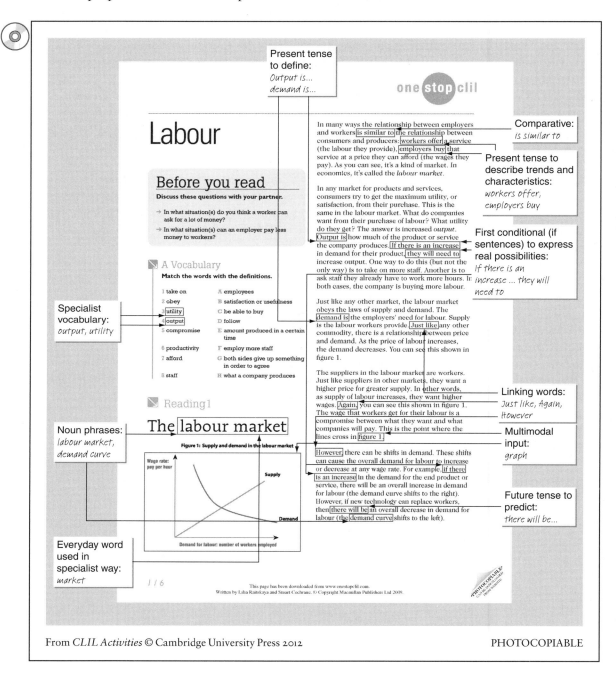

Present tense to define:
Output is...
demand is...

Comparative:
is similar to

Present tense to describe trends and characteristics:
workers offer,
employers buy

First conditional (if sentences) to express real possibilities:
If there is an increase ... they will need to

Specialist vocabulary:
output, utility

Noun phrases:
labour market,
demand curve

Linking words:
Just like, Again, However

Multimodal input:
graph

Future tense to predict:
there will be...

Everyday word used in specialist way:
market

Labour

Before you read

Discuss these questions with your partner.

→ In what situation(s) do you think a worker can ask for a lot of money?

→ In what situation(s) can an employer pay less money to workers?

A Vocabulary

Match the words with the definitions.

1 take on	A employees
2 obey	B satisfaction or usefulness
3 utility	C be able to buy
4 output	D follow
5 compromise	E amount produced in a certain time
6 productivity	F employ more staff
7 afford	G both sides give up something in order to agree
8 staff	H what a company produces

Reading 1

The labour market

In many ways the relationship between employers and workers is similar to the relationship between consumers and producers: workers offer a service (the labour they provide), employers buy that service at a price they can afford (the wages they pay). As you can see, it's a kind of market. In economics, it's called the *labour market*.

In any market for products and services, consumers try to get the maximum utility, or satisfaction, from their purchase. This is the same in the labour market. What do companies want from their purchase of labour? What utility do they get? The answer is increased *output*. Output is how much of the product or service the company produces. If there is an increase in demand for their product, they will need to increase output. One way to do this (but not the only way) is to take on more staff. Another is to ask staff they already have to work more hours. In both cases, the company is buying more labour.

Just like any other market, the labour market obeys the laws of supply and demand. The demand is the employers' need for labour. Supply is the labour workers provide. Just like any other commodity, there is a relationship between price and demand. As the price of labour increases, the demand decreases. You can see this shown in figure 1.

The suppliers in the labour market are workers. Just like suppliers in other markets, they want a higher price for greater supply. In other words, as supply of labour increases, they want higher wages. Again, you can see this shown in figure 1. The wage that workers get for their labour is a compromise between what they want and what companies will pay. This is the point where the lines cross in figure 1.

However, there can be shifts in demand. These shifts can cause the overall demand for labour to increase or decrease at any wage rate. For example, if there is an increase in the demand for the end product or service, there will be an overall increase in demand for labour (the demand curve shifts to the right). However, if new technology can replace workers, then there will be an overall decrease in demand for labour (the demand curve shifts to the left).

Figure 1: Supply and demand in the labour market

Wage rate: pay per hour

Supply

Demand

Demand for labour: number of workers employed

116

3. Sample language and content aims for economics and business studies

Speaking

Learners' CEFR level	Sample aim
A1	Learners can name six key types of industry illustrated in pictures.
A2	Learners can explain three ways a local company competes for customers in a one-minute presentation.
B1	Learners can argue for or against a minimum wage for 16-year-olds in a five-minute video clip.
B2	Learners can present a business plan to three potential investors, asking for an investment in their company.

Writing

Learners' CEFR level	Sample aim
A1	Learners can label a poster showing different types of economic resources.
A2	Learners can describe the key features of a simple graph showing company profits for an annual report.
B1	Learners can provide advice for teenagers in a brochure on how to negotiate a rise in pocket money with their parents.
B2	Learners can produce a report on the costs of a school trip, explaining why the budget should be increased in the following year.

Grammar

Learners understand the use of the present continuous to emphasise trends on a webpage about the share market.

Learners know how to form the present continuous using *to be + -ing* (*the interest rate is rising rapidly*).

Learners can use the past simple and present perfect tenses in a report on company profits.

Vocabulary

Learners can understand the meaning of the following words: *wages, salary, labour costs, supply of labour, demand for labour*.

Learners can use specialised words when they describe a graph (*increase, decrease, peak, trough*).

Learners can distinguish words with specialised meanings in economics and business studies (*scale, production, demand*).

Learners can give the verb and noun word forms for these words (*analyse, convert, inflate, fail, save*).

Geography

1. The language of geography

Geography uses language to explain, study and analyse the earth. Physical geography is concerned with landscapes; human geography looks at who lives on our planet and how we interact with it. Input for geography is often multimodal: it includes photographs and videos, diagrams such as graphs and tables and field trips. In geography, learners need to be able to understand information and subject-specific vocabulary from these sources, as well as to organise information in order to speak and write. Geography offers good opportunities to work on many aspects of language, and on language for thinking skills, in particular. As they develop knowledge and understanding of the subject, CLIL learners can be taught how to think, talk and write like geographers.

Examples of input (spoken, visual and written information) in geography include the following:

- teacher explanations, instructions and demonstrations about physical or human geography
- written texts: facts, figures, numbers; websites showing how geographical features develop, books providing facts about the natural world
- video or audio input: a podcast about global warming, a documentary about a natural event
- objects and models: rocks, plastic relief models, weather instruments and meters
- hands-on work: measuring temperatures or rainfall
- visuals: atlases, maps with keys, tables, charts, diagrams, ground and aerial photographs.

The language of geography uses a variety of language functions, genres and text-types. For example:

- It recounts – i.e. retells events in chronological order: it uses past and present perfect tenses (*how a town has developed*), the passive voice (*rivers were formed*), phrases to place an event in time (*in the Jurassic period*), words for periods of time (*for three years*), organising words for time (*first*).
- It describes and informs – i.e. describes geographical places, including physical and human features: it uses the present tense for characteristics (*Deserts are dry*), prepositions to describe location (*on the steppe*), specialised language to describe location (*latitude and longitude*), adjectives (*cool*), comparatives and superlatives (*The more population growth there is, the more*

food we need), linking words for comparison (*similarly*), adverbs of frequency (*usually*), facts, figures and numbers (*About 2.6 billion people have only about £1 to live on a day*).

- It explains – for example, how or why processes work: it uses present tenses (*the plates move apart*), time phrases (*as the vapour cools, it condenses*), causal linking words and phrases about the results, effects or consequences of events (*Consequently, villages become depopulated*), causal nouns (*result*), verbs to show effect (*resulted in*), numbering words (*number of influences*), linking words for processes (*first of all*).

- It persuades – i.e. attempts to convince someone of a point of view about a geographical issue: it uses linking words to support ideas (*therefore*) or build an argument (*in addition*), judgement words (*appalling*), figures and data to support arguments (*The average temperature has risen by 1%*), numbering words (*There are three main reasons why the dam should be built*).

- It discusses – i.e. presents reasoned argument from different points of view: it uses impersonal language in the third person (*others argue*), tentative verbs (*suggest*), abstract nouns (*deforestation*), conditionals (*If the ice cap melts, the sea level will rise*), linking words to show logical relationships – contrast (*alternatively*), reinforcement (*in addition*) and effect (*therefore*), opinion verbs (*I prefer*), verbs to show value judgements (*would rather*), linking words for conclusions or recommendations (*finally*).

- It predicts and hypothesises: it uses future tenses to forecast (*The population will certainly rise*) or modals to predict (*This ecosystem may disappear*), conditionals (*If the ice cap melts, global temperatures will rise*), modals to recommend (*Future policy should take these factors into account*).

- It uses specialist low-frequency words (*abrasion*) and everyday words in specialist ways (*depression*).

CLIL Activities

2. Sample text and comments for geography

The main purpose of this text is to describe the characteristics of the ecosystem in the Amazon rainforest.

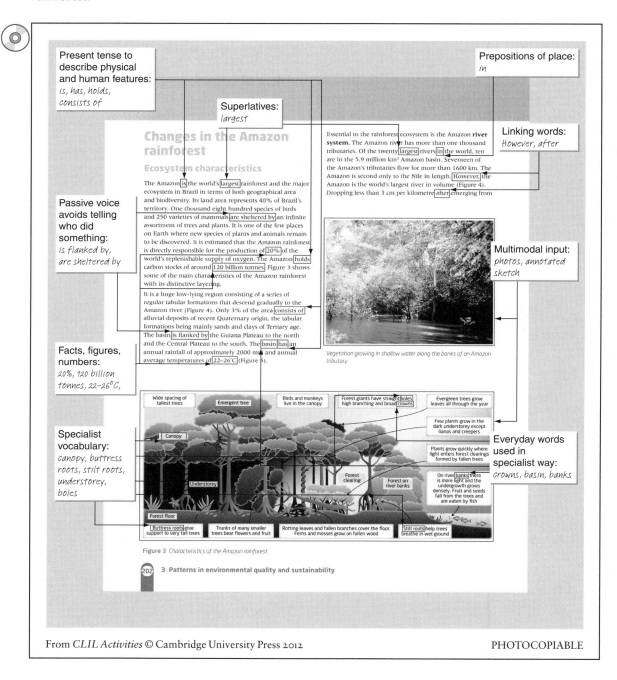

Present tense to describe physical and human features:
is, has, holds, consists of

Superlatives:
largest

Prepositions of place:
in

Linking words:
However, after

Passive voice avoids telling who did something:
is flanked by, are sheltered by

Multimodal input:
photos, annotated sketch

Facts, figures, numbers:
20%, 120 billion tonnes, 22–26°C,

Specialist vocabulary:
canopy, buttress roots, stilt roots, understorey, boles

Everyday words used in specialist way:
crowns, basin, banks

Changes in the Amazon rainforest

Ecosystem characteristics

The Amazon is the world's largest rainforest and the major ecosystem in Brazil in terms of both geographical area and biodiversity. Its land area represents 40% of Brazil's territory. One thousand eight hundred species of birds and 250 varieties of mammals are sheltered by an infinite assortment of trees and plants. It is one of the few places on Earth where new species of plants and animals remain to be discovered. It is estimated that the Amazon rainforest is directly responsible for the production of 20% of the world's replenishable supply of oxygen. The Amazon holds carbon stocks of around 120 billion tonnes. Figure 3 shows some of the main characteristics of the Amazon rainforest with its distinctive layering.

It is a huge low-lying region consisting of a series of regular tabular formations that descend gradually to the Amazon river (Figure 4). Only 3% of the area consists of alluvial deposits of recent Quaternary origin, the tabular formations being mainly sands and clays of Tertiary age. The basin is flanked by the Guiana Plateau to the north and the Central Plateau to the south. The basin has an annual rainfall of approximately 2000 mm and annual average temperatures of 22–26°C (Figure 5).

Essential to the rainforest ecosystem is the Amazon **river system**. The Amazon river has more than one thousand tributaries. Of the twenty largest rivers in the world, ten are in the 5.9 million km² Amazon basin. Seventeen of the Amazon's tributaries flow for more than 1600 km. The Amazon is second only to the Nile in length. However, the Amazon is the world's largest river in volume (Figure 4). Dropping less than 3 cm per kilometre after emerging from

Vegetation growing in shallow water along the banks of an Amazon tributary.

Wide spacing of tallest trees

Emergent tree

Birds and monkeys live in the canopy

Forest giants have straight boles, high branching and broad crowns

Evergreen trees grow leaves all through the year

Few plants grow in the dark understorey except lianas and creepers

Canopy

Plants grow quickly where light enters forest clearings formed by fallen trees

Forest clearing

Forest on river banks

On river banks there is more light and the undergrowth grows densely. Fruit and seeds fall from the trees and are eaten by fish

Understorey

Forest floor

Buttress roots give support to very tall trees

Trunks of many smaller trees bear flowers and fruit

Rotting leaves and fallen branches cover the floor. Ferns and mosses grow on fallen wood

Stilt roots help trees breathe in wet ground

Figure 3 *Characteristics of the Amazon rainforest.*

202   3 Patterns in environmental quality and sustainability

3. Sample language and content aims for geography

Speaking

Learners' CEFR level	Sample aim
A1	Learners can use five adjectives to describe the weather in a pair-work class activity.
A2	Learners can explain a poster they have made about a capital city.
B1	Learners can describe the effects of tourism on an inhabitant of a mountain village in a debate about the possibility of building a ski resort in the village.
B2	Learners can present arguments for and against their country accepting or declining migrant workers in a TV discussion programme.

Writing

Learners' CEFR level	Sample aim
A1	Learners can write a postcard home telling some basic facts about a European capital city they have learned about.
A2	Learners can describe an animal which lives in a warm desert in a paragraph on a website for children aged 8.
B1	Learners can write a short article in a local newspaper about the impact of a new hospital complex.
B2	Learners can write an article for a weekly news magazine explaining the human and environmental causes of global warming.

Grammar

Learners understand how conditionals are used to predict events related to global warming.
Learners know how to form the first conditional using *if* + present tense, + *will* (*if sea levels rise, some low-lying islands will disappear*).
Learners can use the third person -s to describe the processes in precipitation.

Vocabulary

Learners can match words relating to symbols on a map (*contour line, church, main road, river, cycle route, coniferous wood, mixed wood, heliport*).
Learners can use specialised words when they talk about plate tectonics (*ring of fire, plate boundary, magma, hot spots, lava, erupt*).
Learners know all the word forms and some common collocations for a word such as *populate*. (nouns: *population, depopulation*; verbs: *to populate, to depopulate*; common collocations: *population growth, population increase, rural population, human population, world population, ethnic population*; prepositions: *populated by*).

History

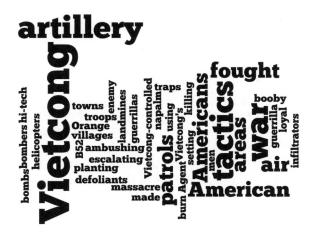

1. The language of history

History uses language to narrate, illustrate, explain and analyse past events. Input for history lessons is often multimodal: it includes paintings, artefacts, field trips to historical sites and museums and historical performances. History lessons – perhaps more than most – also rely heavily on texts, sometimes written in archaic language. History offers good opportunities to work on many aspects of language in combination with other types of input. It involves more than simply narrative: it also requires learners to evaluate primary and secondary sources, look at events from different standpoints and to argue a point of view. As they build up knowledge of the chronology of historical events, CLIL learners experience how historians talk and write about the past and learn themselves how to think, talk and write like historians.

Examples of input (spoken, written and visual information) in history include the following:

- teacher explanations, instructions and demonstrations
- written texts: primary sources – e.g. written accounts of historical events such as letters, diaries, newspaper articles, (auto-)biographies; secondary sources – e.g. reference books
- video or audio input: online games about history, documentaries, podcast of a famous speech
- performances: dramatisations of historical events
- hands-on work: visiting historical places, museums
- visuals: photographs, tapestries, paintings, objects, pictures, maps.

The language of history uses a variety of language functions, genres and text-types. For example:

- It recounts – i.e. retells events from the past in chronological order in autobiographies, biographies, reference books, text books, news articles, primary sources: it uses the past simple and present perfect tenses (*Religion changed under the Tudors*) and past perfect tense (*He told us he had buried three of his parishioners who had died of hunger the day before*), process verbs to show time passing (*ceased*), words and phrases to place an event in time (*in 1931*), words or phrases for periods of time (*when the first world war started*) and organising words for time (*firstly*).

- It describes and informs – i.e. describes characteristics of people, the objects they used and their daily lives in a historical period: it uses the simple past to describe past habits (*They farmed the land using basic tools*), the passive voice (*these events were seen to be*), the language of classification (*Roman villas consisted of*), comparison and contrast using comparatives and superlatives (*This period was much richer than the decade before*), ordering words to link ideas (*nonetheless*).

- It explains – for example, how or why historical events happened: it uses past tenses to explain cause and effect (*led to, caused, resulted in*), determining verbs (*led to*), passive structures (*was caused by*), causal nouns (*factor*), numbering words (*two reasons*), causal linking words (*as a result*).

- It persuades – i.e. attempts to convince someone of a point of view about a historical issue: it uses judgement words (*significant*), linking words to build ideas (*in addition*), numbering words (*There are three main reasons why it was justifiable to use gas in WWI*).

- It discusses – i.e. presents reasoned arguments from different points of view: it evaluates, argues and gives opinions by using, for example, emotionally loaded words (*terrifying*), words which show how much (*very*), words which indicate probabilities (*were likely to*), verbs of opinion (*agree*), linking words to show evaluation (*nevertheless*).

- It uses archaic texts and vocabulary with outdated grammar in primary sources, e.g. subjunctives (*were he alive today, he might say …*) or very long, complex sentences (*We certify to having ourselves seen herds, not of cattle, but of men and women, wandering about the fields between Rheims and Rhétel, turning up the earth like pigs to find a few roots; and as they can only find rotten ones, and not half enough of them, they become so weak that they have not strength left to seek food*).

- It uses specialised terms for particular historical periods (*the Age of Enlightenment*), names of historical objects (*the trenches*), abstract concepts (*democracy*); combines everyday words to create specialised terms (*cold war*); uses everyday words in specialist ways (*depression, capital*) and culturally specific references (*eating tulip bulbs in the Netherlands*).

- It uses nouns to replace verbs (*invasion – invade*).

CLIL Activities

2. Sample text and comments for history

The main purpose of this text is to recount and explain the reasons for pilgrimage to Mecca. It also describes the characteristics of people and the objects they used.

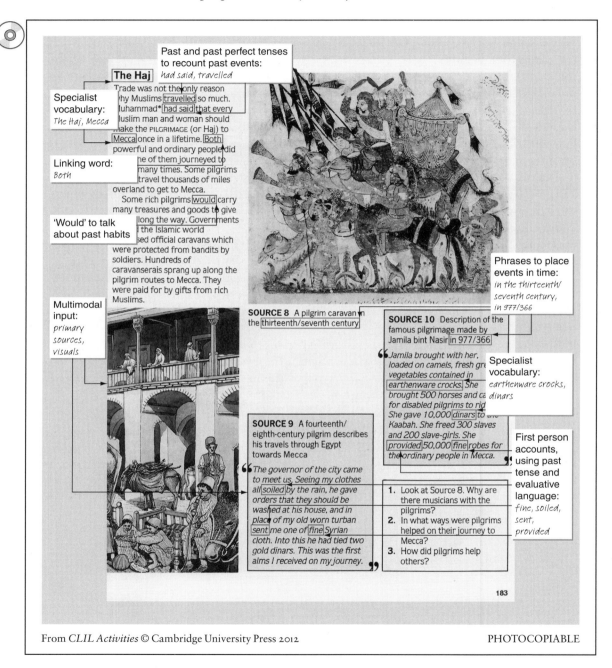

Past and past perfect tenses to recount past events: *had said, travelled*

Specialist vocabulary: *The Haj, Mecca*

Linking word: *Both*

'Would' to talk about past habits

Multimodal input: *primary sources, visuals*

The Haj

Trade was not the only reason why Muslims travelled so much. Muhammad* had said that every Muslim man and woman should make the PILGRIMAGE (or Haj) to Mecca once in a lifetime. Both powerful and ordinary people did – some of them journeyed to many times. Some pilgrims travel thousands of miles overland to get to Mecca.

Some rich pilgrims would carry many treasures and goods to give along the way. Governments in the Islamic world used official caravans which were protected from bandits by soldiers. Hundreds of caravanserais sprang up along the pilgrim routes to Mecca. They were paid for by gifts from rich Muslims.

SOURCE 8 A pilgrim caravan in the thirteenth/seventh century

Phrases to place events in time: *in the thirteenth/ seventh century, in 977/366*

SOURCE 10 Description of the famous pilgrimage made by Jamila bint Nasir in 977/366

Jamila brought with her, loaded on camels, fresh gre vegetables contained in earthenware crocks. She brought 500 horses and ca for disabled pilgrims to rid She gave 10,000 dinars to the Kaabah. She freed 300 slaves and 200 slave-girls. She provided 50,000 fine robes for the ordinary people in Mecca.

Specialist vocabulary: *earthenware crocks, dinars*

SOURCE 9 A fourteenth/ eighth-century pilgrim describes his travels through Egypt towards Mecca

The governor of the city came to meet us. Seeing my clothes all soiled by the rain, he gave orders that they should be washed at his house, and in place of my old worn turban sent me one of fine Syrian cloth. Into this he had tied two gold dinars. This was the first alms I received on my journey.

First person accounts, using past tense and evaluative language: *fine, soiled, sent, provided*

1. Look at Source 8. Why are there musicians with the pilgrims?
2. In what ways were pilgrims helped on their journey to Mecca?
3. How did pilgrims help others?

183

62

3. Sample language and content aims for history

Speaking

Learners' CEFR level	Sample aim
A1	Learners can name the main features of a medieval castle at the start of an audio tour recording.
A2	Learners can explain a poster showing how to defeat a Roman Legion to Asterix and Obelix.
B1	Learners can describe a day in the life of a soldier in a WWI trench in a documentary on the horrors of the trenches.
B2	Learners can present the reasons for and against using gas in WWI to a German general.

Writing

Learners' CEFR level	Sample aim
A1	Learners can label the main events on a timeline leading up to the Russian Revolution for a poster for next year's learners.
A2	Learners can describe the basic living conditions of a Roman soldier in a letter home to his family.
B1	Learners can explain Martin Luther King's contribution to the African-American civil rights movement in an obituary for a newspaper.
B2	Learners can explain the five most important factors in Hitler becoming chancellor in 1933 in an essay for the school magazine.

Grammar

Learners understand how the past perfect tense is used to describe an event in the past before another event (e.g. events leading up to the outbreak of a war).

Learners recognise the difference between regular (*annexed, invaded, influenced*) and irregular past tenses (*told, withdrew, took over*).

Learners can use regular and irregular verbs in the simple past tense when describing a historical figure.

Vocabulary

Learners can recognise words relating to the features of a medieval castle (*ramparts, moat, tower, portcullis*).

Learners can pronounce and spell specialised words correctly when they explain how to defeat a Roman legion (*formation, discipline, flanks, infantry, cavalry*).

Learners can use words which explain causes and effects of the discovery of America appropriately (*as a result of, due to, because, as, so, therefore*).

Information and communication technology (ICT)

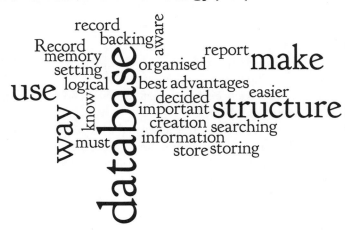

1. The language of ICT

ICT uses language to develop and apply technical computing skills. Learners practise how to find, develop, analyse and present information, and they learn how to model situations, solve problems and evaluate their solutions. There are many opportunities for CLIL ICT teachers to support their learners' understanding of key ICT concepts and skills through the use of physical objects, visuals, demonstrations and hands-on practice. It is these visual elements of the subject that makes ICT a good one for learners who are new to CLIL. However, since ICT lessons may often concentrate on technical skills or involve learners sitting silently behind a computer, the challenge for ICT teachers is to create opportunities for CLIL learners to think for themselves, to speak and to practise communicating in writing. ICT is ideal for cross-curricular work: learners can use the content of their subject lessons to carry out ICT tasks in another language. As they develop ICT knowledge and skills, CLIL learners can be taught how to think, talk and write like ICT specialists.

Examples of input (spoken, written and visual information) in ICT include the following:

- teacher explanations, instructions and demonstrations: digital slide show presentations, demonstrations of software
- written texts: webpages – dense text which says a lot in 'screens', e.g. online tests or explanations, email, social networking sites
- video or audio input: online games, podcasts, radio items on ICT developments
- objects and models: software tools, simulations and models
- hands-on work: working on the computer
- visuals: photographs, graphics, clip art, animations, databases, spreadsheets, graph plotters, charts, diagrams.

The language of ICT uses a variety of language functions, genres and text-types. For example:

- It recounts – i.e. retells events (ICT developments) in chronological order on webpages and in reference books: it uses compact language (text is designed to be read in 'screens'), uses very immediate language in past tenses which is often related to information which goes out of date quickly (*Yesterday's concert was a disaster*), and often uses factual, informative language, rather than flowing, literary or flowery language.

- It describes and informs – i.e. describes computer software and hardware in brief, concrete language with no storyline: it describes characteristics using the present tense (*It has a flat screen and built-in speakers*); uses numbering words (*It has three com ports*), the passive voice (*It has been developed using the latest technology*), linking words (*so*), abbreviations instead of words (*JPEG*), adjectives to show importance (*main*); compares and contrasts products or services (*greater than*).

- It instructs – for example, how to carry out tasks in logical steps (how to install a software programme), how to interact (online tests); it uses imperatives (*Place the cursor over the triangle*), action verbs (*turn on*), question forms in all tenses to check understanding of instructions (*what do you do next?*), linking words to number steps (*finally*).

- It explains – for example, how or why things related to computers work: it uses present tenses to explain cause and effect (*how an image on a website is effective*), verbs to show effect (*resulted in*), linking words to order (*and, so*), to summarise (*therefore*) and to sequence ideas (*firstly, lastly*).

- It persuades – i.e. attempts to convince someone of a point of view about an ICT issue: webpages use bias in text and images to influence, persuade and create emotion in the reader (a pop-up advertisement or poll), linking words to support ideas (*this programme is more effective because*).

- It discusses – i.e. presents reasoned arguments from different points of view: it evaluates, argues, analyses and gives opinions (review of different virus checkers); it might present opinions as facts; it uses linking words for contrasting ideas (*on the one hand … on the other*), verbs of opinion (*it seems*), linking words for conclusions (*to conclude*).

- It predicts and hypothesises: it uses conditionals and modals to discuss and hypothesise, for example conditionals (*if we use this image, then we create the idea that*); it uses data to support a hypothesis, verbs and words to talk tentatively (*I wonder, maybe*) and modal verbs to do the same (*It may be*).

- It uses supporting visuals (logos, banners), music and spoken text (video clips), graphs, spreadsheets in Excel, formulae, data, charts.

- It uses figures with little or no language (spreadsheets) or in combination with language to explain relationships and concepts (a teacher explanation about the peaks and troughs of a graph).

- It can be either very informal (emails) or formal (government website) and distinguishes less than paper text between the two; it is – perhaps more than other sources of input – clearly directed at an audience.

- It includes many technical terms (*hyperlink*) and uses everyday words in specialist ways (*mouse, bold, chat, cell, control, web*).

2. Sample text and comments for ICT

The main purpose of this text is to describe and instruct. It describes word processing software and instructs how to use formatting features.

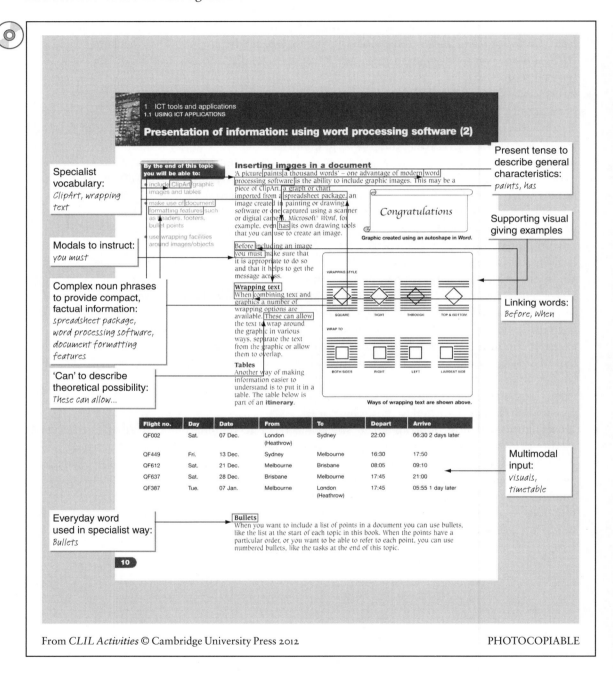

3. Sample language and content aims for ICT

Speaking

Learners' CEFR level	Sample aim
A1	Learners can say the names of computer parts in a game of memory.
A2	Learners can give instructions to a fellow learner on how to use a simple IT facility (insert a picture in a document, create a watermark).
B1	Learners can explain the dangers of displaying personal details on social-networking sites in a presentation for younger learners.
B2	Learners can explain a flowchart of the processes and outcomes of a school drama production.

Writing

Learners' CEFR level	Sample aim
A1	Learners can label a screenshot of a software program.
A2	Learners can write instructions for classmates on how to produce an effective slide presentation.
B1	Learners can write a brochure for school children giving advice on how to use the Internet safely.
B2	Learners can write a report presenting data they have gathered on pupils' preferences for new sports facilities at schools.

Grammar

Learners understand how superlatives are used to describe extreme qualities (*the fastest processor*).

Learners know how to form regular superlatives using the *-est* and irregular superlatives (*the worst*).

Learners can use superlatives in a review of software.

Vocabulary

Learners can recognise words relating to a software program (word processing: *file*, *edit*, *format*, *tools*).

Learners can use specialised words when they give instructions (*insert*, *click*, *add*, *delete*).

Learners can distinguish words with specialist meanings in ICT (*mouse*, *cell*, *control*, *browse*, *chart*, *search*, *column*, *store*).

Learners know all the word forms and most common collocations for a word such as *screen* (noun: *screen*; verb: *to screen*; common collocations: *screenshot*, *blank screen*, *screen capture*, *LCD screen*, *screen background*; prepositions: *on the screen*, *at the top of the screen*, *in the bottom right-hand corner*).

Maths

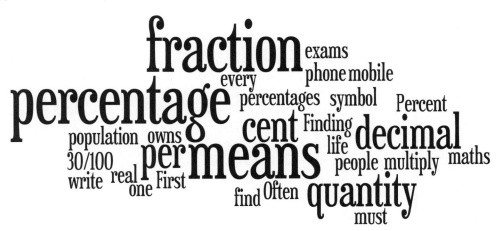

1. The language of maths

Mathematics, or maths, is often described as being a special language in itself. CLIL maths teachers are, therefore, teaching mathematical content as well as the two new 'languages' – that of maths and the target language. The language of maths consists of symbols, visual representations and specialised terminology. There is less textual input in maths than in most other subjects, and learners often spend time during lessons solving maths problems at their desks or listening to teachers explaining mathematical concepts. The challenges for the maths teacher, therefore, are to support learners in understanding mathematical concepts as well as to create opportunities for learners to use both the specific language of maths and the target language. In CLIL maths lessons, teachers can encourage learners to use spoken language to verbalise what they are learning, to talk about solutions to problems, to hypothesise and speculate about possibilities and to justify their answers. A further challenge for CLIL maths teachers is to create opportunities for writing. As they develop mathematical knowledge and understanding, CLIL learners can be taught how to think, talk and write like mathematicians.

Examples of input (spoken, written and visual information) in maths include the following:

- teacher explanations, instructions and demonstrations for solving mathematical problems
- written texts: everyday situations described in terms of mathematical problems (*Francine comes from Belgium and is going to Wales on holiday soon. If the exchange rate is 10 euros to £8.38, how much money would Francine get for the 60 euros she wants to take to Wales?*), mathematical problems, facts, figures, numbers
- video or audio input: interactive games online, a video clip about where we encounter maths in our lives
- objects and models: three-dimensional objects, protractor, compass
- hands-on work: measuring objects in and outside the classroom
- visuals: visual information and symbols (numbers, charts, tables, graphs, formulas (e.g. $C = \pi \cdot d$), photographs).

The language of mathematics uses a variety of language functions, genres and text-types. For example:

- It describes and informs – i.e. describes characteristics: it uses factual, informative, technical language with no storyline; it defines (*In a parallelogram the opposite sides are parallel and equal*), uses numbering words (*a triangle has three sides*), the simple present (*6 plus 4 is*), the passive voice (*x is subtracted from y to produce 13*), comparatives (*more than*) and linking words (*therefore*); it represents information in different kinds of graphs or in symbols instead of words (*0.75%*) and uses prepositions (*into, by*).

- It instructs – for example, how to solve mathematical problems: it uses infinitives and imperatives (*To calculate the surface of a square, multiply the length by the breadth*) and linking words to number steps (*first, then, finally*).

- It explains – for example, how or why a mathematical problem is worked out: it uses present tenses to explain symbols, visuals and data ($C = \Pi \cdot d$ *means to calculate the circumference of a circle, multiply the diameter by pi*), uses linking words to order (*secondly*) and causal linking words (*unless*).

- It predicts and hypothesises: it uses future tenses (*The answer will be less than 4*), conditionals (*if … then*), modals to predict (*will*), modals to recommend (*you should calculate y first*).

- It uses complex sentences or many words to give learners information (*You have just moved into a new house and want to retile the bathroom. It is 5 metres wide and 4 metres deep. The walls are 2.20 metres high and there is a shower area which is 90 cm square.*).

- It shows information with algebraic and graphic representations with few or no words.

- It uses mathematical symbols in different ways in different cultures (e.g. in the UK and the USA, a full stop is used to represent a decimal point – *3.1*, whereas in Europe a comma is used – *3,1*).

- It uses culturally specific symbols (*€20, £20.00, $20*).

- It uses specialist vocabulary used only in mathematics (*vector, quotient, congruent, highest common denominator*), everyday words in a specialised way (*table, round, volume, root, factor, prime, sign, similar, average, mean, plane*), Latin- or Greek-based words (*polygon, hexagon, kilometre*), everyday words used in other ways in different subjects (*solution in science, chord in music*); it combines everyday words to form specialist terms (*square root, set square*) and uses words with similar meanings in different grammatical ways (*subtract, take away, minus, decrease, remove, discount*).

- It forms compound nouns (*highest common factor*).

- It uses compact and concise language, i.e. uses very few words to give learners information (*Calculate how many 400 × 400 mm tiles are needed to tile a bathroom measuring 2,1 m × 4 m × 5 m (h)*).

2. Sample text and comments for maths

The main purpose of this text is to describe and explain. It describes the characteristics of algebraic equations and explains how to solve equations. The problems contain instructions.

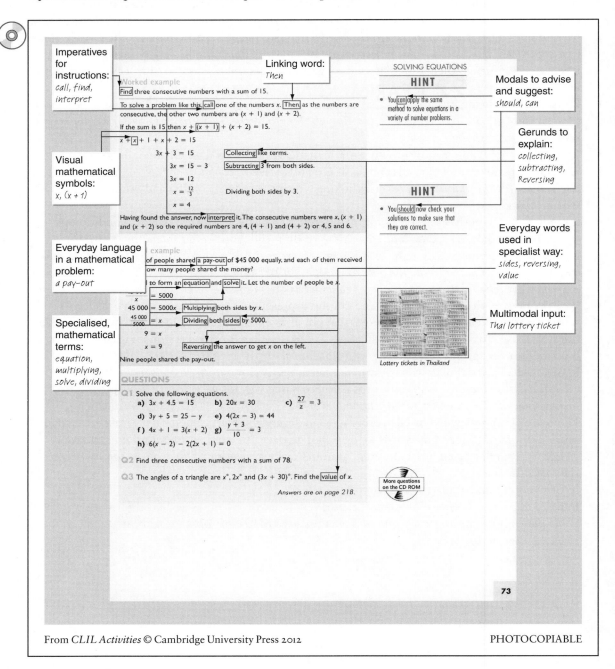

Imperatives for instructions: *call, find, interpret*

Linking word: *Then*

Modals to advise and suggest: *should, can*

Gerunds to explain: *collecting, subtracting, Reversing*

Visual mathematical symbols: $x, (x + 1)$

Everyday language in a mathematical problem: *a pay-out*

Everyday words used in specialist way: *sides, reversing, value*

Specialised, mathematical terms: *equation, multiplying, solve, dividing*

Multimodal input: *Thai lottery ticket*

SOLVING EQUATIONS

Worked example

Find three consecutive numbers with a sum of 15.

To solve a problem like this, call one of the numbers x. Then, as the numbers are consecutive, the other two numbers are $(x + 1)$ and $(x + 2)$.

If the sum is 15 then $x + (x + 1) + (x + 2) = 15$.

$$x + x + 1 + x + 2 = 15$$
$$3x + 3 = 15 \quad \text{Collecting like terms.}$$
$$3x = 15 - 3 \quad \text{Subtracting 3 from both sides.}$$
$$3x = 12$$
$$x = \frac{12}{3} \quad \text{Dividing both sides by 3.}$$
$$x = 4$$

Having found the answer, now interpret it. The consecutive numbers were x, $(x + 1)$ and $(x + 2)$ so the required numbers are 4, $(4 + 1)$ and $(4 + 2)$ or 4, 5 and 6.

HINT
- You can apply the same method to solve equations in a variety of number problems.

HINT
- You should now check your solutions to make sure that they are correct.

Worked example

... of people shared a pay-out of $45 000 equally, and each of them received ... ow many people shared the money?

... to form an equation and solve it. Let the number of people be x.

$$\frac{45\,000}{x} = 5000$$
$$45\,000 = 5000x \quad \text{Multiplying both sides by } x.$$
$$\frac{45\,000}{5000} = x \quad \text{Dividing both sides by 5000.}$$
$$9 = x$$
$$x = 9 \quad \text{Reversing the answer to get } x \text{ on the left.}$$

Nine people shared the pay-out.

Lottery tickets in Thailand

QUESTIONS

Q1 Solve the following equations.

a) $3x + 4.5 = 15$ b) $20x = 30$ c) $\frac{27}{z} = 3$

d) $3y + 5 = 25 - y$ e) $4(2x - 3) = 44$

f) $4x + 1 = 3(x + 2)$ g) $\frac{y + 3}{10} = 3$

h) $6(x - 2) - 2(2x + 1) = 0$

Q2 Find three consecutive numbers with a sum of 78.

Q3 The angles of a triangle are $x°$, $2x°$ and $(3x + 30)°$. Find the value of x.

Answers are on page 218.

More questions on the CD ROM

73

3. Sample language and content aims for maths

Speaking

Learners' CEFR level	Sample aim
A1	Learners can name the two-dimensional mathematical shapes they see in a picture.
A2	Learners can explain how they calculated the surface area of a floor.
B1	Learners can explain a graph they have constructed in a presentation to the class.
B2	Learners can provide a voice-over commentary on a video recording for the class below them of a learner demonstrating how to approach a mathematical problem.

Writing

Learners' CEFR level	Sample aim
A1	Learners can label a graph using the correct terminology.
A2	Learners can write a maths problem about money for peers using everyday language.
B1	Learners can write a paragraph addressed to their school, explaining a pie graph in a report on sales of sweets in the school canteen.
B2	Learners can write a report for a safety committee, including visuals on an investigation into the average distance learners in their year travel to school every day.

Grammar

Learners understand the meaning of modal verbs to express probability (*will*, *may*, *might*, *could*, *should*).

Learners know how to use the present real conditional using *if* + present tense, + present (*if you decrease the value of y, the line on the graph falls*).

Learners can use modals to discuss possible solutions.

Vocabulary

Learners can match these names to shapes: *triangle*, *square*, *rectangle*, *circle*, *polygon*, *ellipse*.

Learners can use these specialist words accurately when they explain their graphs: *y-axis*, *x-axis*, *coordinates*, *row*, *column*, *intersect*.

Learners can distinguish words with similar but distinct meanings (*subtract*, *take away*, *minus*, *decrease*, *remove*, *discount*).

Learners know all the word forms and most common collocations for a word such as *triangle* (noun: *triangle*; verb: *to triangulate*; adjective: *triangular*; common collocations: *right-angled triangle*, *equilateral triangle*; key term: *hypotenuse*).

Music and drama

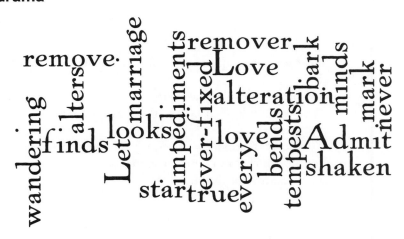

1. The language of music and drama

Music and drama teachers develop learners' ability to use language to understand, evaluate, create and perform their own and others' work. Work in class is frequently practical: watching and listening to performances, singing, playing instruments or acting. Demonstrations and the use of props help learners to follow spoken instructions and explanations: communication is both verbal and non-verbal. Music and drama are good subjects for learners who are new to CLIL, since new language is introduced in a clear context with visual support or physical reinforcement. An extra element of both music and drama is culture: learning about culturally specific musical and dramatic traditions. Both subjects give outstanding opportunities for learners to produce a wide variety of spoken language and to experiment with expressing emotions. CLIL drama teachers can also create plenty of opportunities for learners to read and write a range of texts as well as to develop linguistic creativity. However, CLIL music teachers need to create opportunities for learners to speak and write about as well as to play music. In music, work on reading, speaking and writing needs, therefore, to be consciously planned. As they develop their knowledge and skills in music and drama, CLIL learners can be taught how to think, talk and write like music and drama specialists.

Examples of input (spoken, written and visual information) in music and drama include the following:

- teacher explanations, instructions and demonstrations, such as role plays, playing music for the class, singing
- written texts: texts in magazines, newspapers or on the Internet, in CD in-lay notes, reviews about drama or musical performances, plays, short stories, poetry
- video or audio input: dialogues, plays, films, TV series poetry readings, CDs, songs, pieces of music
- objects and models: props, hats, furniture, musical instruments
- performances: plays, sketches, concerts
- hands-on work: performing music, role play, drama performances
- visuals: photographs of people or famous performances, drawings, musical notation.

The language of music and drama uses a variety of language functions, genres and text-types. For example:

- It recounts – i.e. retells events in chronological order in biographies and descriptions of musical or drama developments, plays, films and concerts: it uses all the past tenses (*Mozart had already been playing the piano for five years when he performed at the age of eight*), phrases to place an event in time (*in 1996*), words for periods of time (*in the 70s*), organising words for time (*next*).
- It describes and informs – i.e. describes characteristics of musical and dramatic works: it uses the simple present (*The base line for the guitar starts with a 4/4 beat*), numbering words (*There are four sections with eight bars*), the passive voice (*is often referred to as*), comparison and contrast (*Compared with an earlier symphony, this one is much more complex*).
- It instructs – for example, how to play an instrument or piece of music, act in a role play: it uses imperatives (*straighten your back*), modal verbs for requirements (*You should whisper*), action verbs (*stand, turn*), adverbs (*strongly*), qualifiers (*That's much better*), comparatives (*Sing as quietly as you can*) and linking words to number steps (*then*).
- It explains – for example, how or why musical and dramatic processes work: it uses present tenses and enabling verbs, verbs to show effect (*The bass creates a dramatic undertone*), linking words (*because, even though*), time phrases (*As the curtains open, the sound of a single drum echoes*), linking words for processes (*in the end*).
- It persuades – i.e. attempts to convince someone of a point of view about a piece: it uses emotive adjectives (*fascinating, thrilling*), linking words to support ideas (*I think the scenery at this point changes because*); numbers examples (*One example of this can be heard in the second movement*); describes mood and emotion with reflexive verbs (*it makes me feel*).
- It discusses – i.e. presents reasoned arguments about works and performances from different points of view: it evaluates, argues and gives opinions (*The lyrics in hip-hop appeal to teenagers because they use street language*); it uses conditionals (*If you lowered your voice, you would sound more manly*), linking words to show logical relationships – contrast (*on the one hand*), reinforcement (*indeed*) and effect (*therefore*), opinion verbs (*in my opinion*), verbs to show value judgements (*prefer*), linking words for conclusions or recommendations (*finally*).
- It includes body language (nodding, eye contact, facial expression).
- It uses different tones and kinds of expression (pace, intonation).
- It uses technical terms (*crotchet, quaver, semibreve, proscenium arch, agitprop*), slang, flowery and ungrammatical language (*I can't get no satisfaction*), Latin- and Greek-based words (*allegro, piano, forte, symphony, saxophone, xylophone*), everyday words in specialist ways (*note, bar, beat, conduct, key, blue*).

2. Sample text and comments for music and drama

The main purpose of this text is to explain what chords are and what they consist of. It also explains how important the rhythm and bass are in a steel band.

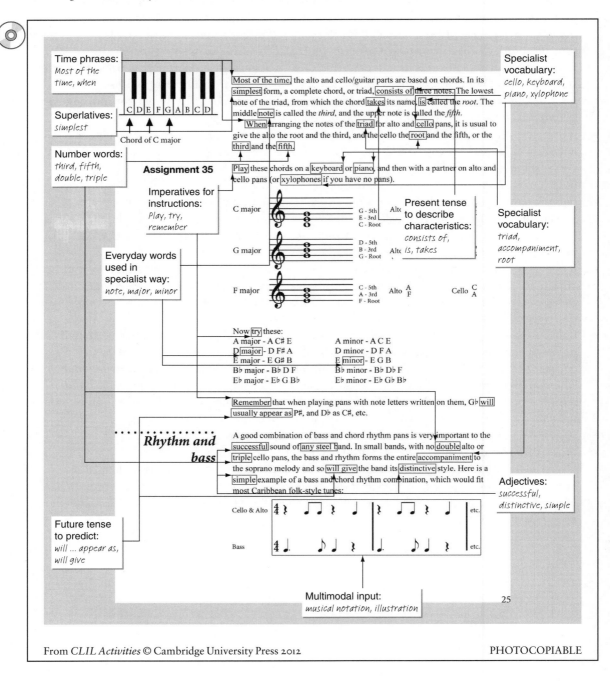

3. Sample language and content aims for music and drama

Speaking

Learners' CEFR level	Sample aim
A1	Learners can name key musical or dramatic techniques in a class game.
A2	Learners can give reasons why they prefer one musical or dramatic piece above another in a class discussion in small groups.
B1	Learners can give a short presentation for a music station or TV programme explaining the key musical or dramatic features of a song or scene.
B2	Learners can compare and contrast dramatic or musical techniques in two pieces in a presentation for the director of a concert or a theatre producer.

Writing

Learners' CEFR level	Sample aim
A1	Learners can label CDs or DVDs with appropriate genre titles.
A2	Learners can write a short description of a piece of music or drama for an advertising leaflet.
B1	Learners can write a review of a concert or performance for a school magazine.
B2	Learners can write an obituary in a newspaper for a musician or performer, critically appraising their contribution to music or drama.

Grammar

Learners understand how the present simple and continuous tenses are used in a spoken commentary on a piece of music (*the drums keep a steady beat, the violins are playing quietly*). Learners can form questions using who, what, where, why in the present and past tense when performing an interview in a role play.
Learners can use comparatives and superlatives when writing a review of two pieces of music.

Vocabulary

Learners know the meaning, pronunciation and spelling of the following words: *percussion, bass drum, bongos, castanets, celeste, cowbell, cymbals, glockenspiel, gong, kettledrum, maracas, marimba, snare drum, timpani, triangle, vibraphone, xylophone.*
Learners can use several of the following words in a music review to describe tone colour: *metallic, jangling, reverberant, vibrant, piercing, hollow, booming, rattling, brittle, rasping, shimmering, tinkling, shattering, silvery.*

Physical education (PE)

1. The language of PE

PE develops learners' ability to participate in and understand the effects of physical activities. Work in a PE class is mainly physical and practical, and done in large spaces, so communication is both verbal and non-verbal. Demonstrations and the presence of objects make it easier for learners to follow spoken instructions and explanations. This makes PE a good subject for learners who are new to CLIL. PE offers good language learning opportunities because new vocabulary and grammar structures are introduced in context, with visual support and physical reinforcement. Misunderstandings can be seen and immediately corrected. Learners practise their listening skills, since they hear how words are pronounced and used in concrete situations. It can, however, be tempting for PE teachers to do much of the talking themselves, which limits the range of language skills learners practise. Work on reading, speaking and writing, therefore, needs to be consciously planned if PE teachers in CLIL classrooms want to support language development in skills other than listening.

Examples of input (spoken, written and visual information) in PE include the following:

- teacher and learner explanations, instructions and demonstrations about gymnastics, ball techniques, a basketball pass
- written texts: texts to demonstrate techniques or rules, magazine or newspaper articles on sport or sports personalities
- video or audio input: videos to demonstrate techniques or rules, video clips of famous sports personalities or examples of a good performance
- objects and models: equipment in the gym, different kinds of balls, hockey stick
- performances: gym demonstrations, sports matches (between schools or of national teams)
- visuals: photographs showing good techniques, drawings, diagrams.

The language of PE uses a variety of language functions, genres and text-types. For example:

- It instructs – for example, how to do sports or exercises: it uses imperatives for commands (*freeze*), time words (*then*), prepositions (*behind, above*), adverbial phrases (*Make sure the head is kept still over the feet, with a slight lean forward*), question forms in all tenses to check understanding of instructions (*Where do you throw the ball?*), questions by learners to clarify understanding (*Do I have to jump now?*), long adverbial phrases (*in a long, smooth upward direction*) and long noun phrases (*heel-to-toe relationship*), action verbs (*skip*) and phrasal verbs (*roll off*), adjectives (*quick, slow*) and adverbs (*fast, strongly*), qualifiers to describe adjectives (*slightly bent*), comparatives (*as high as you can*) and superlatives (*the lowest score*), linking words to number steps (*first*).

- It explains – for example, how or why sports techniques work: it uses linking words for cause and effect (*so the ball goes faster, because you may fall over*), time phrases (*As you lean forward, put your weight on your right leg*), gerunds as nouns (*Shooting is easier if you stand still*), present tenses to describe actions (*He's doing a brilliant somersault*), the passive voice to describe techniques (*when the leg is bent and then extended, this gives the player more power*).

- It predicts and hypothesises: it uses future tenses and conditionals to predict or warn (*You will fall over if you lean forward too much*), conditionals to give advice (*If you lift your arm, you will be able to push further*), modals to advise (*Bending your knees as you land might help you keep your balance*).

- It uses specialist terms for techniques (*jump shot, one-hand shot*) and equipment (*racket, harness, carabiner*), and everyday words in specialist ways (*stick, fit, field, pitch, defend, cue, foul*).

CLIL Activities

2. Sample text and comments for PE

The main purpose of this text is to instruct how to shoot in basketball. The text also explains how shooting techniques work and gives advice.

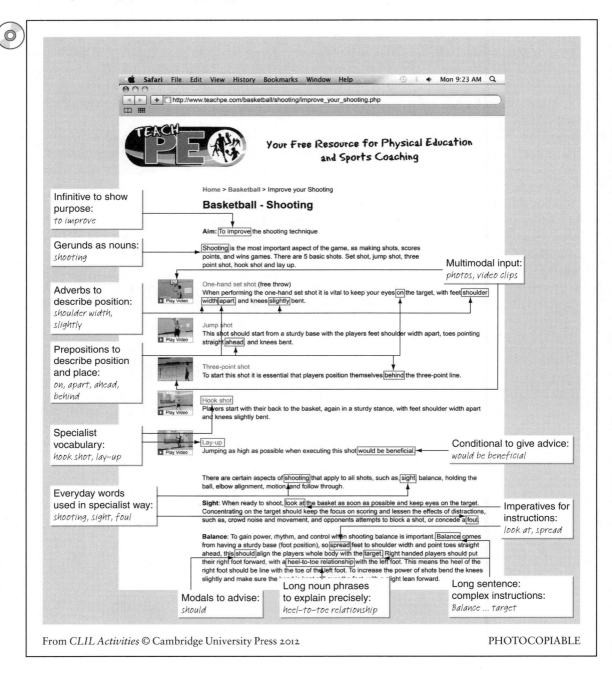

Infinitive to show purpose:
to improve

Gerunds as nouns:
shooting

Adverbs to describe position:
shoulder width, slightly

Prepositions to describe position and place:
on, apart, ahead, behind

Specialist vocabulary:
hook shot, lay-up

Everyday words used in specialist way:
shooting, sight, foul

Multimodal input:
photos, video clips

Conditional to give advice:
would be beneficial

Imperatives for instructions:
look at, spread

Modals to advise:
should

Long noun phrases to explain precisely:
heel-to-toe relationship

Long sentence: complex instructions:
Balance ... target

Safari   File   Edit   View   History   Bookmarks   Window   Help   Mon 9:23 AM   Q

http://www.teachpe.com/basketball/shooting/improve_your_shooting.php

TEACH PE

Your Free Resource for Physical Education and Sports Coaching

Home > Basketball > Improve your Shooting

Basketball - Shooting

Aim: To improve the shooting technique

Shooting is the most important aspect of the game, as making shots, scores points, and wins games. There are 5 basic shots. Set shot, jump shot, three point shot, hook shot and lay up.

Play Video

One-hand set shot (free throw)
When performing the one-hand set shot it is vital to keep your eyes on the target, with feet shoulder width apart, and knees slightly bent.

Play Video

Jump shot
This shot should start from a sturdy base with the players feet shoulder width apart, toes pointing straight ahead, and knees bent.

Play Video

Three-point shot
To start this shot it is essential that players position themselves behind the three-point line.

Play Video

Hook shot
Players start with their back to the basket, again in a sturdy stance, with feet shoulder width apart and knees slightly bent.

Play Video

Lay-up
Jumping as high as possible when executing this shot would be beneficial

There are certain aspects of shooting that apply to all shots, such as, sight balance, holding the ball, elbow alignment, motion and follow through.

Sight: When ready to shoot, look at the basket as soon as possible and keep eyes on the target. Concentrating on the target should keep the focus on scoring and lessen the effects of distractions, such as, crowd noise and movement, and opponents attempts to block a shot, or concede a foul.

Balance: To gain power, rhythm, and control when shooting balance is important. Balance comes from having a sturdy base (foot position), so spread feet to shoulder width and point toes straight ahead, this should align the players whole body with the target. Right handed players should put their right foot forward, with a heel-to-toe relationship with the left foot. This means the heel of the right foot should be line with the toe of the left foot. To increase the power of shots bend the knees slightly and make sure the heel is kept still over the foot, with a slight lean forward.

From *CLIL Activities* © Cambridge University Press 2012   PHOTOCOPIABLE

78

3. Sample language and content aims for PE

Speaking

Learners' CEFR level	Sample aim
A1	Learners can name the equipment and main verbs used in a sport in a class quiz.
A2	Learners can give tips on how to improve a sports technique in a feedback session.
B1	Learners can give a short presentation explaining warm-up techniques for a sport.
B2	Learners can explain the advantages and disadvantages of particular sports for different groups of people in a sports school.

Writing

Learners' CEFR level	Sample aim
A1	Learners can label illustrations of sports on a poster.
A2	Learners can write instructions for a short sports exercise.
B1	Learners can write a brochure encouraging fellow students to join a sports club.
B2	Learners can write a report for their school giving reasons why the budget for sports equipment should be doubled.

Grammar

Learners understand how modals are used to give advice (*could, should, need to*).
Learners know how to form the present continuous using *to be + -ing* (*he's jumping over the mat*).
Learners can explain how to improve a somersault using modal verbs.

Vocabulary

Learners can recognise words relating to the objects used in a PE lesson.
Learners can use specialised words when they give instructions (*shot, net, bounce, defend*).
Learners can distinguish words with similar but distinct meanings(*bat, racket, club, stick*), or terms that they regularly interchange (*skip, jump, hop*).
Learners know all the word forms and most common collocations for a word such as *throw* (noun: *throw, throwing*; verb: *throw, threw, thrown*; common collocations: *throw a ball, a good throw, a short throw, a two-handed throw, throw over arm, throw under arm*; prepositions following *throw*: *throw up, down, away, forward, back, into, in, out*).

Science

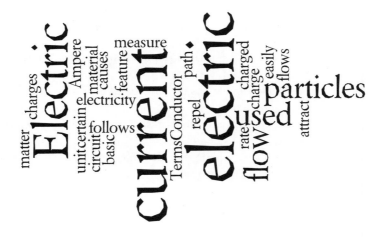

1. The language of science

Science subjects use language to describe, explain and analyse scientific phenomena. Science classes provide a lot of multimodal input and thus support understanding in a variety of ways. By showing learners how to use the visuals accompanying input, teachers can help them to develop strategies for understanding science. Through learning about science, learners develop language for thinking skills, such as reasoning, questioning, creative problem-solving and evaluating. As the language and subject matter become more challenging through the years, learners can become skilled at expressing complex scientific ideas more formally and academically in both speaking and writing. As they develop scientific knowledge and understanding, CLIL learners can be taught how to think, talk and write like scientists.

Examples of input (spoken, written and visual information) in science include the following:

- teacher explanations, instructions and demonstrations related to scientific experiments, processes and concepts
- written texts: scientific articles, laboratory reports, instructions for experiments
- video or audio input: websites on scientific topics, scientific models on the Web (of a heart beating, of a flower opening), online games
- objects and models: animals, plants, scientific equipment, model of atoms and molecules
- hands-on work: experiments, fieldwork and demonstrations, visit to scientific museum
- visuals: pictures, photographs, models, video, diagrams, graphs and charts, the periodic table.

The language of science uses a variety of language functions, genres and text-types. For example:

- It recounts – i.e. retells factual events in chronological order in laboratory reports: it uses past tenses (*the gas evaporated*), organising words for time (*next*), the passive voice (*3 ml of water was poured into the test tube*).
- It describes and informs – i.e. describes scientific phenomena: it uses factual, informative, technical language with no storyline; it explains characteristics (*a carbon molecule consists of*); it uses long, complex sentences with sub-clauses (*So whilst all cells have the same features, such*

as cell membrane, *nucleus and cytoplasm, their appearance can be very different*), numbering words (*it has two chambers*), prepositions (*above*), ordering words (*first, finally*), the language of comparison and contrast (*The greater the amount of light, the more the plant grows*).

- It instructs – for example, how to do experiments: it uses imperatives (*Pour 3 ml of water into the test tube, then add the crystals*), question forms in all tenses to check understanding of instructions (*What do you do next?*), questions by learners to clarify understanding (*Do I have to light it now?*), linking words to number steps (*first, then*).

- It explains – for example, how or why scientific processes work: it uses the present tense to explain cause and effect using time phrases (*As it dissolves, the colour changes*), causal linking words (*because*), determining verbs (*caused it to bubble*), listing words (*thirdly*), verbs to show conclusion (*this shows*).

- It persuades – i.e. attempts to convince someone of a point of view about a scientific issue: it uses numbering words (*There are four main reasons*), data to support arguments (*The survival rate increased by 5%*), the third person (*research shows*), linking words to build an argument (*moreover*).

- It discusses – i.e. presents reasoned arguments on scientific issues from different points of view: it evaluates, argues and gives opinions; uses tentative verbs (*Those in favour of nuclear power claim*), linking words for contrasting ideas (*On the one hand, on the other hand*), linking words for conclusions (*to sum up*).

- It predicts and hypothesises: it uses future tenses (*The water will take longer to boil*), conditionals (*If an object is submerged completely, it displaces its own volume of fluid*), modals to predict (*could*), to emphasise tentativeness (*the flower might grow*) and to recommend (*future studies should*), qualifying words or phrases (*these results might mean*), linking words for effects (*since*).

- It uses figures, symbols or abbreviations with few or no words (e.g. in diagrams, equations).

- It uses abbreviations and symbols derived from Latin (Pb for Lead), Greek (π for pi) or English (He for Helium, f for Force, P for Power).

- It uses many technical terms (*alkali, capacity, molecule*), many Greek- and Latin-based words (*photosynthesis, hydrochloric acid*), everyday words in specialist ways (*table, cell, tissue, action*), words to describe concepts that are difficult to visualise or understand (*power, energy, atom*), similar words with different meanings (*dissolve, solution, solubility, soluble*).

- It uses nouns instead of verbs and adjectives (*motion – moves*), long noun phrases (*water retention rates*) and adjective phrases (*dissolving this acid*).

2. Sample text and comments for science

The main purpose of this text is to describe and explain. It describes the characteristics of animal cells and explains cell processes.

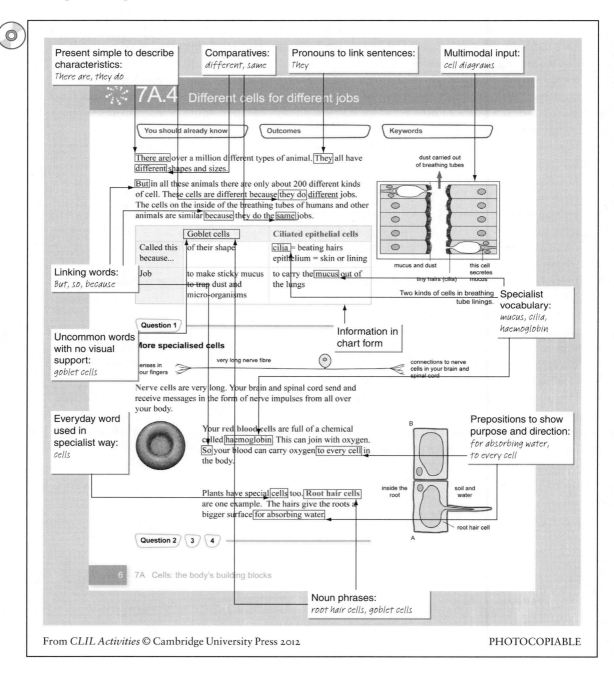

Present simple to describe characteristics:
There are, they do

Comparatives:
different, same

Pronouns to link sentences:
They

Multimodal input:
cell diagrams

7A.4 Different cells for different jobs

You should already know | Outcomes | Keywords

There are over a million different types of animal. They all have different shapes and sizes.

But in all these animals there are only about 200 different kinds of cell. These cells are different because they do different jobs. The cells on the inside of the breathing tubes of humans and other animals are similar because they do the same jobs.

dust carried out of breathing tubes

	Goblet cells	Ciliated epithelial cells
Called this because...	of their shape	cilia = beating hairs epithelium = skin or lining
Job	to make sticky mucus to trap dust and micro-organisms	to carry the mucus out of the lungs

mucus and dust | this cell secretes mucus

tiny hairs (cilia)

Two kinds of cells in breathing tube linings.

Linking words:
But, so, because

Specialist vocabulary:
mucus, cilia, haemoglobin

Question 1

Uncommon words with no visual support:
goblet cells

More specialised cells

...enses in our fingers

very long nerve fibre

connections to nerve cells in your brain and spinal cord

Information in chart form

Nerve cells are very long. Your brain and spinal cord send and receive messages in the form of nerve impulses from all over your body.

Everyday word used in specialist way:
cells

Your red blood cells are full of a chemical called haemoglobin. This can join with oxygen. So your blood can carry oxygen to every cell in the body.

B

Prepositions to show purpose and direction:
for absorbing water, to every cell

inside the root | soil and water

Plants have special cells too. Root hair cells are one example. The hairs give the roots a bigger surface for absorbing water.

root hair cell

Question 2 3 4

A

6 7A Cells: the body's building blocks

Noun phrases:
root hair cells, goblet cells

3. Sample language and content aims for science

Speaking

Learners' CEFR level	Sample aim
A1	Learners can name the parts of a flower in a class quiz.
A2	Learners can give instructions on how to carry out an experiment on surface tension.
B1	Learners can explain the difference between speed and velocity in a short presentation.
B2	Learners can discuss the advantages and disadvantages of nuclear power in a debate.

Writing

Learners' CEFR level	Sample aim
A1	Learners can label a diagram of a simple electric circuit in an instruction booklet.
A2	Learners can write instructions for an experiment on solids, liquids and gases for their classmates.
B1	Learners can provide advice for diabetes patients in an A5 flyer.
B2	Learners can evaluate the arguments for and against the use of fossil fuels in a report for Greenpeace.

Grammar

Learners understand how the passive voice is used in a laboratory report when the actor/agent is not important (*I added salt* vs. *salt was added*).

Learners know how to form the passive in the simple past, using *was/were* + past participle.

Learners can use the passive in a report on a class experiment.

Vocabulary

Learners can recognise words relating to the structure of organisms (*organ, tissue, cell*).

Learners can use specialised words when they recount an experiment on gases (*exert, force, Styrofoam cup, tongs, bubble, suspension, collapse*).

Learners can distinguish words with similar but distinct meanings, (*membrane* and *skin*), or terms that they regularly mix up (*cell wall* and *cell membrane*).

Learners know all the word forms and most common collocations for a word such as *test* (noun: *test*; verb: *test*; common collocations: *test tube, blood test*; preposition following test: *tested for*).

Part 3: Practical activities

1 Activating

1.1 Finish the sentence

Outline	Learners activate prior knowledge by completing sentences.
Thinking skills	Recalling
Language focus	Present tenses, vocabulary
Language skills	Writing
Time	10–15 minutes
Level	A2 and above
Preparation	Think of a key word on an aspect of your topic. It must be a word that you can use as the start of a sentence and be a word which learners actually have ideas about – i.e. nothing too abstract. Write the word as the start of a sentence 10 times on the board or on a worksheet (see Box 1.1).

Procedure

1 Explain to the learners that you want to find out what they already know on the topic you are about to start.
2 Give one handout like the one in Box 1.1 to each learner. They have to complete all 10 sentences quickly. Learners should be encouraged not to give up and to complete all the sentences, adding more if possible. As they think harder, they will come up with more ideas.
3 Pair the learners and ask them to compare their answers and improve their own, in terms of both ideas and language.
4 Elicit some answers from the whole class, picking up on the ideas which link to your content and language aims.

Box 1.1: Finish the sentence

The desert

Write a different ending for each sentence. Two examples are done for you.

1. The desert is dry and hot.
2. The desert sometimes freezes at night.
3. The desert ...
4. The desert ...
5. The desert ...

---

6. The desert …
7. The desert …
8. The desert …
9. The desert …
10. The desert …

Subject examples
Art, design and technology: Chairs …
Economics and business studies: Inflation …
History: Stalin …
ICT: A flowchart …
Maths: Triangles …
PE: Hockey …

Note
Use words which have several meanings as the first word of the sentences. This highlights how words have different meanings in different contexts. For example:

- *Cell*: in everyday language it is a small room, as in a prison; in ICT terms, cells are the small boxes in a spreadsheet in which you enter data or text; in biology a cell is the basic unit of living material.
- *Depression*: in everyday language this is an emotion that people feel when they are sad; in geography it describes the weather; in history and economics, it is a period of economic decline.
- *Table*: in maths or economics a table can be a times table or a chart; in art, design and technology, a table is a piece of furniture; in ICT a table is a function in a word-processing program.

💡 **Tips for cross-curricular cooperation between subject and language teachers**

Before the lesson: The language teacher can brainstorm vocabulary on the topic in advance and remind learners about the present tenses, focusing on the final *s* on the third person (*the desert freezes*) and the placing of frequency adverbs (*never*, *occasionally*, *sometimes*, *often*, *always*, etc.).

1.2 Graphic organisers for activating (1): Venn diagram

Outline	Learners complete a Venn diagram.
Thinking skills	Remembering, understanding, comparing
Language focus	Simple present tenses, past tenses, vocabulary
Language skills	Writing (making brief notes) and informal speaking
Time	15 minutes
Level	A2 or above
Preparation	A Venn diagram is a useful tool to focus learners and to activate prior knowledge. It helps to highlight similarities and differences related to a topic. Prepare a handout of a Venn diagram for each learner (see Box 1.2 and Activity 2.4: *Graphic organisers* for some examples). Your chosen topic needs to be one with which the learners are fairly familiar.

Procedure

1   Give out the Venn diagrams or draw one on the board for learners to copy. Learners work individually or in pairs.

2   Learners note down similarities between the topics in the middle (overlapping) space and differences in the outer spaces.

3   Walk around and give hints to learners who get stuck: *Have you thought about (rhythm)?*, *Have you written anything down about (climate)?*

4   Gather the information from the class in one Venn diagram on the board. Encourage learners to use comparatives and linking words (*Plastic is harder than wood*; *Mammals give birth to live young, but reptiles lay eggs*).

Box 1.2: Graphic organisers for activating (1) – Venn diagram

a) Art, design and technology

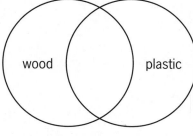

b) History

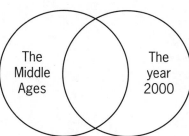

From *CLIL Activities* © Cambridge University Press 2012   PHOTOCOPIABLE

Subject examples
Economics and business studies: needs/wants
Geography: New York / London
ICT: Facebook/MSN
Maths: triangles/parallelograms
Music and drama: classical and jazz music
PE: rugby/football
Science: mammals/reptiles

Note

You can, of course, use Venn diagrams at other stages of your lessons (see Activity 2.4: *Graphic organisers*).

💡 Tips for cross-curricular cooperation between subject and language teachers

Before the lesson: The language teacher can work on comparatives and superlatives (*-er than*, *-est*) and linking words related to comparisons (e.g. *on the one hand …, on the other hand …; but; whereas*).

After the lesson: In the language lesson, learners can work in pairs to find out 10 differences between two pictures related to the topics.

1.3 Graphic organisers for activating (2): target practice

Outline	Learners complete a target image with ideas and people related to a topic.
Thinking skills	Remembering, understanding
Language focus	Vocabulary
Language skills	Writing (making brief notes) and informal speaking
Time	15 minutes
Level	A2 or above
Preparation	Provide a handout of a target for each learner like the one in Box 1.3.

Procedure

1 Give the targets out, one per learner. In the middle of the target, learners write your chosen topic.
2 In the other circles, they note down how it affects themselves (*Me*), their town (*My town*), their country (*My country*) and the world.
3 Pair the learners and ask them to compare their answers and improve their own, in terms of both ideas and language.
4 Elicit some answers from the whole class.

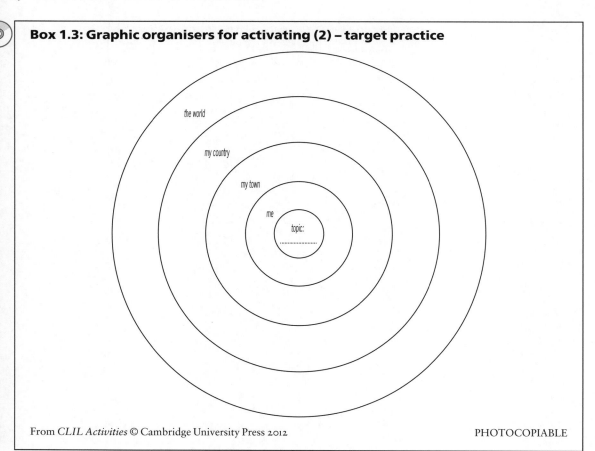

Box 1.3: Graphic organisers for activating (2) – target practice

the world

my country

my town

me

topic:
....

From *CLIL Activities* © Cambridge University Press 2012   PHOTOCOPIABLE

Variation
Divide the class up into groups; each group completes a different target on a different sub-topic.

Subject examples

Geography: poverty (partially completed)

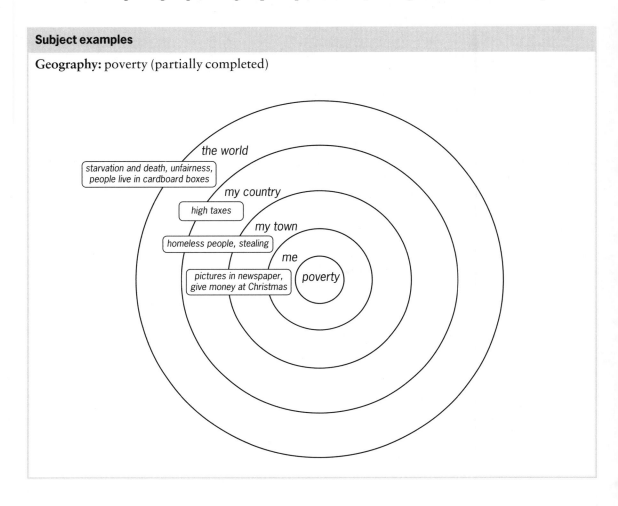

1.4 Graphic organisers for activating (3): spider diagram

Outline	Learners and teachers brainstorm on a topic and make a spider diagram together.
Thinking skills	Remembering, ordering, classifying
Language focus	Vocabulary
Language skills	Speaking and writing
Time	20 minutes
Level	A1 and above
Preparation	Before your lesson, decide on your topic and also think of a number of sub-categories for a spider diagram. Keep the ideas for sub-topics to yourself. See Box 1.4 for an example.

Procedure

1 Tell the learners the new topic and write it in the middle of the board. Ask them to call out ideas or words which they already know related to the topic. As they do so, write the ideas clearly but randomly around the topic in the centre of the board. Help the learners to think of more ideas by asking questions like, *And have you thought about …? What about this aspect of the topic?*

2 When all the ideas are on the board, ask the learners if they can see sub-topics. Write these on the board and suggest your own ideas if necessary.

3 Ask the learners to make a spider diagram using the sub-topics, each arm of the spider relating to a sub-topic. Learners can also add more ideas to the diagram.

4 Once learners have made a number of spider diagrams, you can ask them to do steps 1, 2 and 3 themselves or in small groups.

Box 1.4: Graphic organisers for activating (3) – spider diagram

Physics: electricity

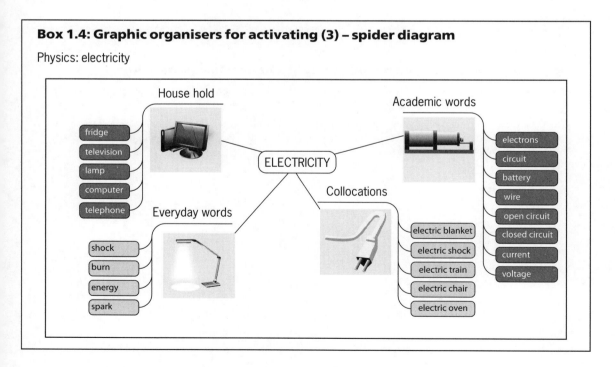

Geography: rivers

A brainstorm related to rivers might elicit: *tributary, Thames, estuary, delta, flood plain, Nile, Amazon, river-bed, meander, mouth, river bank, wildlife, fish, birds, crocodile,* etc.

Possible themes you can provide for grouping the brainstormed words: *features, inhabitants, names, processes.*

Maths: shapes

A brainstorm related to shapes might elicit the following: *triangle, rectangle, pentagon, octagon, circle, cone, parallelogram, rhombus,* etc. Possible themes you can provide for grouping the brainstormed words: *symmetrical and asymmetrical shapes.*

Note

Another way of working on words for any topic is to ask learners to brainstorm the following four aspects of any topic:

- academic words which are special to your subject (*electrons*)
- words which 'collocate with' (or often accompany) your main theme (*electric blanket, electric fence*)
- everyday words which are used in your subject and may have different meanings in other contexts (*energy*)
- everyday words (*fridge*).

> **Tips for cross-curricular cooperation between subject and language teachers**
>
> Before the lesson: The language teacher can work on the language of suggestions and opinions, helping learners with phrases such as *What do you think (about) …?; What about …?; In my opinion …; I think …*
>
> After the lesson: The learners can write a short piece which includes at least 20 of the words or phrases in their mind map, e.g. a very short news article for a popular newspaper about the topic they have discussed. The language teacher gives them feedback on their writing.

1.5 Guessing the lesson

Outline	Learners guess what the lesson is going to be about from a set of clues on the blackboard.
Thinking skills	Guessing, hypothesising
Language focus	Nouns or questions related to the topic you are about to learn
Language skills	Speaking
Time	15 minutes
Level	A2 or above
Preparation	Think of 10 to 20 key words or phrases which are related to the topic you are going to cover and which learners need to know. Your learners should know the words, half know them or be able to guess them with some help from you.

Procedure

1 Randomly write your chosen key words about the new topic on the board. Explain to the learners that you are going to play a guessing game to see how much they already know about the next topic or unit.

2 Learners look at the words and answer questions such as the following:
   • What do you think the lesson will be about?
   • Which words can you add to these?
   • Which words do you know?
   • Which words don't you know?
   • How can you guess the meaning of the words you don't know?
   • What do you think the lesson is going to be about?

3 Learners look up and write a definition for one word of their choice. Learners read aloud their definitions; the other learners write down which word is being described.

Subject examples

ICT: use and misuse of data

Possible words: *Data Protection Act, EPOS (electronic point of sale), verification, security, bar codes, feedback, online, mailshot, junk mail, hacking*

PE: athletics

Possible words: *Achilles tendon, hamstring, quadriceps, triceps, aerobic, anaerobic, interval training, fartlek, endurance, power*

Variations

1 *Questions*: Write the topic of the lesson on the board. Learners work in pairs and write down 10 questions about the topic – at least 4 should begin with *Who? What? How?* and *Why?* For example, for the topic 'The Slave Trade', learners might produce questions such as:
   • Where did slaves come from?
   • Were all slaves men?
   • Who owned slaves?
   • What happened to children born into slavery?

- How were slaves treated?
- Why was slavery acceptable to people at the time?
- Where did the slaves come from?

Collect the questions from the class and use them later to see if learners have learned everything they wanted to at the end of the topic.

2 Use Wordle (http://www.wordle.net/) or another program to create a word cloud from a text. Project this onto a (digital) whiteboard and ask learners to guess the topic of the lesson. See Box 1.5 for an example of a word cloud from a text about the digestive system, created using Wordle.

Box 1.5: Guessing the lesson

💡 **Tips for cross-curricular cooperation between subject and language teachers**

Before the lesson: The language teacher can help learners with strategies for guessing the meaning of words, for example by considering the formation of the word (nouns often end in *-ion*, while *in-* and *im-* at the start of a word often mean the opposite); words with the same roots (e.g. photograph, photographer); or punctuation, e.g. a capital letter, which often indicates places or names.

After the lesson: The subject or language teacher asks learners to organise 20 key words from the lesson into five categories and explain why they have chosen these categories.

1.6 Hands-on discovering

Outline	Discover something about the topic of the lesson through a hands-on activity.
Thinking skills	Classifying, comparing and contrasting: looking for similarities and differences
Language focus	Simple present tense, adjectives, giving opinions
Language skills	Speaking
Time	15–20 minutes
Level	B2
Preparation	Prepare about six or seven objects, photographs or pictures related to a topic you are teaching. Label each one with a number; create a chart for learners to complete while discussing the objects or pictures. See Box 1.6 for an example for a science lesson on the properties of substances.

Procedure

1 Ask your class to speculate on a question related to the topic you have prepared in advance, e.g. *How many substances do you think there are in the world?* (science says that the answer is about 5 million).
2 Divide the class into groups and give each group one object or picture. (For the science example in Box 1.6, this could be materials in transparent pots: sugar, methylated spirits (ethyl alcohol), white vinegar, iron filings, alcohol, a piece of wood, salt, peanut butter.)
3 Give each learner a copy of a chart like the one in Box 1.6. Explain that they should complete the chart with the name of the object or picture or photograph in the middle column. They should also write describing words in the right-hand column (e.g. *transparent, liquid*). Do one example together.
4 Learners work in groups and complete their charts. Walk around and help with words that learners are struggling to find.
5 When the groups have completed the chart related to one object or picture, they pass it on to another group until they have completed the entire chart.
6 Provide the class with a synthesising question/task about all of the objects or pictures together. For the example in Box 1.6 this might be to write down as many general properties of materials as they can. Ask each group to discuss the synthesising task before writing. You could discuss what the word *properties* means – the things (qualities) that make something what it is, that make it unique and recognisable, e.g. colour (sugar is white), smell (sugar smells slightly sweet), solidity (sugar is solid, not liquid).
7 Ask the whole class to stand up. Each learner should have the answer to the synthesising task in their head. One learner says his or her answer and the learners with the same one sit down. Continue until all the learners are sitting down.

Box 1.6: Hands-on discovering

Number	Substance	Describing words
1	sugar	crystalline, white, solid, …
2	white vinegar	clear, liquid, has smell, …
3		

Subject examples
Art, design and technology: nineteenth-century painting techniques
Materials: copies of paintings from the nineteenth century illustrating different techniques
Economics and business studies: food kilometres from producer to consumer
Materials: map of the world, food samples
Geography: the features of rocks
Materials: different rocks, crystals, stones
History: primary and secondary sources
Materials: paintings, statues, coursebook texts, letters, diary entries
ICT: the features of an effective homepage
Materials: a number of different webpages
Maths: two- and three-dimensional shapes
Materials: silhouettes or cut-outs of two-dimensional shapes; photographs of buildings or places which include two- or three-dimensional shapes.
Music: musical instruments
Materials: pictures of musical instruments
Science: biology – plant classification
Materials: types of leaves or flowers

Note

Asking learners to sort and classify examples using physical objects or images is effective in CLIL because (a) it engages the learners by asking them to use language to think actively about the content and (b) it appeals to different learning styles (in this case particularly visual and kinaesthetic).

 Tips for cross-curricular cooperation between subject and language teachers

Before the lesson: The language teacher can work on adjectives to describe objects, e.g. by asking questions such as *How would you describe sugar in some detail? How would you describe a violin?*

After the lesson: In the language lesson, the learners can write short descriptions of substances or objects on cards and read them out, without revealing which object or substance they are describing. Other learners guess the object or substance.

1.7 KWL (know, want, learn) grid

Outline	Learners write notes about what they Know (K), Want to know (W) and have Learned (L) in a KWL grid.
Thinking skills	Recalling, predicting
Language focus	Note-taking, prediction
Language skills	Writing (notes) and speaking
Time	15–20 minutes
Level	A2 and above
Preparation	Decide on a topic you are going to work on with your learners and a written or spoken task you want them to complete about the topic. Prepare and copy a KWL grid – one for each learner (see Box 1.7).

Procedure

1 Give the learners a KWL grid, like the one in Box 1.7. If you prefer, learners can complete a KWL grid in pairs.
2 In the first column, learners write what they already know about the topic.
3 In the second column, learners write questions about what they want to know about the topic.
4 When the work is completed (after a number of lessons), learners can fill in the third column of their KWL grids, outlining what they have learned.

Box 1.7: KWL (know, want, learn) grid

Topic: ....

Know	Want	Learned

From *CLIL Activities* © Cambridge University Press 2012   PHOTOCOPIABLE

Subject examples

Economics and business studies

Topic: cash flow and solvency		
Know	**Want**	**Learned**
Cash flow means something to do with cash	What is cash flow? Is it something to do with banks?	

PE

Topic: muscle training		
Know	**Want**	**Learned**
We have many muscles: in our arms and legs and stomachs. Some people have lots of muscles, others don't.	How long will it take me to get a 'six pack'? Why do some people have better muscles than others?	

Note

To use this activity effectively and to focus the learners' attention, it is important that they are clear about the final product (e.g. presentation, brochure, poster), since it is hard to complete a KWL grid without an explicit aim.

Tips for cross-curricular cooperation between subject and language teachers

Before the lesson: The language teacher can remind learners about questions in the present and past tenses, particularly in the second person singular. Pay attention to the present perfect tense.

After the lesson: The language teacher can give the learners exercises in question formation in the areas in which learners made most mistakes.

1.8 Newsy newspapers

Outline	Learners find headlines from newspapers in their own language and English in order to identify key issues relating to the topic and to see the link between the subject and real life.
Thinking skills	Identifying, classifying, categorising, evaluating
Language focus	Reading: understanding the language of newspaper headlines
Language skills	Listening, watching, reading, speaking or writing
Time	20 minutes
Level	A1 or above
Preparation	Choose a topic in the news to focus on in class. Collect a variety of recent newspapers and magazines in English and your own language and ask learners to do the same. Think of four categories under which learners can classify the information in the news: learners will look for headlines related to these sub-topics. Prepare four posters as in step 1; the title of each poster is a phrase or question related to your topic. Have some extra blank posters ready for step 7.

Procedure

1 Hang four large sheets of paper in front of the classroom. Each poster has a title – a category linked to your chosen topic.
2 Learners write down individually '*At least five things I know about (topic)*'.
3 Hand out copies of newspapers and magazines and ask learners to get out the newspapers and magazines they have brought from home.
4 Learners work in pairs. They sift through the newspapers and magazines to find headlines relating to the topic and the four categories on the posters. Each pair writes their headlines on the appropriate poster.
5 Discuss the headlines, the meanings of the different categories and whether the categories cover all the topics in the headlines. Highlight the issues you want to cover in your lessons.
6 Learners refer to the notes they made in step 2 and add any other ideas or points they have thought of that are not yet on the board.
7 Discuss in which categories the learners would put these ideas. Create new sub-topics on the blank posters if these ideas are not covered by the original four posters.

Subject examples

ICT: new technological developments

Poster titles: social networking, telecommunication, hardware

Maths: numbers in the news

Poster titles: percentages, integers, ordinals

♀ Tips for cross-curricular cooperation between subject and language teachers

Before the lesson: The language teacher can teach a lesson on the language of newspaper headlines, which has its own particular grammar (e.g. short, snappy words; alliteration, rhyming and assonance; few auxiliary verbs; no articles).

After the lesson: Learners can write short newspaper articles in the language lesson with appropriate accompanying headlines about the topic they are working on.

1.9 Placemat

Outline	Learners write ideas about a topic individually and then compare and combine their ideas.
Thinking skills	Combine, compare, contrast
Language focus	Various, depending on topic
Language skills	Speaking
Time	20 minutes
Level	A2 and above
Preparation	Give one very large (A2 / poster size) piece of paper to each group of four learners and a marker pen to each learner (preferably four different colours). Choose a topic that you would like to brainstorm with your learners – one that they know something about already. Prepare a synthesising or 'sponge' question that integrates the learners' initial ideas (see step 5).

Procedure

1   Learners sit in groups of four (maximum) around a table with a large sheet of poster paper between them and one marker pen each.
2   One of the learners makes a 'placemat' on their poster paper, like the one in Box 1.9.
3   Provide the learners with a question or issue. They write this in the middle of their placemat. Each learner then writes as many comments or opinions as they can in their own space on the placemat. The learners don't talk to each other at this stage, but work individually.
4   By turning the placemat around or moving around themselves, the learners read what everyone has written in their own space.
5   Provide a 'sponge' question. This is a question that combines, categorises or synthesises the ideas from step 3 and that provokes group discussion. It is vital to have a fresh question at this stage which further processes the ideas from step 3. Each group writes the answer to the 'sponge' question in the open space in the centre of the placement.
6   Discuss and compare the groups' answers as a whole class, until the class agrees on the ideal answer.

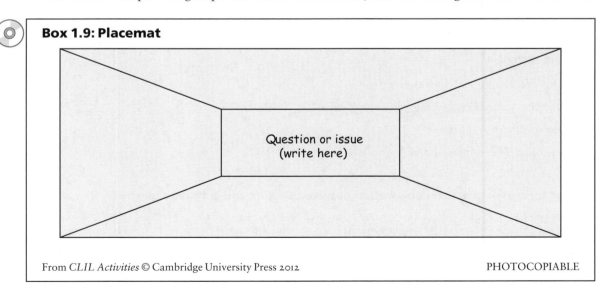

Box 1.9: Placemat

Question or issue
(write here)

From *CLIL Activities* © Cambridge University Press 2012   PHOTOCOPIABLE

Subject examples

Art, design and technology

Step 3: Write down what you know about Surrealism and its artists.

Step 5: What is Surrealism? Write a short definition. ('sponge' question)

Economics and business studies

Step 3: What do you think happens when a currency is devalued?

Step 5: What do you believe to be the one main reason for and the main effect of devaluation? ('sponge' question)

Geography

Step 3: What are the main geographical features of Scandinavia?

Step 5: Which three geographical features represent Scandinavia best? ('sponge' question)

ICT

Step 3: Think of a favourite webpage that you visit often. Why is it so attractive? What makes you return to it again and again?

Step 5: Which five features make a webpage most effective? ('sponge' question)

Science (physics)

Step 3: Write down as many things that produce or use energy as you can think of (e.g. a kettle, a catapult).

Step 5: How could you group these into different categories and what name would you give each one (e.g. kinetic, thermal, sound, chemical, electrical, gravitational potential)? ('sponge' question)

1.10 Quickest, most, best

Outline	Learners participate in a competition to interest and motivate them on the topic.
Thinking skills	Brainstorming, remembering, identifying
Language focus	Variable
Language skills	Writing (note taking) and speaking
Time	10 minutes
Level	A2 or above
Preparation	Decide on the topic of your lesson and on some competitive tasks.

Procedure

1   Write the topic of the lesson on the board.
2   Give learners a competitive task. If you use grammatical terminology, you might like to remind them, for example, what a verb or a noun is. Some example tasks you might consider are:
   • Who is the first pair to write down 10 verbs related to the topic?
   • Who is the first group to write down the most nouns related to the topic?
   • Who can write down the most words related to the topic in one minute?
   • Who can write down the most famous people related to the topic in one minute?
   • Who can write the best definition of (a topic) in exactly 20 words?
   • Who can create the best drawing of (concept, idea) in two minutes?
3   Use the words they suggest to launch your topic.

Subject examples

Economics and business studies
Quickest: Which group can make a diagram about the product cycle the quickest?
Most: Which group can write down the most nouns relating to finance in five minutes?
Best: Which group can give the best definition of supply and demand in two minutes (books closed)?

Music and drama
Quickest: Which group can write down 10 nouns to describe parts of a stage the quickest?
Most: Which learner can write down as many names of all the notes and their symbols on the music stave (e.g. *crochet*, *semibreve*) as possible?

♀ Tips for cross-curricular cooperation between subject and language teachers

Before the lesson: The language teacher can work on both superlatives with *-est* and those including most/best.

After the lesson: The language teacher can ask learners to complete a short paragraph about themselves, which must include 10 superlatives

1.11 Red and green circles

Outline	Learners decide whether statements about a new topic are true or false.
Thinking skills	Remembering, evaluating, reasoning
Language focus	Present and past tenses
Language skills	Speaking
Time	10 minutes
Level	A1 and above
Preparation	Create a list of 10 true and false statements about a topic you are going to cover, for yourself. Each learner receives one red and one green cardboard circle.

Procedure

1 Give each learner one red and one green cardboard circle.
2 Read your true/false statements out, one by one.
3 The learners each have to decide if the statement is true (green circle) or false (red circle), and once the statement is read out, hold up a green or red circle. In classrooms with interactive whiteboards and voting software, learners can vote electronically.
4 After each statement, you can discuss their answers, or leave them open and repeat the activity once the lesson is over. In this (latter) way, you can check learning.

Subject examples

Economics and business studies: recession and depression
1 Recessions and depressions are related. (T)
2 A recession is the same as a market in decline. (T)
3 It is possible to predict the length of a recession. (F)
4 If wages drop and people buy less, money becomes plentiful. (F)
5 A depression is a short recession. (F – it's a prolonged recession)
6 A symptom of a depression is that unemployment rises. (T)
7 A stock market crash is a symptom of a depression. (T)
8 The Great Depression in the USA happened in 1930. (F – 1929)
9 The Great Depression ended as the Second World War began. (T)
10 In a recession, all (or most) of the sectors that make up the economy start declining at the same time. In a real recession, these sectors must suffer longer than a month or two. (T)

Music and drama: jazz music
1 Jazz was created in New Orleans. (T)
2 Jazz really started to be popular in the 1920s. (T)
3 All the following words have something to do with jazz: *improvisation, syncopation, rhythm, blue notes, melody, harmony.* (T)
4 The 'call-and-response pattern' in jazz originated in South American music. (F – African)
5 A blues scale usually has seven notes. (F – five notes)
6 Jazz played a part in the feminist movement. (T)
7 Duke Ellington played the trumpet. (F – piano)

8   Louis Armstrong played brass instruments and sang. (T)
9   Miles Davis was addicted to heroin. (T)
10 A typical jazz instrument is the oboe. (F)

Science: classifying animals
1   A dog is an insect. (F)
2   A spider is an insect. (F)
3   A crocodile is a mammal. (F)
4   A fish is a reptile. (F)
5   A whale is a fish. (F)
6   A dolphin is a mammal. (T)
7   A snake is a reptile. (T)
8   A crab is a fish. (F)
9   A worm is an insect. (F)
10 An elephant is a mammal. (T)

Variations

1   You can also do this activity with agree/disagree statements, particularly if, for example, your topic is an ethical one and you wish to motivate learners and hold their interest.
2   You can review the answers to the questions at the end of the lesson, to help learners evaluate what they have learned.
3   The activity can also be used for revision.

♀ Tips for cross-curricular cooperation between subject and language teachers

Before the lesson: The language teacher can work on the present simple tense with learners, asking them to find examples of present simple tenses in a text, for example, and to explain why the present simple tense and not the present continuous is used.

After the lesson: Learners can write their own true/false statements for each other in a language lesson

---

1.12 Researching the lesson

Outline	Learners bring their own text or image in as input.
Thinking skills	Reasoning, evaluating, categorising
Language focus	Variable
Language skills	Reading and speaking
Time	10 minutes for homework, 20 minutes in class
Level	A2 or above
Preparation	For homework, ask half of your learners to bring a picture and the other half to bring a text of maximum 50 words related to your new topic. It is handy if you have a mixture. The texts and pictures must be large enough for other learners to be able to read or see at the back of the classroom.

Procedure

1   At the beginning of the lesson, ask learners to stick their images and texts on the blackboard with magnets or tape and then sit down, or use a digital whiteboard to display them.
2   The learners all look at the images and texts. Their task (in pairs) is to think of four or five main categories into which all the texts and/or images could be placed.
3   Each pair shares their ideas for groupings.

Subject examples
This activity can be done with any topic.

1.13 Scrambled eggs

Outline	Learners focus on a topic in a first lesson by putting a sentence or text into the right order.
Thinking skills	Ordering, organising
Language focus	Word order, paragraph organisation, text organisation
Language skills	Speaking
Time	5–15 minutes
Level	Any
Preparation	Choose one sentence or question which is relevant (humorous, interesting, controversial) to your topic and mix it up. Create small cards, one word per card (see Box 1.13).

Procedure

1 Give the learners a set of words, individually, in pairs or in small groups (see Box 1.13 for an example from a science lesson on nuclear power).

2 Ask the learners to create one sentence from your mixed-up words and to share it with the class. If it is a question, you can discuss their answers.

3 Learners recreate the sentence. Once they have completed that task, initiate a discussion based on the sentence, e.g. for the science example in Box 1.13, they could discuss how science might prove or disprove this claim.

Box 1.13: Scrambled eggs

A science lesson on nuclear power

Nuclear	environmentally	is
the		most
energy	power	of
means	friendly	generating

Subject examples

Art, design and technology
A pile of bricks bought by the Tate Gallery in 1972 is considered to be experimental art.

History
There are some legitimate reasons for allowing torture.

ICT
Governments should be able to block certain websites for children under 12.

Maths
The square on the hypotenuse is equal to the sum of the squares on the other two sides.

Variations
- Scramble a paragraph or a complete text. Make cards or a handout of the mixed-up sentences or paragraphs and ask the learners to reconstruct the text or paragraph.
- Provide a number of scrambled sentences, one per group. The sentences should make up a whole paragraph. For example, if you have six groups, groups firstly scramble their own sentences and share them with the class: the teacher writes them on the board. Then, the whole class can make the complete text from the six sentences.

> ⚲ **Tips for cross-curricular cooperation between subject and language teachers**
>
> Before the lesson: The language teacher can work on word order and get learners to unscramble sentences or jigsaw reading texts. They can also do work on signal words and connectives (linking words) which indicate how text is organised.

1.14 Vital visuals

Outline:	An interesting visual is used to introduce a topic.
Thinking skills	Guessing, hypothesising, evaluating
Language focus	Asking and answering questions, mostly in the present tense. For more in-depth questions, conditionals
Language skills	Speaking or writing
Time	15–20 minutes
Level	A2 and above
Preparation	Select a visual – a photograph, cartoon, DVD or other image – which is strongly related to your topic and create a task around the visual. The task introduces your learners to the topic of the lesson and gets them talking. Make a list of questions or a pile of questions on cards for learners to work with. Ensure that all the learners can see the visual clearly. See Box 1.14 and *Subject examples* for some ideas. See also Activity 2.12: *Skinny and fat questions and thinking skills*.

Procedure

1   Give learners a copy of the list of questions/a set of question cards on the visuals you have chosen. Ask them to answer the questions about the image in pairs, on paper or speaking together.

2   Gather some ideas together as a class.

Note

More ideas for working with images can be found in Goldstein (2008).

💡 **Tips for cross-curricular cooperation between subject and language teachers**

Before the lesson: The language teacher can do an information gap activity. One learner stands at the front of the class with an intriguing image; the rest of the class guesses what the scene on the image is. The teacher pays attention to question forms, using different question words: *what*, *why*, *who*, *how*, *when*, *where*, etc.

After the lesson: Learners can write a title for the photograph or an accompanying article in the language lesson.

Box 1.14: Vital visuals

Physics: radiation
Image of people wearing a hazmat suit (garment worn for protection against hazardous substances)

What?
What is the image of?
What are the people doing in the image?
What are they wearing? / What do they look like?
What is the relationship between the people in the image?
What do you think the message of the image is?
What is the image trying to tell or explain to the viewer?

Where?
Where is the image taken?
Where do the people come from?
Where are they going?

When?
When (time of day or year) was the image taken?
When did the people meet each other?
When did they start this activity?
When are they going to stop?

Who?
Who is in the image?
Who or for what event was the image taken for?
Who created the image?

Why?
Why do you think the image was created?

Why are the people dressed as they are?
Why is this image important?

In-depth/other
Write down two questions you would like to ask the person who created the image.
Imagine the image is in a textbook: what is its title?
If this image was the cover for a ....(subject) book, what would the title be?

If the image was illustrating a ....(subject) article, what would the title be?

Subject examples

Geography: a model of a river landscape or painting of a river

What?
What is the model/painting of?
What features of a river do you see in the model/painting?
What do the features look like?
What are the relationships between the geographical features you can see and the features of the river?
What do you think the person who made the model/painting wanted to show the viewer about rivers?

Where?
Where is the river?
Where does it come from?
Where is it going to?

When?
When was the model/painting made?

Who?
Who was the model/painting made for?
Who is the designer/ artist?
Who can you see in the model/painting?

Why?
Why do you think the model/painting was made?
Why does it show these features?
Why is this model/painting important?

In-depth/other
Write down the questions you would like to ask the designer/artist.
Imagine the model/painting in a museum: what is its title?
If this model/painting was the cover for a geography book, what would the title be?
If the model/painting was illustrating a newspaper article, what would the title be?

1.15 Word wall

Outline	Learners find key vocabulary in a chapter and help each other to understand and spell it.
Thinking skills	Classifying, deciding, evaluating
Language focus	Vocabulary of a future unit in a coursebook
Language skills	Reading and speaking
Time	45–50 minutes
Level	B1 or above
Preparation	Prepare 20 or 30 rectangular cards (15 × 10 cm) or sticky labels for words and definitions. You will need two marker pens for each group of three or four learners. You will need to have a source (i.e. dictionaries or – if available – the Internet) ready so that learners can find out the meanings of words. Learners need their coursebooks, too. Prepare enough copies of Word wall 1 for each learner and enough copies of Word wall 2 for each group of learners.

Procedure

1 Explain to learners that they will be creating a 'word wall' of unfamiliar key vocabulary that appears in the next chapter in their coursebook. They will also help each other to understand and spell the vocabulary.

2 Each learner looks through the chapter individually and completes Word wall 1 (see Box 1.15a) to create a personal list with five words from the chapter they are going to start. These should be words that they do not know but that they feel it is important to learn.

3 In groups of three or four, learners compare personal lists and agree on a group master list. They complete Word wall 2 (see Box 1.15b) to create a group master list of 10 unfamiliar words.

4 Distribute 10 cards or sticky labels and markers to each group. Learners print the key words in large letters on the cards or sticky labels, leaving room for a definition of the word.

5 Gather the cards or sticky labels and put the words up on the board alphabetically. Remove any that are duplicated.

6 As a class, ask learners to speculate on the meaning of the words. Discuss the meaning of prefixes like *ex-*, *in-*, *im-* or suffixes like *-tion*, *-able*.

7 Hang the word wall on the classroom wall during the lessons dealing with the chapter.

Box 1.15a: Word wall

Word wall 1: personal list of five unfamiliar words

My name: _____

1. _____

2. _____

3. _____

4. _____

5. _____

From *CLIL Activities* © Cambridge University Press 2012   PHOTOCOPIABLE

Box 1.15b: Word wall

Word wall 2: group master list of 10 unfamiliar words

Group members:
1
2
3
4

1. _____
2. _____
3. _____
4. _____
5. _____
6. _____
7. _____
8. _____
9. _____
10. _____

PHOTOCOPIABLE

Follow-up

Divide the words on cards chosen by the class between the groups and ask each group to add:

(a) a clear meaning for each word on the cards or sticky labels in smaller letters;

(b) a sentence including the word which makes its meaning clear. Here is an example of a card:

hurdle (noun)

a difficult problem to be overcome; an obstacle

The last hurdle before leaving school was her French exam.

The groups then present their words to the rest of the class and put them back on the word wall.

2 Guiding understanding

2.1 Expert groups

Outline	Learners read different texts and work in a group to answer questions about the same topic.
Thinking skills	Comparing and contrasting, reasoning
Language focus	Asking and answering questions
Language skills	Speaking and reading
Time	Depends on length of text
Level	Any
Preparation	Prepare four different texts (A, B, C, D) of a similar length about different aspects of the same topic. Make sure that the texts you choose are short, free-standing and of approximately the same length and difficulty. Short encyclopaedia entries on roughly the same topic can work well here, e.g. on different ways of solving global warming (geography) or different types of sustainable energy production (physics). Prepare a set of questions about the topic which cover the information in all four texts equally (see Box 2.1). Decide on your groupings before the lesson starts – i.e. which learners will work together in the first part of the lesson using the same text and which learners will work together in the second part of the lesson when groups use three or four different texts.

Procedure

1 Divide the class into groups of four. Tell the learners that you have four different texts and that each group of four learners is going to work together to answer questions on one of these texts.
2 Give each group their text and questions. Before they begin, tell them that they will not find answers to all the questions in the text, so where not given, they must work together to try and guess the answers to questions. Explain that everyone needs to take notes, since later in the lesson they will be working in different groups. Allow learners 10–20 minutes, depending on the length of the texts.
3 Divide the class into new groups of four so that each group is made up of one learner from each of the four original Groups A-D. Since each group member has worked on a different text, the new groups should be able to complete all of the questions for the different texts by sharing their answers.

Box 2.1a: Expert groups

Darwin: start of text A

Charles Darwin was born on 12th February two hundred years ago. He hated school, especially learning Latin, but he loved reading and studying the details of the natural world. He had a famous grandfather who was a radical thinker. Erasmus Darwin was the doctor of George III, an inventor of engines and very interested in natural philosophy. In fact, Erasmus had influenced the ideas of Mary Shelley who wrote *Frankenstein*. His mother, Susannah, was the daughter of Josiah Wedgwood. The Wedgwood pottery was very advanced for its time. The Wedgwoods were radical, technological minded business people. [...]

Darwin: start of text B

Some ideas in science are difficult to understand, because our intuitions don't like them very much. Some scientists argue that this may be because our brains have not evolved fast enough, and are better designed to work for small groups of hunter/gatherers. This is what most of us were doing four to five thousand years ago. So, for instance, we think we have a good chance of winning the National Lottery, we see significance in coincidences and we read astrology predictions and only remember when they come true. [...]

Darwin: start of text C

Before Darwin was born, most people in England thought that species were not linked in a single 'family tree'. They were unconnected, unrelated and unchanged since the moment of their creation. Earth itself was thought to be 6,000 years old. There would not have been time for species to change. People were not part of the natural world; they were above and outside it. They had been created to rule over the animals. Many also believed that there were superior races created to rule over inferior races. Before 1800, only a handful of naturalists in England and France had given the idea of evolution serious consideration. [...]

Darwin: start of text D

Natural selection is a simple mechanism that causes populations of living things to change over time. In fact, it is so simple that it can be broken down into five basic steps: V.I.S.T.A.: Variation, Inheritance, Selection, Time and Adaptation. Members of any given species are seldom exactly the same, either inside or outside. Organisms can vary in size, colour, ability to fight off diseases and countless other traits. These traits arise from spontaneous mutation and enable the organism to survive and pass them to future generations. [...]

These partial texts are reproduced with permission from http://www.collaborativelearning.org/darwinsbirthday.pdf

Box 2.1b: Expert groups

Charles Darwin: question sheet

1. Name two or more historical events that happened in Darwin's lifetime.	2. How did Darwin earn his living?	3. Why was Darwin slow to publish his ideas?	4. How do viruses survive?
5. How do we pass on our traits to our offspring?	6. How was the earth and the origins of life viewed before Darwin?	7. What are vestigial features and can you think of some examples?	8. How did Darwin's ideas influence social change?
9. How do analogies help us to understand difficult concepts?	10. What stimulated Darwin to think about evolution?	11. How did Darwin's views undermine the idea of slavery?	12. Why are Darwin's theories still considered controversial?

From *CLIL Activities* © Cambridge University Press 2012   PHOTOCOPIABLE

Subject examples

Any texts and topic can be used for this activity.

Variation

In order to differentiate, you can provide texts of differing difficulty or length and think in advance who to give the texts to.

2.2 Gist statements

Outline	Learners match and answer statements about a text before reading for detail.
Thinking skills	Understanding
Language focus	Depends on the text
Language skills	Reading or listening
Time	20 minutes
Level	A2 and above
Preparation	Select a text you will be dealing with in class. This could be a written or a spoken text (e.g. your own presentation or a video). Read through or listen to the text to identify three to five main points. For each point, formulate a true/false statement. Break up each statement or question into two halves and mix them up. See Box 2.2 for an example for history.

Procedure

1 Introduce the topic of the text with a brief warm-up activity (for ideas, see Chapter 1 of Part 3). Do not give out the text or play the video yet.
2 Hand out the jumbled-up true/false statements. Learners work individually to make complete true/false statements.
3 Learners work in pairs, check their statements and decide together if they think their statements are true or false.
4 Hand out the text or play the video and ask the learners to read or listen and find the answers to the questions. They should try to ignore any words they do not know and focus on finding the answers to the questions.
5 Learners compare their answers with those of their neighbour.
6 Check the answers briefly in class.

Subject examples

Any text can be used for this activity.

Follow-up

After the learners have read or heard a text and understood the main points, you can move on to more detailed work with the text, e.g. using graphic organisers (see Activity 2.4: *Graphic organisers*). Learners could write their own gist questions for future texts and bring them to the next lesson for their classmates to answer.

Note

Helping CLIL learners to read for a purpose and to focus only on the main points in a text the first time they read or listen trains them in good reading habits such as skimming, scanning and sometimes skipping unfamiliar words in order to understand a complete paragraph or text.

Box 2.2: Gist statements

Example text: speech by William Wilberforce (campaigner for the abolition of slavery)

'I must speak of the transit (transport) of the slaves in the West Indies. This I confess, in my own opinion, is the most wretched part of the whole subject. So much misery condensed in so little room, is more than the human imagination had ever before conceived … A trade founded in iniquity, and carried on as this was, must be abolished, let the policy be what it might, – let the consequences be what they would, I from this time determined that I would never rest till I had effected its abolition.'

Reproduced with permission from: https://www.bbc.co.uk/scotland/education/hist/abolition/?section=abolitionists&page=wilberforce&mainContent=read

---

True/false statements

Wilberforce feels:

The worst thing about slavery is the way slaves are caught.

Transporting so many slaves together in such a small space created more misery than people had ever thought of before.

Slavery is so evil that it should be stopped, but not if it costs too much money.

Jumbled statements

Wilberforce feels		T/F
The worst thing about slavery	but not if it costs too much money.	
Transporting so many slaves together in such a small space	is the way slaves are caught.	
Slavery is so evil that it should be stopped,	created more misery than people had ever thought of before.	

2.3 Graffiti

Outline	Learners read texts, answer questions on posters and give short presentations.
Thinking skills	Reasoning, giving opinions, evaluating, identifying
Language focus	Various, depending on topic and questions
Language skill	Speaking and writing
Time	45 minutes or more
Level	B1 or above
Preparation	Make four copies of six or more different texts or visuals (e.g. graphs, pieces of art, sets of photographs) which relate to the same subject. Before the learners come into the classroom, hang up six posters around the wall. At the top of each poster, write a question relating to the texts you have chosen to use. These ('fat') questions (see Activity 2.12: *Skinny and fat questions and thinking skills*) should help the learners to understand the text they read as well as get them thinking: they should not be too easy.

Procedure

1 Make groups of four and give each learner a number from 1 to 4. This is to ensure that every learner participates: they will not know the role for their number until later.

2 Give each group a colour name (e.g. red, blue, black, green) and a marker of that colour. The group will keep that marker as they move to a different poster and topic.

3 Now give each group a different article to read. Learners skim through their articles for a few minutes.

4 Learners stand next to a poster in their groups. They read the question and then have three minutes to write their group's responses on the first poster. Number 1 will write on the first poster, number 2 on the second poster, and so on.

5 When the three minutes are up, groups move to a different poster and answer the question on that poster. They can also add comments, questions, extra points or question marks. (Learner number 2 writes the answers this time.)

6 Repeat step (5) six times so that every group has answered a question on each poster.

7 When learners have finished, they can sit down. Now explain that each group should return to the poster they began with, take it off the wall and prepare a short presentation using the answers on the poster. Tell the learners you might call on anyone to give the presentation, so they should all be prepared.

8 Learners give the presentation.

Subject examples

ICT: writing for the Web
1. List some different ways of organising hypertext on a webpage.
2. List some criteria for effective headlines.
3. How can you 'hook' your readers' attention and make them take notice of your webpage?
4. How can you hold their interest and keep them reading your page?
5. Write down some rules web writers should follow about language on a webpage.
6. What should you avoid when writing for the Web?

Music and drama

This task is based on a play called *His Dark Materials*, written by British playwright Nicholas Wright and adapted from Philip Pullman's trilogy of fantasy novels of the same title. All learners must have read the play so that they go around the posters expressing their own ideas.
1. What do you think the title of the play means?
2. Describe Lyra in as much detail as you can (both appearance and character).
3. What are daemons? How are they different from humans? Write notes here to describe them.
4. Who are the armoured bears and what is their role in the play?
5. Are Lord Asriel and Mrs Coulter friends or enemies? How and in what way?
6. If you were to write an email to Philip Pullman about this play, what would you like to ask him?

2.4 Graphic organisers

Outline	Learners complete a chart or table to represent information from a text visually.
Thinking skills	Ordering, classifying, understanding, analysing
Language focus	Depends on text
Language skills	Reading
Time	10 minutes depending on length and complexity of text
Level	A1 and above
Preparation	Select a text and read through it to identify its main structure. Choose a graphic organiser which would help learners to structure the information in the text visually. See Box 2.4 for some examples. Alternatively, an internet search using the search terms 'your subject + graphic organiser' (e.g. history + graphic organiser, art + graphic organiser) will generate plenty of examples. Adapt the graphic organiser you have chosen to the information in your text by completing a model graphic organiser yourself. Photocopy your empty graphic organiser. You will need one graphic organiser and one text per pair of learners.

Procedure

1 Introduce the topic of the text briefly. Give each learner a copy of the graphic organiser you have designed, and ask them to work in pairs to see how much information they can complete before they read the text.
2 Give each pair a copy of the text and ask them to correct and complete their graphic organiser using the information in the text.
3 Use a (digital) whiteboard to discuss and agree on a complete final version as a class.

Box 2.4: Graphic organisers

Text structure	Graphic organiser
Cause and effect	Flowchart
Sequence of events	Timeline
Parts of a whole	Tree map, fishbone map, spider map
Compare and contrast	Venn diagram
Classification	Table/chart

a) Flowchart

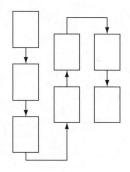

b) Timeline

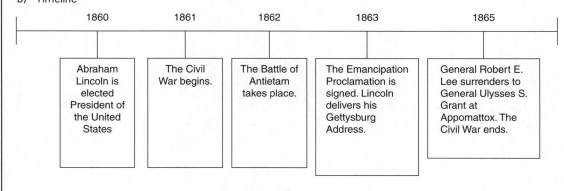

c) Spider map

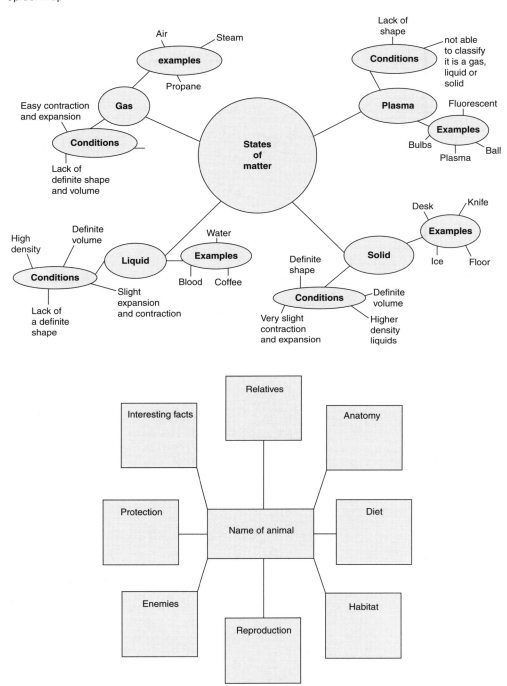

d) Tree map

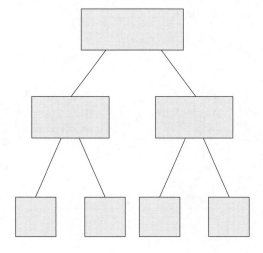

e) Fishbone map

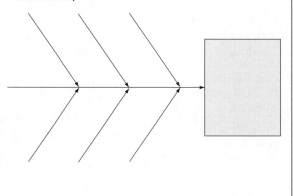

f) Venn diagram

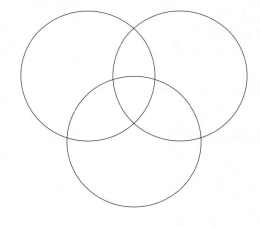

g) Chart

K	W	H	L
What do we know?	What do we want to find out?	How can we find out what we want to learn?	What did we learn?
Attributes or characteristics we expect to use:			

PHOTOCOPIABLE

Subject examples

Art, design and technology: naïve art – Henri Rousseau's paintings
Text: a video on Rousseau
Graphic organiser: a table for classification of key features

Henry Rousseau
As you watch the video, fill in this table.

	Title of painting	When painted	Where is it now (museum, city)?	Main colours used	Adjectives used in description of painting
Example 1	The dream	1910	Museum of Modern Art (MOMA), New York	light green, dark green, purple, flesh colour …	sharp, moonlit, wild …
2					
3					
4					

History: the Great Fire of London
Text: coursebook description of events leading up to and during the Great Fire of London
Graphic organiser: timeline

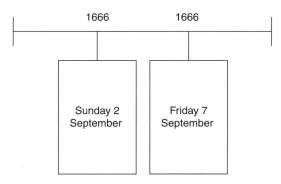

Biology: digestion
Text: description of digestion processes
Graphic organiser: flowchart of journey of food from mouth to anus

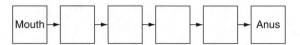

Physics: Newton's laws of motion
Text: coursebook explanation of Newton's laws
Graphic organiser: tree map

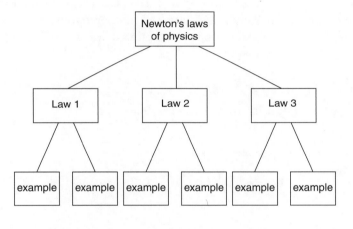

Follow-up
Once learners are familiar with different types of graphic organisers, they can also design their own.

Variation
It is possible to give learners more or less support by partially completing the graphic organisers you provide.

Note
Graphic organisers help CLIL learners by scaffolding their learning. Giving learners frameworks like these helps them to understand not only what the main points in a text are, but also how different texts are structured. This helps them become good independent readers and listeners.

2.5 Interactive PowerPoint®

Outline	Learners interact with a PowerPoint presentation.
Thinking skills	Predicting, reasoning
Language focus	Various
Language skills	Speaking
Time	10–20 minutes
Level	Any
Preparation	Prepare a number of PowerPoint slides which cover your topic. For each slide, prepare a task or question which learners can discuss in pairs. For example, for geography: *Who is affected by logging? What does deforestation mean for the world climate?* This keeps them actively involved during the presentation.

Procedure

1 Introduce your new topic briefly.
2 Show your first slide (a task or question) and ask learners to discuss their answer(s) in pairs.
3 Give some input (perhaps with some other slides you have prepared) about the topic.
4 Show a following slide – a task or question – and again ask learners to discuss their ideas in pairs.
5 Continue until the end of the presentation.

Subject examples

Economics and business studies: inflation (example slide)

- What is inflation?
- What effect does inflation have on:
    a) your family?
    b) prices?

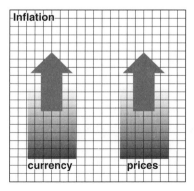

Geography: the rainforest (example slide)

Animals in the rainforest

- Name all the animals you can see in this picture.
- Talk about other animals that you think might live here.

History: the Vikings (example slide)

Which country did the Vikings NOT come from?

a) Sweden
b) Finland
c) Denmark
d) Norway

2.6 Interview as input

Outline	Learners interview a person and use this as input on a topic.
Thinking skills	Understanding
Language focus	Forming questions
Language skills	Speaking and listening
Time	20 minutes
Level	B1 and above
Preparation	When preparing to start a new topic in your subject, find out first of all whether the learners can gather information on this topic from people they know. Assuming this is possible, plan to introduce the topic a week or two before you want to start work on it. Prepare enough copies of the questionnaire in Box 2.6 for learners to refer to when creating their own questionnaire.

Procedure

1 Write the subject topic on the board. Ask your learners to tell you any (English-speaking) people they know who might be able to provide information on this topic, e.g. a relative, a friend of the family, neighbour, colleague of a family member, someone at school, employee at a local business.

2 Ask learners to work in pairs and write down five questions they could ask one of these people about the topic.

3 Ask learners to write their questions on the board. Discuss the questions together, e.g. which questions will give the learners the most interesting information? Are all the questions appropriate (why/why not)? What makes a good interview question?

4 Together, decide on 5 to 10 interesting questions suitable for an interview. Explain to learners that you would like them to interview someone on this topic (preferably in English) and make notes on their answers (see Box 2.6 for an example questionnaire). They should bring their notes with the answers to class or upload them to an electronic shared work space. (Allow some time, i.e. at least a week, for the learners to arrange and carry out the interview.) If the learners have audio-recording devices, they can also record the interviews and upload them to a shared work space for other learners to listen to.

5 In the first lesson on the new topic, ask learners to share the information they found out in interviews and discuss the variety of answers they have to the questions.

Follow-up
Learners come to the classroom with their answers and can compare them. They could make graphs about their information, or do some writing.

Variation
It is also possible to provide your learners with a ready-made list of questions.

Note
Obviously, the choice of appropriate topic will depend on the context in which you teach – it is important to be sensitive about personal or controversial issues so that learners are not placed in a difficult situation when they carry out the interview.

Box 2.6: Interview as input

History: 1960s

Interview framework about the sixties

First, ask your interviewee if you may ask some questions about them and their life in the 1960s. Write the answers to their questions on this form.

My name_____

Name of person I interviewed_____

Date of birth of person I interviewed _____

Date_____

Interview questions

1. How old were you in 1965?
2. Where did you live then?
3. What was your house like?
4. What were you doing in the 1960s? (Were you at school, did you work, etc.?)
5. What was music like during the 60s?
6. What did your parents do in the 60s?
7. What was the worst thing that happened to you in the 60s?
8. How have things changed for the better since the 60s?
9. How have things changed for the worse since the 60s?
10. How has food and drink changed since the 60s?
11. (Write your own question here and ask it)
12. (Write your own question here and ask it)

From *CLIL Activities* © Cambridge University Press 2012   PHOTOCOPIABLE

Subject examples

Art, design and technology: interview about someone's experience of art – favourite pieces of art or artists

Geography: interview about geographical events which someone remembers in the news

ICT: interview about use of ICT – number of hours, what kind of programs, favourite applications, etc.

Maths: interview about attitudes to maths: likes, dislikes, types of maths, maths lessons

PE: interview about sports and lifestyle

Science: interview about electric household appliances

2.7 Jumbles

Outline	Learners put text or pictures into the right order.
Thinking skills	Ordering, reasoning
Language focus	Linking words
Language skills	Reading and listening
Time	10 minutes or more depending on length of text
Level	A1 or above
Preparation	Copy a text for each group of three learners. Jumble the text on paper by putting parts of the text in the wrong order to prevent learners putting the text together like a jigsaw. Cut up each photocopy of the text into sections (words or sentences or paragraphs) and put a jumbled version of each text into an envelope. You will need one envelope per group of three learners containing the jumbled text and one copy of the original text per group.

Procedure

1   Explain that you have a text for the learners to read, but that it is in the wrong order. Depending on the level of your learners, you could give a reason why the text is mixed up (e.g. a gremlin got into your drawer last night and went crazy with a pair of scissors or a virus got into your computer).

2   Learners work in groups of three. Give each group of three learners one envelope containing the jumbled text and ask them to read the text and put it in the correct order. Tell the learners they need to read the text carefully to look for clues which will help them know what the right order is. You can also instruct them to highlight or circle the information in the text which they use to recreate the original order.

3   When the learners have finished, give out the original text so they can check whether they put it back together in the correct order.

4   To help the learners understand the text better, give them some further activities to do such as the following: 2.1: *Expert groups*, 2.12: *Skinny and fat questions and thinking skills*, 2.3: *Graffiti*, 2.4: *Graphic organisers*.

Subject examples

Any text can be used for this activity. Here are some ideas.

Maths: order words in a jumbled maths problem: the jumbled words *128 is 80 of five-eighths* becomes 80 is five-eighths of 128.

Science: physics and chemistry – order the steps in an experiment.

Variation

It is possible to create a similar ordering activity using images. Copy images of the main points in a text and give them to learners. As they listen to a presentation or watch a video, they put the images in the order in which they are mentioned.

Note

Depending on the level of the learners and the length of the text, you can jumble words in a single sentence, sentences in a paragraph or paragraphs in a longer text. This is a fun activity which trains CLIL learners to look for markers and connectives in texts too.

2.8 Learner-generated questions

Outline	Learners design their own questions and discuss the characteristics of good questions for CLIL.
Thinking skills	Comparing and contrasting, reasoning, creative thinking, evaluating
Language focus	Questions
Language skills	Reading and writing
Time	60 minutes
Level	B1 and above
Preparation	Choose a page from your coursebook which your class is familiar with but that is proving challenging for them. There needs to be a lot of information on the page. You will need coloured card (in at least two different shades for the *Variation* option).

Procedure

1 Elicit the question words in English, i.e. *what, when, who, why, how, how many,* and revise the formulation of questions, highlighting, if possible, any important differences between English and the learners' first language.

2 Explain that you are going to practise creating 'good' questions about the texts you have been reading. Elicit their ideas about what makes a 'good' question.

3 Give the learners one coloured card each. Learners look at the chosen page and write down one 'good' question about the information on the page on their coloured card.

4 Ask the learners to stand up and move the furniture to one side. They then circulate, asking and answering the questions they have written on their cards.

5 Carry out a class discussion about questions for content and language learning, e.g. What makes a good question? Which question do you think was the best? Why? Which questions were more interesting? Which questions were easier/more difficult? Why? Which questions were more difficult to formulate in English and why? Which question was written in the best English? (see also Activity 2.12: *Skinny and fat questions and thinking skills*).

Subject examples

This activity can be done with most texts.

Variations

- Learners work in groups of three or four. Distribute all the cards that the learners have made and ask them to rank them from easiest to most difficult.
- Learners work in groups of three or four. Distribute all the cards that the learners have made. Give out different coloured cards. Each group writes the answer to one question on each new card to make pairs of questions and answers (i.e. answers on a second colour). Collect in the sets of questions and answers and redistribute them to each group. The groups then match the answers and the questions.

Follow-up

Collect all the questions which the learners have provided and use a number of them in a test related to the material.

2.9 Listening questions

Outline	Learners complete a focus task as they listen to a presentation or watch a video.
Thinking skills	Ordering, understanding
Language focus	Depends on presentation/video
Language skill	Listening
Time	15–20 minutes, depending on length of presentation/video
Level	A2 and above
Preparation	Select a presentation or video which you will use in class. Write down 6 to 10 important points you want the learners to remember. Put the points in random order, using letters of the alphabet (a–k). Make sets of cards with each point on a separate card, one set per learner or pair of learners.

Procedure

1   Introduce the topic of the presentation or video briefly and give each learner or pair of learners a set of cards.
2   Tell learners that these points are not in the correct order. Ask them to read through the points on the cards and discuss with a partner the order in which they think they will occur on the video.
3   Ask the learners to listen to the presentation or watch the video and – as they listen – check if they have put the cards in the correct order.
4   After the presentation or video, check their answers.

Subject examples
Any presentation/video can be used for this activity.

Variations

- Instead of jumbling the main points, you could make statements – some correct and some inaccurate. Learners first predict whether the statements are true or false, and then listen to see if they were correct.
- Give out a partially completed or empty graphic organiser (see Activity 2.4: *Graphic organisers* for ideas). Learners complete the graphic organiser as they listen or watch.
- Give out a gapped text about the presentation or video. Learners fill in the gaps as they listen or watch.

Note

It is important in CLIL to see listening activities as learning opportunities and to get learners actively involved in listening – either to you as you present a topic, or to a video or audio presentation. Providing a task before listening helps them to learn to predict, whereas providing a task while they listen helps them to listen actively.

2.10 Mind the gap

Outline	Learners fill in the missing words in a text.
Thinking skills	Reasoning, understanding, evaluating
Language focus	Subject-specific vocabulary
Language skill	Reading
Time	10–15 minutes, depending on the level of difficulty of the text
Level	A2 and above
Preparation	Select a short (up to 300 words) text. It is easiest if you have a digital version but if not, use a photocopy of the text. Delete a number of important subject-specific words (no more than 10–15 words per page) from the text you have chosen. Delete only words for which there are clues in the text that will help learners guess each word. This is called a cloze text. Number the gaps for easy reference and ensure the gaps are not too close together so that learners can use the context to guess the words. (Another gap-filling activity is 3.1: *Academic word list.*)

Procedure

1 Learners work in pairs and write down five words they would expect to read or hear in a text about the topic. The learners share the words they have listed with the class.
2 Explain to the learners that they are going to read a cloze text (i.e. a reading passage in which words have been deleted and that they need to fill in).
3 Hand out one copy of the text to each pair, and ask learners to fill the gaps in the text. The words they listed at the beginning of the lesson may help them.
4 Encourage the learners to discuss how they worked out the correct missing words, i.e. which clues in the text did they use to help them?
5 Allow learners to compare their answers with the complete original text.

Subject examples

Any text can be used for this activity.

Follow-up
Learners can make cloze exercises for each other using texts from the coursebook or the Internet.

Variations
* List the words you have deleted in random order at the end of the text.
* Provide the first letter of each missing word.
* Leave the first letter of each missing word in the text and give the learners a list of synonyms for the missing words.
* Delete certain types of words (e.g. prepositions, verbs, articles, linking words).
* Delete words at random (e.g. every tenth word).
* On a digital whiteboard, project a four-line text. Students take it in turns to read the text aloud. Each time, delete one word, until the final student must reproduce the whole text from memory.
* Use an audio or video text. Learners fill in the missing words as they listen.
* Providing extra words that do not fit the text will make the activity more difficult.

2.11 Running commentary

Outline	Teachers give a running commentary on their actions as they give instructions to the class.
Thinking skills	Understanding
Language focus	Any
Language skills	Listening
Time	10–20 minutes
Level	A1 and above
Preparation	Select a practical classroom activity for which you can give instructions in class. Write out your instructions in simple, detailed steps: e.g. *Take a piece of A4 paper and fold it in half. Take a blunt knife and hold it in between the two halves of paper.* Jumble the instructions up and make photocopies of them for each learner.

Procedure

1 Give each learner a photocopy of the jumbled instructions.
2 Tell the learners to listen while you read the instructions. As they listen they should put the instructions in the right order.
3 Do one example together to make sure all the learners understand what they have to do, and then give your instructions.
4 Learners compare their answers in pairs.
5 Check the answers.
6 Ask the learners to carry out the instructions themselves.

Subject examples

Any instructions can be used for this activity

Art, design and technology: instructions for making a sculpture

Economics and business studies: instructions about how a bank account works

---

Follow-up
Learners could write instructions for each other

Variations
• Learners could match two halves of sentences, instead of putting instructions in the correct order.
• You could also put the instructions on cards so that learners put them into the right order as they listen.

Note
This technique is most appropriate for learners completely new to CLIL. It is important that learners hear and see a lot of input at all stages. A running commentary gives them written and spoken input to accompany hands-on demonstrations. This activity also gives learners a good reason to listen and will help them to concentrate better, too.

2.12 Skinny and fat questions and thinking skills

Outline	Learners change 'skinny' questions into 'fat' questions.
Thinking skills	Comparing and contrasting, reasoning, creative thinking, evaluating
Language focus	Questions
Language skills	Reading and writing
Time	30 minutes
Level	B1 and above
Preparation	Skinny questions usually require factual, short answers; fat questions help learners to think more and use more language than skinny ones, so they are great for CLIL. Choose a text with skinny questions or write five skinny questions to accompany the text. See Box 2.12 for some examples.

Procedure

1 Draw a 'skinny' question mark on the board, and ask learners a subject question which requires a short, factual answer (e.g. geography: *What is the average temperature in summer in your country?*).

2 Draw a 'fat' question mark on the board, and ask learners a subject question which requires a longer answer, and makes them think (e.g. geography: *How does the average temperature change during a typical year in your country?*). Discuss the difference between the two questions with your class, and introduce the terms *skinny* and *fat questions*.

3 Put learners into pairs and hand out the text and skinny questions. Ask the learners to change each skinny question into a fat question. They should also write their own model answers for each fat question on a different piece of paper. The answers to the questions might be found in the text, or between the lines.

4 Form groups of four from two pairs. The pairs give their fat questions to each other, keeping the answers to themselves. They answer each other's fat questions.

5 The pairs give their answers to each other and discuss any differences between their answers.

6 Ask each group to choose the best question (i.e. the question that really made them think and use lots of language in their answer). Share and discuss these together.

Box 2.12: Skinny and fat questions and thinking skills

Skinny questions (lower-order thinking skills, short answers)	Fat questions (higher-order thinking skills, longer answers)
What happened when I added the acid?	Can you explain the shape of the graph?
What is electricity?	How could we use our work on electricity to design a winter lighting system for a greenhouse?
What is the greenhouse effect?	How might the greenhouse effect affect the lives of your children and grandchildren?
Give me 10 different words starting with *in-*.	What do you think the prefix *in-* means? How many other prefixes can you think of which mean the same?
Have you read Chapter 8?	What is your opinion of Chapter 8?
What did David Livingstone discover?	How do you think David Livingstone's early life affected his career? Describe a day in the life of David Livingstone in Africa.

Subject examples

Most texts can be used for this activity.

Follow-up

Learners write their own fat questions about a different text.

💡 Tips for cross-curricular cooperation between subject and language teachers

Before the lesson: The language teacher practises question forms with the learners.

After the lesson: The language teacher gives feedback on common mistakes made in formulating questions.

2.13 Subheadings

Outline	Learners use subheadings to ask and answer questions about a text.
Thinking skills	Predicting, reasoning
Language focus	Question forms
Language skills	Reading
Time	10 minutes
Level	A2 and above
Preparation	Select a text with subheadings and illustrations. Photocopy the text, and then blank out all the main text, leaving only the subheadings and illustrations. You will need one copy of the subheadings and illustrations handout and a copy of the complete original text for each pair of learners.

Procedure

1 Write the title of the text on the board and ask learners to suggest illustrations or subheadings they might expect to see in a text with this title. Write their suggestions on the board.
2 Form pairs, and distribute one copy of the handout of subheadings and illustrations to each pair.
3 Ask the learners to look at the subheadings and illustrations and to make up two questions per subheading that they think the missing text may answer.
4 Hand out one copy of the complete text to each pair and ask them to see if they can find the answers to their questions in the text.
5 Discuss briefly how they can use this reading strategy themselves to help them to understand and remember subject information.

Subject examples
Any text can be used for this activity

Note
This activity can be done with an interactive whiteboard.

2.14 Understanding new words

Outline	Learners use existing vocabulary knowledge to help them understand new words.
Thinking skills	Reasoning
Language focus	Vocabulary
Language skill	Reading
Time	10 minutes
Level	A2 and above
Preparation	Select any text you want to use in class. Make one copy per learner. You will need a set of coloured highlighter pens for each pair of learners.

Procedure

1 Carry out an understanding for gist activity (e. g. Activity 2.2: *Gist statements*) to introduce the text to your learners.
2 Learners work in pairs and underline all the words in the text that one or both of them already know.
3 Learners use a pink highlighter pen to mark all the words which look like words from their first language.
4 Learners use a green highlighter pen to mark all the words which contain affixes that they know (*un-*, *im-*, *-tion*, *-able*).
5 Learners use a blue highlighter to mark any words which contain Latin or Greek roots.
6 Learners use a yellow highlighter to mark other words in the text which are new, but that they think they can guess.
7 Learners draw a line with a pencil through any remaining words that they think they need to know to understand the text. Can they understand the text without these words?
8 How many of the remaining words do the learners think they should look up in a dictionary?

Subject examples
Any text can be used for this activity.

Note

Depending on your learners, and the text, you may decide not to use *all* of the categories we suggest in the procedure. We have included all of them, so you can choose those that are relevant. These analysis techniques do have their limitations, for example learners may not be able to work out the meaning of a word from the affix, if they do not know the root. They may also not be familiar with Greek or Latin. However, in some circumstances, these techniques can help learners to unlock the meanings of words, and showing learners how they can use their knowledge of how language works to help them understand texts is an important CLIL teaching technique.

Variation

This can also be carried out as a class activity with a digital whiteboard.

2.15 What was the question?

Outline	Learners create questions about a text from the answers.
Thinking skills	Reasoning, creative thinking
Language focus	Question forms
Language skills	Reading and writing
Time	20–30 minutes depending on the length of text and level of difficulty
Learners' level	A2 and above
Preparation	Select a text from your coursebook with accompanying questions and model answers. If you do not have ready-made questions and answers, make up your own to go with the text. Keep the text separate from the questions and answers. You will need enough copies of the text for half the class and enough copies of the answers for the other half.

Procedure

1 Introduce the topic of the text. Briefly brainstorm learners' ideas about what themes might be discussed in the text and write them on the board.
2 Divide the class into two halves. Give each learner in one half of the class a copy of the text, and give a copy of the answers to each learner in the other half of the class.
3 Explain that someone has lost the questions that accompany the text they are going to read, but that the answers are available. Their task is to work out together what the original questions were.
4 Discuss all the questions as a class, and then agree on one final version of each of the original questions. You could then give out the original questions for the learners to compare their versions with those on the original list.

Subject examples
Any text can be used for this activity.

Follow-up

Learners can make up their own questions and answers for any text and give the answers to another learner to work out the questions.

Variation

You could introduce this activity to A1 learners as a matching exercise. In that case, you mix up the questions and answers and ask the learners to match the question to the answer.

3.1 Academic word list

Outline	Learners work on their academic vocabulary by completing gaps in a text.
Thinking skills	Remembering, reasoning, understanding
Language focus	Vocabulary
Language skills	Reading
Time	10–20 minutes
Level	B1 and above
Preparation	For this activity, you will need a digital text and copies of the gapped text or texts generated for your learners. Log on to the Academic Word List (AWL) site at http://www.nottingham. ac.uk/~alzsh3/acvocab/index.htm and click on the AWL gapmaker. Paste your chosen text into the box, choose a level from 1 (easiest) to 10 (hardest) and submit your text to the site. Assess the text generated; if it's too difficult or too easy, try another level until you produce a gapped text you are happy with. You can also differentiate between your learners by producing gapped texts at different levels. Copy and paste your gapped text and the words into a document, number the gaps for ease of reference and make enough copies for your learners. See Box 3.1 for an example for science.

Procedure

1 Brainstorm some examples of academic vocabulary on the board and discuss the difference between academic and general vocabulary, for example:

General vocabulary	Academic vocabulary (from the AWL sublist)
happen	occur
main	major
work	labour
show	indicate
meaningful	significant

2 Give out your gapped text or texts, one copy per pair of learners.
3 Check that your learners understand the vocabulary which they must use to fill in the gaps. Work through the first example with them, helping them with vocabulary-guessing strategies, e.g. *Is the word a noun? Is it singular or plural? How do you know?*
4 Learners complete the gaps in pairs.
5 Give out a completed version of the text.

Box 3.1: Academic word list

Science: electricity

(original text from Wikipedia http://en.wikipedia.org/wiki/Electricity)

Electricity is a general term that encompasses a variety of phenomena resulting from the presence and flow of electric charge. These include many easily recognisable phenomena, such as lightning and static electricity, but in addition, less familiar concepts, such as the electromagnetic field and electromagnetic induction.

In general usage, the word 'electricity' is adequate to refer to a number of physical effects. In scientific usage, however, the term is vague, and these related, but distinct, concepts are better identified by more precise terms:

Electric charge – a property of some subatomic particles, which determines their electromagnetic interactions. Electrically charged matter is influenced by, and produces, electromagnetic fields.
Electric current – a movement or flow of electrically charged particles, typically measured in amperes.
Electric field – an influence produced by an electric charge on other charges in its vicinity.
Electric potential – the capacity of an electric field to do work on an electric charge, typically measured in volts.
Electromagnetism – a fundamental interaction between the magnetic field and the presence and motion of an electric charge.

Gapped text produced at level 4

Words to complete the gaps:

adequate   concepts   distinct   identified
interaction   interactions   physical   potential

Electricity is a general term that encompasses a variety of phenomena resulting from the presence and flow of electric charge. These include many easily recognisable phenomena, such as lightning and static electricity, but in addition, less familiar 1. ...., such as the electromagnetic field and electromagnetic induction.

In general usage, the word 'electricity' is 2 .... to refer to a number of 3 .... effects. In scientific usage, however, the term is vague, and these related, but 4 ...., concepts are better 5 .... by more precise terms:

Electric charge – a property of some subatomic particles, which determines their electromagnetic 6 .... Electrically charged matter is influenced by, and produces, electromagnetic fields.
Electric current – a movement or flow of electrically charged particles, typically measured in amperes.
Electric field – an influence produced by an electric charge on other charges in its vicinity.
Electric 7 .... – the capacity of an electric field to do work on an electric charge, typically measured in volts.
Electromagnetism – a fundamental 8 .... between the magnetic field and the presence and motion of an electric charge.

Subject examples

Any academic text can be used for this activity.

Variation
Learners can find their own texts and generate gapped texts for each other, or to practise themselves.

Note
See Activity 2.10: *Mind the gap* for another gap-filling activity. The Academic Word List (AWL) was developed by Averil Coxhead at the Victoria University of Wellington in New Zealand; online activities have been developed by the University of Notthingham in the UK. The AWL contains 570 sublists (word families) of the most common academic words.

> 💡 **Tips for cross-curricular cooperation between subject and language teachers**
>
> Before the lesson : The language teacher works with learners on the vocabulary-guessing strategy of looking at the context surrounding a word in order to guess it, e.g. is the missing word a noun, a verb or something else?

3.2 Bingo

Outline	Learners play the game of Bingo with vocabulary they have learned.
Thinking skills	Understanding, defining
Language focus	Vocabulary
Language skills	Listening and speaking
Time	10 minutes
Level	Any
Preparation	List 12 words learners need to learn and prepare definitions for them. Make Bingo cards using nine of the words in three rows of three, one different card per learner. See Box 3.2 and *Subject examples*.

Procedure

1 Give each learner a Bingo card.
2 Use your list of 12 words. Call out your definition of nine of them, at random.
3 Learners cross out the word if they think the definition matches a word on their card.
4 The learner with a completed card shouts 'Bingo!'
5 Check that the learner has crossed out the correct words on their card.
6 Continue until three learners shout out 'Bingo!'

Box 3.2: Bingo

Art, design and technology: architectural detail

arch	porch	architrave
doorway	window	moulding
gate	stanchion	carving

From *CLIL Activities* © Cambridge University Press 2012   PHOTOCOPIABLE

Subject examples

Maths

Draw numbers from a pack of cards from 1 to 100.

square number	multiple of 7	cube number
factor of 24	prime number	triangular number
negative number	multiple of 4	factor of 42

4	56	27
8	37	15
−2	20	7

You can also use Bingo cards for equivalences between fractions, decimals and percentages. For example, call out a decimal (0,3); learners cross out the equivalent percentage (30%).

Variation

Bingo can be used for any matching exercise, e.g. pictures and words, examples and names (vinegar is an example of ethanoic acid).

 Teaching tip

Learners take it in turns to read the definitions for the rest of the class, instead of the teacher reading them.

3.3 Guess the word

Outline	Learners have one minute to guess as many words as possible from a pile of cards.
Thinking skills	Remembering, defining, creative thinking
Language focus	Vocabulary
Language skills	Speaking
Time	10 minutes
Level	Any
Preparation	Make a list of about 20 words. Write each word on a separate card. Put all the cards upside down in a pile at the front of the class.

Procedure

1   Divide the class into two teams, A and B.
2   Ask a learner from Team A to pick up a card from the pile and describe it for their team, without, of course, mentioning the word. Team A must try to guess the word being described. When they have guessed the word, the learner picks up a new card and continues. The team has one minute to guess as many words as possible.
     Each word guessed correctly is one point.
3   After one minute, it's Team B's turn.

Subject examples

This game can be used with any list of words.

Variation
Instead of describing the word, learners can draw the words on the board.

 Teaching tip

Use words from the learners' own personal vocabulary files (see Activity 3.10: *Personal vocabulary file or glossary*) to encourage learners to actively use their files.

3.4 Hot seat

Outline	Learners ask someone in the hot seat questions to find out the subject word or phrase on a card.
Thinking skills	Creative thinking, evaluating
Language focus	Questions
Language skills	Speaking and listening
Time	20 minutes
Level	A2 and above
Preparation	Identify 10–20 key subject words or phrases related to your current topic which you want your learners to remember and understand. Write them on separate cards. Copy one set of cards per group of six learners.

Procedure

1 Divide the class into groups of six. Nominate one of the learners to sit in the 'hot seat'.
2 Give each learner in the hot seat one card you have prepared. Tell them to look at the first card, without letting anyone else in the group see it.
3 Tell the remaining five members of the group that they must take it in turns to ask questions to find out the word or phrase on the card. Their questions may be open or closed, but learners may not ask what is on the card directly.
4 The learner in the hot seat must answer the questions. The first learner to guess the words on the card then takes the hot seat, and the activity continues until all the cards have been used up.
5 If necessary, practise guessing the word on one card together as a class.

Subject examples
Any topic can be used for this activity.

Variation

It is also possible to use the cards to play the game '20 questions': learners may only ask questions which can be answered 'yes' or 'no'. They may guess the contents of the card after any question, but must stop after 20.

3.5 Matching trios

Outline	Learners match three or four sets of cards.
Thinking skills	Classifying
Language focus	Recycling subject-specific vocabulary, giving opinions
Language skills	Speaking
Time	10 minutes
Level	Any
Preparation	Make sets of cards where learners match three different items together, for example a word, its academic equivalent and a definition. See Box 3.5 for a maths example.

Procedure

1   Learners work in groups. Give each group a pile of cards.
2   Learners match the cards with each other, making as many sets of cards as possible.

Box 3.5: Matching trios

Maths: revision of linear formulae, quadratic formulae and inversely proportional formulae. Learners match four different aspects of maths together. Learners match the name of the formula with the name of the graph, the appropriate table and formula(e).

Set 1: names of formulae

linear formula	quadratic formula	inversely proportional formula
linear formula	quadratic formula	inversely proportional formula
linear formula	quadratic formula	inversely proportional formula

Set 2: names of graphs

straight line	parabola	hyperbola
straight line	parabola	hyperbola
straight line	parabola	hyperbola

Set 3: measurements on axes

A			
X	0	1	2	3
Y	15	17	19	21

B			
X	0	1	2	3
Y	3	5	11	21

C			
x	0	1	2	3
y	6	6,5	8	10,5

D			
X	0	1	2	3
Y	0	24	12	6

E			
x	0	1	2	3
y	41	36	31	26

✂

Set 4: formulae

F	G	H
$y = 2x + 15$	$xy = 24$	$y = -5x + 41$
I	J	K
$y = 2(x + 7\frac{1}{2})$	$y = \frac{1}{2}x^2 + 6$	$y = 2x^2 + 3$

✂

KEY

Table A	Table B	Table C	Table D	Table E
Formulae F and I	Formula K	Formula J	Formula G	Formula H
Linear formula	Quadratic formula	Quadratic formula	Inversely proportional	Linear formula
Straight line	Parabola	Parabola	Hyperbola	Straight line

Subject examples

Economics and business studies: Learners match word (*inflation*), definition (*rise in cost of living*), illustration (e.g. graph).

Art, design and technology: Learners match materials (piece of plastic), names of materials (*plastic*) and a picture showing something made of the material (plastic cup).

Variation

Learners could create their own matching activities for each other.

3.6 Mind maps

Outline	Learners create a mind map for vocabulary.
Thinking skills	Ordering, defining, classifying
Language focus	Vocabulary
Language skills	Speaking
Time	15 minutes
Level	A1 and above
Preparation	Write the name of a topic in the centre bubble of the mind map template (see Box 3.6 for an example). Prepare enough copies for each learner in your class.

Procedure

1 Individually, learners write down about 25 words related to a topic. Ask the class for examples and write 25 to 30 words randomly on the board.
2 Explain that you remember words better if you group them in themes or categories. Ask the learners to work in pairs and think of how they might organise the words into groups (e.g. by sound, by meaning, by colour, by category). Elicit examples from the learners and demonstrate how to create a mind map using some categories they suggest.
3 Hand out a copy of the mind map template to each learner. Ask learners to work individually and create a mind map like the one in Box 3.6 for the words they chose at the beginning of the lesson. They can also use colours or drawings to show words belonging to the same category. Depending on the level of your class, choose several well-worked-out examples to display around the walls of your classroom.

Variation

Write a key word about a topic you would like to revise in the centre of a piece of paper, e.g. *Renaissance*. In the corners of the paper write sub-categories, e.g.

- Art and architecture
- Science and technology
- Explorations
- Why did the Renaissance happen?

Learners create a mind map to brainstorm the knowledge they have on these topics. They can then use arrows to connect the ideas together.

Follow-up

Learners maintain their mind maps in subsequent lessons and review the words regularly.

Box 3.6: Mind maps

Biology: Health

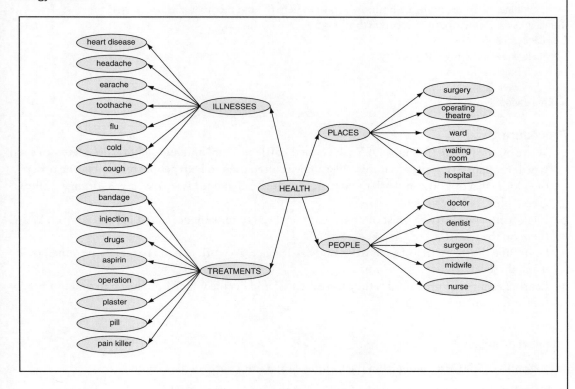

This mind map was generated using Inspiration software.

From *CLIL Activities* © Cambridge University Press 2012   PHOTOCOPIABLE

Subject examples

Any vocabulary can be used for this activity.

⚬ Teaching tip

Various digital mind-mapping tools are available which can be used for this exercise. Inspiration can be found at www.inspiration.com.

3.7 Mnemonics

Outline	Learners make up a funny phrase to help them remember a list of words.
Thinking skills	Remembering, creative thinking
Language focus	Vocabulary
Language skills	Speaking and writing
Time	10 minutes
Level	Any
Preparation	None

Procedure

1 Write on the board, 'Richard Of York Gained Battle In Vain' and highlight the first letter of each word. Explain to learners that this mnemonic is often used to help people remember the order of colours in a rainbow and ask them to guess what each colour is (Answer: red, orange, yellow, green, blue, indigo, violet).

2 Elicit from your learners a list of items that they need to remember related to your subject. Write them on the board.

3 Underline the first letter of each word and ask learners to work in pairs to make up a mnemonic using these letters. Set a time limit.

4 Learners share the mnemonics they have created and decide which one they will find most helpful for remembering the list.

Subject examples

Geography: StalaCtites hang from the Ceiling. StalaGmites are on the Ground.

Music: the notes associated with the five lines of the treble clef using the following mnemonic (from the bottom line to the top):

Every Good Boy Does Fine.

Chemistry: atoms which always pair up:

N	H	Cl	Br	I	O	F
Nitrogen	Hydrogen	Chlorine	Bromide	Iodine	Oxygen	Fluoride

Never Hit Clara's Brother Immediately On Fridays.

Biology: classification:

kingdom phylum class order family genus species

King Philip Came Over For Green Spaghetti.

3.8 Noticing

Outline	Learners find and practise examples of language use in a text.
Thinking skills	Classifying, applying, analysing, evaluating
Language focus	Grammar, vocabulary
Language skills	Reading
Time	20 minutes
Level	A2 and above
Preparation	Survey your coursebook and select several examples of a text-type that is often used in your subject (see Part 2: *Subject pages* for ideas). Identify some language which is used frequently in the text (e.g. types of linking words, verbs, adjectives). Select two texts that contain a number of examples of this type of language, Text A and Text B. Leave Text A complete, but delete all examples of the language feature you want to highlight from Text B. You can make the activity more, or less, difficult by providing the missing words in random order, mixing up the letters in the words, providing the first letter of the missing word, or giving no words at all. You can also do this activity on a smart board. Make one copy of the text for each pair of learners.

Procedure

1 Highlight some of the characteristic language features of Text A, either on the board or using a projection. Explain and give an example of the language (*We use the imperative to tell people what to do – Sit down, Take your coats off*).

2 Hand out examples of a similar text with gaps (Text B) and ask learners to fill them in. Alternatively, create another task to help them notice the language (see the physics task in Box 3.8).

3 Set a writing exercise where learners will need to use your chosen language feature.

Box 3.8: Noticing

Physics: lab reports

The language of laboratory reports, which uses a lot of passive forms, is sometimes difficult for CLIL learners. This noticing task guides them to look at the passive tenses in an authentic laboratory report.

Instructions

Laboratory reports are often written in the passive tense (e.g. *The test tube <u>was filled</u>, The liquid <u>was measured out</u>*), to make them more formal and less personal. You can recognise passive-voice expressions because the verb phrase always includes a form of *be*, such as *am, is, was, were, are* or *been*. However, the presence of a form of *be* does not necessarily mean that the sentence is in the passive voice. You can also recognise passive-voice sentences since they often include a '*by the …*' phrase after the verb, or suggest one: for example, *The man <u>was bitten by the</u> dog*).

Here is a part of a real laboratory report. Highlight or underline all the examples of the passive tense in the text. How many are there?

1. six   2. seven   3. eight   4. Nine

Subject examples
History: linking words for time
Music and drama: adjectives in reviews of concerts

Note
Learners can notice two things: firstly, the meaning (what language is used) and secondly, the form (how the language is used). For example, if learners come across a sentence like *On Jan. 21, 2008, stock prices tumbled around the world* (from a text for economics and business studies), they might notice the meaning, i.e. that *tumbled* means 'fell', or the form, i.e. that *tumbled* (ending in *-ed*) is a regular past tense, which is often used in combination with a specific time (*Jan. 21, 2008*).

 Teaching tips

Here are some ideas related to noticing which can be done in a few minutes:

- Explain and draw attention to a particular form. For example, *If we look at this text, we see a number of imperatives. For instance <u>measure</u>, <u>fill</u>, <u>add up</u>, <u>empty</u>, <u>dissolve</u>.*
- Recycle a structure frequently and consciously in spoken or written language. For example, as a teacher, use these words yourself, put them into tasks and write them on the board.
- Learners do tasks which highlight or underline a structure, to draw attention to it. For example, *Adjectives are words used to describe nouns. They are words like <u>small</u>, <u>hairy</u>, <u>bald</u> and <u>long-legged</u>. There are quite a few adjectives in this text. Use a highlighter pen to highlight all the adjectives in this text.*
- Learners do a task that requires them to be aware of a structure in order to complete it. For example, *Here are some instructions for an experiment. Complete the instructions with the 10 words (imperatives) provided below.*
- Learners change words from one form to another: for example, *How many related words can you make from the word <u>unemployment</u>?* (employment, to employ, employable, employability).

 Tips for cross-curricular cooperation between subject and language teachers

Before the lesson: The language teacher and subject teacher select a suitable text together. The language teacher helps the subject teacher with grammar questions.

After the lesson: For homework, learners find 10 examples of the structure they have been working on from the Internet or television.

3.9 Odd one out

Outline	Learners discuss which word or picture is the odd one out.
Thinking skills	Comparing and contrasting, reasoning
Language focus	Vocabulary
Language skills	Speaking
Time	20 minutes
Level	A2 and above
Preparation	Scan a chapter in your coursebook. Select groups of four words/concepts/ideas which can be linked in several ways (e.g. *table*, *chair*, *bed*, *sofa* or *emancipation*, *segregation*, *integration*, *assimilation*). There should NOT be an obvious odd one out in your groups of four, but several possibilities. Make a table like the one in Box 3.9 for each group of four words. You will need a copy of the table for each group of three learners.

Procedure

1   Write four words on the board. Discuss with the class which word could be the odd one out and why. Encourage the learners to think creatively and to come up with a variety of reasons. These might be to do with meaning, colour, number of letters, pronunciation, etc.
2   Divide the class into groups of three. Give each group a copy of the table you prepared (Box 3.9).
3   Ask the learners to circle the word they feel is the odd one out and to write their reason in the final column.
4   Ask the groups in turn to explain some of their choices to a partner or the rest of the class.

Box 3.9: Odd one out

				Reason
table	chair	bed	sofa	
red	blue	yellow	white	
scissors	knife	saw	scalpel	
tape measure	ruler	calliper	compass	
oils	watercolours	crayons	charcoal	

From *CLIL Activities* © Cambridge University Press 2012   PHOTOCOPIABLE

Subject examples

Economics and business studies: *inflation, deflation, recession, crisis*

Geography: *volcano, earthquake, tsunami, flood*

Note
This activity is adapted from Leat (2001).

3.10 Personal vocabulary file or glossary

Outline	Learners create and organise their own personal vocabulary list or glossary in a notebook or on the computer.
Thinking skills	Ordering, defining, classifying
Language focus	Vocabulary
Language skills	Vocabulary learning strategies
Time	15 minutes
Level	A1 and above
Preparation	Learners need a notebook or file which they use as their personal vocabulary book or file for all the subjects taught in English. It helps if all the teachers use the glossaries in a similar way.

Procedure

1 Ask each learner to write down the 10 words they most want to remember from this lesson.
2 Elicit an example of a word a learner has written down. Use the word to show learners on the board which information they can note down in a vocabulary list (see Box 3.10 for an example).
3 Ask learners to complete similar vocabulary records for each of the words they have chosen.
4 Depending on the level of your class, choose several well-worked-out examples to display around the walls of your classroom. Update these regularly to suit the topic you are working on.

Box 3.10: Personal vocabulary file or glossary

Form: spelling and pronunciation   acid   /ˈæsɪd/

Picture

Meaning   'A substance (usually liquid) which reacts chemically with other materials and sometimes dissolves them.'

Use in a sentence   The <u>acid</u> made a hole in the plastic cup.

Related words   acidic/acidify

From *CLIL Activities* © Cambridge University Press 2012   PHOTOCOPIABLE

Subject examples
Any vocabulary can be used for this activity.

Follow-up
Learners maintain their glossary in subsequent lessons and review the words regularly.

Variation
There are a number of less elaborate ways of reviewing words. Here are just a few.

- During the lesson, if learners do not understand a word while doing a task, they go up to the board and write it in the designated space, for example the left-hand side of the board. At an appropriate moment, the teacher discusses all these words or phrases with the whole class. This activity enables learners to decide for themselves which vocabulary they need to know.
- Learners recall two or three words silently inside their head which have been used in the lesson. In random order, ask each learner to say one word. Continue until all the learners have given a word. If a word is used, learners need to think of a new one.
- Learners recall one key word from the lesson silently in their head. Ask one learner to say his/her key word. Ask how many learners had the same word.

♀ Teaching tip
There are websites on the Internet where you can learn and store personal vocabulary online, free.

♀ Tips for cross-curricular cooperation between subject and language teachers
After the lesson: The language teacher and subject teacher use the glossaries as input for various vocabulary games, e.g. hangman, word searches, scrambled letters, twenty questions, memory.

3.11 Ranking

Outline	Learners put a list of words, pictures or sentences in an order.
Thinking skills	Ordering, classifying, comparing
Language focus	Vocabulary and language of comparison
Language skills	Speaking
Time	10 minutes
Level	A2 and above
Preparation	Prepare a list of 8 to 15 points which can be ordered in some way (see *Subject examples* for ideas). Write the points on individual cards and put them in an envelope. Prepare one set of cards per group of three learners.

Procedure

1 Divide the class into groups of three.
2 Give one set of cards to each group of learners.
3 Ask the learners to put the cards in the correct order.

Subject examples

Art, design and technology: 15 paintings from oldest to most recently painted

History: 15 events from most distant past to most recent past

ICT: 15 developments in ICT in the past five years

Maths: 8 names of shapes from least number of sides to most number of sides

Music and drama: 15 notes in order of appearance in a song

PE: 15 verbs in order of use in a sport

Science

Biology: 15 parts of the digestive system in the order they are passed by a piece of food

Physics: 10 words occurring in an electrical circuit in order of the flow of current

Chemistry: 15 verbs involved in an experiment

Variations

It is also possible to rank words in terms of the closeness of their relationship to a concept, such as temperature: e.g. *Put the colours in order from warm to cold*.

 Teaching tip

Learners who enjoy a challenge could guess what order they should put the cards in from looking at the words.

3.12 Snake

Outline	Learners use cards to ask and answer questions to form a 'loop'.
Thinking skills	Remembering, understanding
Language focus	Vocabulary
Language skills	Reading and listening
Time	10 minutes
Level	Any
Preparation	Choose about 15 words or concepts which you want your learners to remember. Write a definition of one of the words on the left-hand side of the card and write another word on the right-hand side. On the next card, write the definition of this word on the left-hand side and a new word on the right-hand side. Continue until you have made cards for all the words. The last card includes a definition of the very first word, so learners can make a circular 'snake' out of all the words and definitions. You will need one set of cards per group. See Box 3.12 for a set of cards for geography.

Procedure

1 Divide the class into groups of four. They deal out their set of cards. Learners can look at their own cards but not show them to others.
2 One learner starts the game by reading out the definition on the first card and placing their card in the centre of the table.
3 The person with the card whose word is defined says the word, and reads aloud the next question, placing the card next to the first card.
4 The game continues until all cards have been placed on the table. The definition on the last card should be the answer to the first card, so that cards make a 'snake'. In this way, the learners can check that they have the answers right.

Follow-up
Learners can create their own loop card games for each other, using words from their personal vocabulary files (see Activity 3.10: *Personal vocabulary file or glossary*).

Variation
Instead of definitions, you can use questions.

 Teaching tip

You can make this game competitive by giving a prize to the first group to finish the snake.

Box 3.12: Snake

A layer of dense plant growth. It contains shrubs and ferns.	Amazonia
Name of a tropical rainforest found in South America.	Brazil
A country this rainforest is found in.	equatorial climate
The types of climate where tropical rainforests grow.	emergents
The tallest trees in the rainforest.	lianas
The name of the vine type plants found in the rainforest.	mahogany, greenheart
Examples of hardwoods	Amerindians
The name of the original inhabitants of Amazonia.	buttress

The name given to large tree roots.	canopy

✂- -

The layer of trees that blocks out the sun from lower layers.	forest floor

✂- -

This layer is usually dark and damp; it contains a layer of rotting leaves.	evergreen

✂- -

The appearance of the rainforest all year round	under canopy

✂- -

A layer of bare trees and lianas found under the canopy.	adaptation

✂- -

The way in which plants and animals survive in the rainforest.	shrub layer

✂- -

Subject examples

Any words and definitions can be used for this activity.

3.13 Sorting

Outline	Learners sort cards describing characteristics into sub-categories.
Thinking skills	Classifying
Language focus	Vocabulary
Language skills	Reading and speaking
Time	20–30 minutes
Level	A2 and above
Preparation	This is a revision activity. Make a table like the one in Box 3.13 of your chosen topics (in capital letters) and characteristics (in very short sentences or phrases). Copy or print the table you have created on to coloured cardboard – a different colour for each group. Copy one set of cards for each group of four learners. Cut out the cards and shuffle them.

Procedure

1 Learners work in groups of four around a table with a pile of cards (of a single colour). Give them the task: 'You have 10 minutes to arrange the cards into three logical columns on your table.'

2 Circulate, asking critical questions and giving hints about the choices learners have made, but not telling them the right answer.

3 Learners should be encouraged to use English only and to discuss why they think a card belongs in a certain column.

4 After 10 minutes, or when each group is ready, the groups rotate. Each group moves to another table and has another five minutes to correct or reorganise the work of another group.

5 After five minutes, the groups go back to their own table and look at the changes the other group made to their work. They reorganise the columns again, depending on whether they agree or disagree with the new order.

6 If learners get stuck, you can do scaffold learning by providing a short text about the three topics (e.g. about veins, arteries and capillaries for the example in Box 3.13) to help them to sort the cards.

7 Discuss the correct answers.

Box 3.13: Sorting

ARTERIES	CAPILLARIES	VEINS
They carry blood away from heart.	They carry blood through tissues and organs.	They carry blood towards heart.
They contain blood at high pressure.	They contain blood at low pressure.	They contain blood at lowest pressure.
They have no valves.	They have no valves.	They have valves to stop blood flowing back.
They have thick muscular walls.	They have very thin walls for escape of fluids.	They have thinner walls with less muscle.
No substances leave or enter this vessel.	Exchange of substances takes place with tissues in this vessel.	No substances leave or enter this vessel.
A pulse is created by heart pumping & contraction of wall muscle.	There is no pulse.	There is no pulse.
They have strong walls.	They have delicate walls which are easily broken.	They have flexible walls which are squashed easily so blood is pushed further along vessel.
They carry oxygenated blood (with one exception).	They carry a mix of oxygenated and deoxygenated blood.	They carry deoxygenated blood (with one exception).

✂

From *CLIL Activities* © Cambridge University Press 2012   PHOTOCOPIABLE

Variation

Make sets of about 20 words or concepts you would like your learners to remember on small cards. Give each of them – or each pair – a set of words. Ask them to group the words into appropriate categories. Have a brief class discussion about the groups and why they chose to group the words in that way.

Follow-up

Ask learners to make a poster showing all the words in the categories they have chosen. They can add titles for each category and illustrations. Hang the posters on the classroom walls.

3.14 Taboo

Outline	Learners play a game with taboo words.
Thinking skills	Creative thinking
Language focus	Vocabulary
Language skills	Speaking
Time	20 minutes
Level	A2 or above
Preparation	Make a set of 'taboo cards' related to a topic you are covering at the moment. Each card includes one word or phrase and a number of associated 'taboo' words. For example, for the topic *CELL*, the card could include *small, smallest, basic, unit, life*. (See *Subject examples*.)

Procedure

1   Divide the class into competing teams. Each team nominates a clue-giver and a checker.
2   Team A's clue-giver turns over the first card and holds it in his or her hand so that only the clue-giver in Team A and the checker from Team B can read it.
3   The clue-giver from Team A describes the word at the very top of the card without saying any (or any part) of the taboo words or phrases printed below it. No rhyming words can be given. No hand motions or sound effects can be added. If the clue-giver from Team A says one of the taboo words, the checker from Team B will say 'taboo' and a new card is turned over. The group must guess the word within 75 seconds.
4   Scoring. Each time a team guesses a word correctly within 75 seconds, their team scores a point and a new card is turned over. If the clue-giver says one of the taboo words or runs out of time, the team loses a point.
5   Team B's clue-giver turns a card over and Team A's checker looks at the card.
6   Once the class has the idea, work in smaller groups to play the game.

Subject examples

Maths

FRACTION
number part whole percentage quarter

Physics

FORCE
influence power mass velocity matter

Note
The original idea for this activity comes from http://www.nps.gov/archive/indu/education/westbeach/taboo.htm.

 Teaching tip

In order to make cards, type your headword into an internet search engine. This makes it easy to find five words which are often used in combination with this word.

3.15 Vocabulary posters

Outline	Learners create posters with useful vocabulary.
Thinking skills	Ordering, creating
Language focus	Vocabulary
Language skills	Writing and speaking
Time	20–30 minutes, depending on size of posters and number of words
Level	Any
Preparation	Review a topic you will be dealing with in class – read through the resources you will be using (coursebook chapter, internet sources), and make a list of the key vocabulary (30 to 40 words) learners will need for this topic. Divide the list up into smaller groups (of 6–10 words) – one per group of three/four learners in your class. For each group you will need to bring the following to class: one word list, A1 paper for posters, coloured pens and pencils, glue, magazines.

Procedure

1 Learners work in groups. Give each group a full set of resources: word list, paper, pens and pencils, glue, magazines.
2 Learners use the resources to create posters which show the meaning of each of the words. Show learners some models – an internet search for vocabulary posters in your subject could help. Discuss how learners can show the pronunciation of a word (e.g. with word stress markings, or phonetic script). Set a time limit.
3 When all the posters are finished, hang them on the wall so that learners can use them for reference when they work on the topic.

Subject examples

Any word list can be used for this activity.

Variations

Learners can also make posters of useful phrases for classroom language (*What does this mean? How do I say …? Could you say that again, please?*), group work language (*What do you think? Why? What do we have to do?*), social talk (*Did you see …? What did you do last weekend? Have you heard …?*). This can help to stimulate the use of English in the class.

 Teaching tip

The types of words for visualisation can be more, or less, challenging depending on the level of your learners (e.g. *democracy* is more difficult to visualise than *table*). Keep any inspiring posters to use in subsequent years.

3.16 Vocabulary strategies

Outline	Learners use word forms and patterns to expand their vocabulary.
Thinking skills	Remembering, analysing
Language focus	Vocabulary
Language skills	Writing and speaking
Time	10–20 minutes
Level	A2 and above
Preparation	Choose a word from your subject which appears in several different forms, e.g. *technology*. Find as many associated words as you can (e.g. *technique, technician, technological, technical, technophobe, high-tech, low-tech, techie*). An online dictionary may help.

Procedure

1 Write your word on the board and ask learners to work in pairs and write down as many words that share its root on the board.
2 Elicit the words the learners have thought of. Write them on the board. Add any words they have forgotten.
3 Check all the learners know the meanings of each of the words and how to pronounce them.
4 Repeat the activity with two or three more words, and then divide the class into two teams. Ask them to choose 10 words and write one sentence using each word.
5 Hold a quiz to see which team can guess the most correct words: Team A reads aloud their sentence, missing out the key word (e.g. *After the Industrial Revolution, came the* .... *revolution.*). Team B supplies the missing word and spells it. If they get the word, its pronunciation and spelling right, they get two points. If they get the word right but mispronounce or misspell it, they get one point. If they get the word wrong, they get no points. The teams take it in turns until all the sentences have been used.

Subject examples

This activity can be used with words in any subject.

Variations

You could use the same technique to ask learners to make words with Latin or Greek roots (e.g. *syn-: synthesis, synthetic, photosynthesis, synthesizer*). They could work out the common meaning of the word and how it is used in each word (*syn-* means bring together, *synthesis* is the process of bringing together, *synthetic* describes materials that are brought together, *photosynthesis* is the process whereby light is used to bring together chemical compounds, a *synthesizer* brings sounds together). They could then hold a quiz on words containing *syn-*.

3.17 Word association

Outline	Learners organise words into categories and explain their choices.
Thinking skills	Classifying
Language focus	Vocabulary
Language skills	Speaking
Time	15 minutes
Level	A2 and above
Preparation	Select some words which you would like learners to recall. Choose some categories, for example shape, colour, animal, place, in which they could place the words (see *Subject examples* for some ideas).

Procedure

1 Write all the words on the board.
2 Introduce the categories you have chosen. Choose one word and ask several learners which category they would place the word in, and why.
3 Ask the learners to work individually and place each of the words into one of the categories.
4 Put learners into pairs and ask them to explain their choices to each other.
5 Monitor the learners' discussions and ask learners to explain the most unusual or surprising choices to the whole class.

Subject examples

Economics and business studies: banking

account   bank   statement   borrow   budget   cash   cashier   cheque
credit card   currency   deposit   savings   withdraw   instalments   receipt
refund   income   pay into   save up   take out   broke   hard-up

We have come across the words above during our lessons over the past few weeks. This task will help you to remember them better.

Write each word under the colour you associate it with and be ready to explain why you have chosen a particular colour for a word.

YELLOW	BLUE	RED	GREEN
cash	savings	withdraw	pay into

Learners might say things such as *I put savings under BLUE because it's the colour of my bank's website*, or *I put withdraw under RED because if you have a negative bank balance you are 'in the red'*.

History: the Industrial Revolution

capital   capitalism   collective bargaining   communism   conservative
enclosure   entrepreneur   exploitation   industrialisation   monopoly
obsolete   oligopoly   oppression   proletariat   radical   strike   union

We have come across the words above during our lessons over the past few weeks. This task will help you to remember them better.

Write each word under the shape you associate it with and be ready to explain why you have chosen a particular shape for a word.

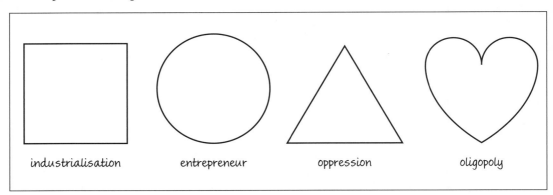

industrialisation   entrepreneur   oppression   oligopoly

Learners might say things like *I put <u>industrialisation</u> under the square because it sounds organised.*

Biology: five senses

(colour) **blind listen tongue bitter hard of hearing tickle   glance   stroke eye
glimpse   rub   look at notice stare   hear   eyesight   scent   stink   sniff   aroma
nose   inhale** mouth sweet deaf   sour   taste buds feel   ear   massage

We have come across the words above during our lessons over the past few weeks. This task will help you to remember them better.

Write each word under the sense with which you associate it.

Possible key

hearing	sight	smell	taste	touch
hear	glance	scent	inhale	feel
listen	eye	stink	mouth	stroke
deaf	glimpse	sniff	tongue	tickle
hard of hearing	look at	aroma	sweet	rub
ear	notice	nose	sour	massage
	stare		bitter	
	(colour) blind		taste buds	
	eyesight			

3.18 Word puzzle

Outline	Learners create word puzzles for each other using key subject words.
Thinking skills	Defining, remembering, understanding
Language focus	Vocabulary
Language skills	Writing
Time	20 minutes
Level	A2 and above
Preparation	None

Procedure

1 Learners think of a word with at least four letters relating to your current topic, e.g. *rise*.
2 Highlight each letter in the word.
3 Learners think of another related word beginning with each of these letters, e.g. *reach*, *increase*, *sharply*, *explode*.
4 Ask learners for one sentence using each of these words, e.g.
   The world population will reach crisis point soon.
   The increase in people living in cities will continue.
   China's export rate rose sharply last year.
   The number of old people is expected to explode.
5. Delete the original word from each sentence, e.g.
   The world population will .... crisis point soon.
   The .... in people living in cities will continue.
   China's export rate rose .... last year.
   The number of old people is expected to ....
6. Learners think of their own word and follow this procedure to produce a word puzzle. Set a time limit.
7. Collect the word puzzles and redistribute them around the class.
8. Learners solve the word puzzle they have been given.

Subject examples

This activity can be used with any word.

♡ Tips for cross-curricular cooperation between subject and language teachers

Before the lesson: The subject teacher supplies subject word lists for the language teacher to do this activity in a language lesson.

During the lesson: The language teacher collects the sentences learners create in the word puzzles and identifies spelling or grammar problems.

After the lesson: The language teacher does follow-up work on any grammar problems which arose in the sentences.

3.19 Word stories

Outline	Learners create a story using subject vocabulary.
Thinking skills	Ordering, defining, classifying
Language focus	Vocabulary
Language skills	Vocabulary learning strategies
Time	15 minutes
Level	A1 and above
Preparation	None

Procedure

1   Ask each learner to write down the 10 words they most want to remember from this lesson and list one learner's words at the side of the board.
2   Write down the first word or phrase of a story (e.g. *Yesterday, Suddenly, Once upon a time*) and ask learners to think of a sentence to follow this, using one of the words in the list.
3   Ask the class to work in pairs and finish this story, making use of all the words. Encourage the learners to be as creative and imaginative as possible. The crazier the story, the better. Set a time limit.
4   Ask learners to create their own individual stories using the 10 words they wrote down at the beginning of the lesson, and then ask some learners to recount their story to the class.
5   Learners read their stories to each other. While one reads, the other writes down the 10 words they think were on their partner's original list.
6   Display some of the best examples on the walls of your classroom and update them regularly to suit the topic you are working on.

Subject examples
Any vocabulary can be used for this activity.

Follow-up
Learners make new stories in subsequent lessons and review the words regularly.

○ Tips for cross-curricular cooperation between subject and English teachers

Before the lesson: The English teacher could introduce vocabulary learning strategies in an English lesson leading up to this activity.

Team teaching: The English teacher could monitor the stories learners create – checking for accuracy.

After the lesson: The English teacher and subject teacher could use the stories as input for various vocabulary games, e.g. hangman, word searches, scrambled letters, 20 questions, pictionary, memory. The drama teacher could also use the stories as input.

---

4 Focus on speaking

4.1 Balloon debate

Outline	The class debates which person (object or solution) should be thrown out of a hot-air balloon.
Thinking skills	Ordering, reasoning, creative thinking
Language focus	Giving opinions
Language skills	Speaking
Time	60 minutes
Level	B1 and above
Preparation	Choose six people (objects or solutions) related to your subject. The class must consider the qualities of each person and then vote for one to be removed on the grounds of being least 'essential'. In order to do this, the class debates about the qualities of each person and then votes for one to be removed.

Procedure

1 Introduce the idea of a balloon debate, describing the situation as follows: *Six people are inside the basket of a hot-air balloon which is quickly losing height. To stay in the air, one of the people must leave the balloon or it will crash.*

2 Divide the class into six groups: each group represents one person in the balloon. Alternatively, a balloon debate can work with items related to your subject, as in the example in Box 4.1.

3 Give each group 10 minutes to prepare a two-minute presentation which persuades the rest of the class why they should remain in the balloon. (Alternatively, learners can research further into the character they are representing as homework.) To ensure participation at this stage, explain that any learner in the group can be called upon to argue the group's case.

4 Set a timer. One random person from each group presents their arguments in two minutes, in turn. Be strict with the timing. During the presentations, each learner notes down which person they feel should be rejected and why.

5 After the presentations, each group discusses which person should be removed from the balloon. This, of course, will not be their own person, object or solution. Give groups five minutes to prepare a one-minute speech to explain who they think should be thrown out of the balloon and why.

6 Set a timer. Each group presents their counter-arguments in one minute, in turn.

7 Groups discuss again which person, object or solution should be removed from the balloon and make a final vote.

Box 4.1: Balloon debate

Reading text

Government Wants to Cut Expenditure on Maintenance of Human Bodies
By our scientific correspondent

Yesterday the government announced measures to economise on the costs of human bodies. The most striking measure is the plan to abolish at least one entire organ system. However, there is still no consensus among government officials which organ system should be done away with. According to reliable sources more details will be announced by next month.

The different organisations for organ systems have been asked for input and comment. The following seven institutes were approached:

- the Association of Circulatory Systems (ACS)
- the Royal Club of Respiratory Systems (RCRS)
- the Friends of Excretion (FE)
- the Digestive Society (DS)
- the Endocrine System Interest Group (ESIG)
- the Nervous Ones (NO)
- the Propagators of Reproduction (PoR)

The above-mentioned interest groups have expressed their concern about the situation, but are not willing to comment at this stage. All agree that talks should be held with each party concerned before opinions can be vented, and that society should not be rushed into such a far-reaching measure.

The following procedure has been proposed. Each of the organisations will send representatives to the talks which will be held at our school. There will be simultaneous meetings, each with one representative of each interest group. The outcome will be discussed in a plenary session. Hopefully, a number of government officials will be present to witness the possible consequences of their proposed policies.

From *CLIL Activities* © Cambridge University Press 2012   PHOTOCOPIABLE

Subject examples
Art, design and technology: six artists or designers; six tools; six artistic movements
Economics and business studies: six important economists / economic theories; six ways of economising in a company making cutbacks
History: six famous leaders; six inventions
Maths: six numbers: 0, ½, 2, 3, 6, 10; six shapes
Music and drama: six musicians or actors; six instruments; six plays or films
PE: six sports; six pieces of sports equipment
Science: six famous scientists; six discoveries

Variations

There are other kinds of situations in which you ask learners to choose one out of a number of people, objects or solutions, such as:

- a sinking ship – which object should be taken into the life boat?
- a time capsule – which object should be chosen to be buried for future generations?
- a 'Back to the Future' moment in a film – which events would you change in the past?
- a computer about to crash – which files would you save?
- papers being blown away by a hurricane – which one should be blown away?
- a spaceship carrying objects to a new planet – which one object should be chosen as most representative of society?
- products for a company – which new product should be developed?
- applicants for a job – who is the best candidate?
- requests for financial backing for projects – which is the least essential?
- government plans to make cutbacks – which is the least essential?

💡 **Tips for cross-curricular cooperation between subject and language teachers**

Before the lesson: The language teacher presents and practises language for giving opinions and formulating arguments.

During the lesson: The language teacher monitors the learners' language use during group work. The subject teacher monitors learners' subject ideas during group work.

After the lesson: The language teacher gives feedback on language use and sets a follow-up writing exercise, such as a written-out speech.

4.2 Describe and draw

Outline	Learners describe a picture to a partner who draws it.
Thinking skills	Ordering
Language focus	Prepositions
Language skills	Speaking
Time	10 to 20 minutes
Level	A2 or above
Preparation	Collect photographs, pictures or illustrations related to the topic you are covering which are simple to draw. Each learner will need a blank sheet of paper, a pencil and an eraser.

Procedure

1 Divide the class into pairs (A and B). Give each pair a different picture and tell them they must keep it secret. Firstly, they make notes of some useful words and expressions for describing the picture.

2 Brainstorm with the class some useful language for explaining the position of objects in their picture, e.g. *on the right-hand side*, *in the left corner*, *below*, *above*, *next to*, *in the middle*, *underneath*. Write these words on the board for reference.

3 Model an example where a pair of learners describe their picture to the class and you draw it on the board.

4 Put the learners in fours, pair A and pair B, and position each pair opposite each other so that they can't see each other's pictures. Pair A describes their picture to pair B, who must draw it carefully. Set a time limit.

5 Swap roles so that pair B describes their picture to pair A.

Subject examples

Art, design and technology: a line drawing which shows perspective

Economics and business studies: a graph or flowchart

Geography: a diagram of how waves generate power

History: a ground plan of a large Roman villa

ICT: a diagram of input devices

Maths: a series of diagrams showing the relationships between height and tangent point

Music and drama: a drawing of a musical instrument

PE: a series of stick figure drawings explaining a physical exercise

Science: biology – diagram of the respiratory system; chemistry – illustration of an experiment; physics – illustration explaining kinetic energy in a slingshot

---

4.3 Eyewitness

Outline	Learners role play a television interview with someone (or something) who has just returned from an amazing journey or event.
Thinking skills	Creative thinking
Language focus	Describing events and phenomena
Language skill	Speaking
Time	40 minutes
Level	B1 and above
Preparation	Find a video clip or short reading text where someone is interviewed about an amazing event or journey (see *Subject examples* for some ideas). Prepare a few short questions about content and interviewing techniques as an introduction to the activity. Prepare enough copies of the 'Events and reaction' table (in Box 4.3) for each learner.

Procedure

1   Introduce the topic of an amazing journey or event, using your chosen video clip or text and prepared questions.
2   Discuss the kinds of questions that interviewers ask to encourage people to give full descriptions of their experiences. List the questions on the board, e.g. *Could you tell me what happened? Where were you? How did that feel? What happened next?*
3   Introduce the event or journey learners will describe. Learners now work in pairs and use the table in Box 4.3 to make notes as preparation for the interview.
4   Learners take it in turns to practise the interview, swapping the roles of interviewer and interviewee. Set a time limit for the interview (between two and four minutes).

Subject examples

Geography: the journey of a piece of cotton from cotton plant to T-shirt

ICT: eyewitness account of the journey of a virus through a computer

Music and drama: eyewitness account of audience reaction to a controversial film or play

PE: eyewitness account of the journey of an Olympic athlete as they train for the competition

Science: biology – eyewitness account of the fertilisation of a mammal's egg from inside the womb

Follow-up

Learners can present their interviews to each other or video record and upload them to a shared workspace for feedback.

Tips for cross-curricular cooperation between subject and language teachers

Before the lesson: The language teacher introduces and practises the language of description, adjectives, present tense, etc.

During the lesson: The subject teacher helps learners with the events column and the language teacher with the reactions column in the table.

After the lesson: The language teacher gives feedback on the use of language (vocabulary, intonation, pronunciation) and the subject teacher on their use of content knowledge (accuracy and the detail of events).

CLIL Activities

Box 4.3: Eyewitness

Event	Reaction

From *CLIL Activities* © Cambridge University Press 2012   PHOTOCOPIABLE

176

4.4 Information gaps

Outline	Learners complete a task together by sharing different bits of information.
Thinking skills	Reasoning, evaluating
Language focus	Question forms
Language skills	Speaking and listening
Time	20 minutes
Level	A2 and above
Preparation	In information gap activities, each learner is missing certain information required to complete a task and has to communicate with another learner or learners to find it out. For example, Learner A has a picture, text or table with certain information removed and Learner B has the same picture, text or table with different information removed. Together they can complete the picture, text or table by asking each other questions. In this way, learners have a real reason to communicate. Make an overview of a topic you want to cover in class. Divide the information into two (or more) incomplete sets for your learners (see Box 4.4 and *Subject examples* for some ideas).

Procedure

1 Practise an example of the information gap activity with the class, discussing with them the type of questions they can ask, such as:
   - What is the name of the artist?
   - Where does he/she come from?
   - How do you spell it? Can you spell that?
   - Does that have a capital letter or a small one?
   - What's the name of a piece of art in this movement?
   - What is the name of the style of art?
   - When was this art movement?
2 Learners work in pairs, A and B. Give Learner A some information and Learner B some different information. They must not show their information to each other, but must complete their information by communicating with their partner.

CLIL Activities

Box 4.4: Information gaps

Biology: cells

Describe and draw: Learner A

Microbes

a) Fungi

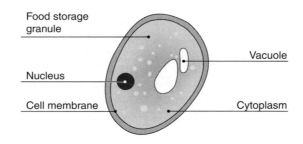

b) Bacteria

c) Viruses

178

Box 4.4: Information gaps (*cont.*)

Describe and draw: Learner B

Microbes

a) Fungi

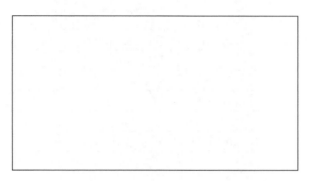

b) Bacteria

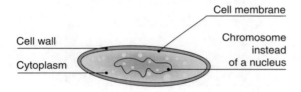

c) Viruses

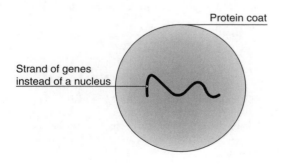

PHOTOCOPIABLE

Subject examples

You can make charts like the one below for many topics in all subjects.

Art, design and technology: twentieth-century art

Learner A's Information:

Artist's name	From	Name of example piece of art	Movement	Dates
1. Henri Matisse	France			
2.	Spain		Cubism	
3. Salvador Dali		Lobster telephone		1920s onwards
4.	Italy		Futurism	
5. William van Alen		Chrysler building in New York		1910–1970s

Learner B's Information:

Artist's name	From	Name of example piece of art	Movement	Dates
1.		Portrait of Madame Matisse (The green line)	Fauvism	1905–1907
2. Pablo Picasso		Le guitarist		1906–1921
3.	Spain		Surrealism	
4. Giacomo Balla		Abstract Speed + Sound		1906–1930s
5.	USA		Art deco	

Variations
- This activity may be set up so that the total information needed to complete the task is divided among three or four learners. They must communicate about the information that they each have in order to carry out the task.
- You can also provide two pictures which contain ten differences and ask pairs to talk to find the differences between them.

 Teaching tip

It is possible to design different kinds of information gaps – factual, personal or opinion. *Factual* information gaps ask learners to exchange facts (e.g. about events in history or stages in the respiration process in biology). *Personal* information gaps ask learners to exchange information about themselves and their personal lives (e.g. about their own experiences with events, people or places). *Opinion* information gaps ask learners to exchange opinions (e.g. about likes or dislikes or controversial issues).

4.5 Living graphs

Outline	Learners plot statements on a graph and justify their actions.
Thinking skills	Justifying, reasoning, explaining
Language focus	*If*-sentences, giving opinions
Language skills	Speaking
Time	20–30 minutes
Level	B1 and above
Preparation	In a living graph, learners are given a graph and a set of related statements to discuss. Learners place the information on a graph and justify its position. Prepare a graph of some data and some numbered statements relating to the graph. Some – or all – of your statements should be ambiguous so that learners have to discuss and justify where to place them. See Box 4.5 and *Subject examples* for ideas.

Procedure

1 Learners work in pairs. Give each pair a graph and the accompanying set of statements. They decide where each statement should go on the graph and mark the place with its number. Learners must be able to explain their choice.

2 Debriefing. Discuss with learners where they have put their statements and why.

Box 4.5: Living graphs

History: the treatment of black South Africans in the 1930s and 1940s

Living graph:

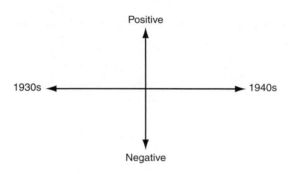

Possible statements:

1. Many whites believed that black South Africans were inferior to them and were not intelligent or hard working.	2. Black South Africans did not have freedom of movement. This meant that they needed to have permission to travel to certain areas.

Subject examples

ICT: graph of noise level at a pop festival

Possible statements:

1. It starts to rain hard.	2. The lead singer plays her guitar lying on the ground.

Music and drama

Use a graph related to a play the learners are working on. Axis X is time and Axis Y is positive/negative emotions.

Possible statements:

1. The family discover that J.C. has an incurable disease.	2. J.C. has a bone marrow transplant.

Variation

Put a very large graph on a poster or the board and give each learner one or two statements on a card. They stick their statements at the appropriate place on the graph. This variation produces one large class graph but probably generates less speaking overall. It can also be done on an interactive whiteboard.

 Tips for cross-curricular cooperation between subject and language teachers

Before the lesson: The language teacher works on the language of giving opinions and arguing your point of view.

After the lesson: The learners write a short paragraph in the language lesson explaining what the graph shows.

4.6 Problems, problems

Outline	Pairs of learners solve two different problems, explain their solution to the other pair, and then try solving the other problem.
Thinking skills	Creative thinking, evaluating
Language focus	Questions
Language skills	Speaking and listening
Time	40 minutes
Level	B1 and above
Preparation	Design two problems for learners to solve in your subject, Problem A and Problem B (see *Subject examples* for ideas). Make enough copies of each problem on cards for half of the class.

Procedure

1 Divide the class into two groups, A and B. Learners within each group then form pairs.
2 Give each pair in Group A a copy of Problem A to solve, and each pair in Group B a copy of Problem B.
3 The learners work in pairs to solve the problem they have been given. Set a time limit. If learners finish early, give them another problem.
4 When all the pairs have finished, form groups of four, consisting of one pair from Group A and one pair from Group B.
5 The pairs cross-question each other about the problem they had to solve – what they did, how they did it and what problems they faced.
6 Now give Problem B to Group A and Problem A to Group B and ask them to solve the new problem, using the experiences of the previous group to help them.

Subject examples

Economics and business studies
Problem A: Design a new, cheaper, more environmentally friendly packaging for a supermarket product.

Problem B: Design a new product for the teenage market.

PE
Problem A: Design a five-minute warm-up which stretches and uses all the muscles in the leg and foot.
Problem B: Design a five-minute warm-up which stretches and uses all the muscles in the stomach.

Note
The idea for this activity is based on Gibbons (2002, p. 31).

4.7 Prove it

Outline	Learners ask and answer questions in order to prove or disprove statements in a game.
Thinking skills	Reasoning, evaluating
Language focus	Question forms and vocabulary
Language skills	Speaking
Time	20 minutes
Level	A2 or above
Preparation	Make a handout which contains 10 statements related to the topic which you are covering in class (see Box 4.7 for an example). You must be able to prove or disprove each statement by asking questions of the other class members. You will need one copy of the statements per learner. Leave some space for them to write notes about their answers.

Procedure

1   Give each learner a list of statements on your topic and explain that they need to prove or disprove all the statements on it. Do one example by asking a question to individual learners about the first statement (for the example in Box 4.7, you could ask: *Do you know the name of Henry Moore's former home?*). Once two learners can answer the question, explain that you have proved the statement.

2   Before learners begin, remind them about question forms. If your learners are reluctant to speak, ask them to write down possible questions in pairs or groups before they start to mingle and ask questions.

3   The aim of the game is for each learner to prove or disprove each statement on their handout. To do this, they will need to stand up and move around the class asking each other questions. They will also need to take notes to support their answers, for example the name(s) of other learners.

4   After about 15 minutes, discuss the answers with them.

Box 4.7: Prove it

Art, design and technology: architecture

Architecture (buildings)	Notes
Prove or disprove all of the following statements by asking your classmates questions. 1. Two people know where Henry Moore's former home is. 2. At least three people can explain what a 'tented structure' is. 3. Half the class can name one building built by Christopher Wren. 4. Two people can name two modern buildings which are built in the form of a pyramid. 5. Five people can name five different kinds of religious buildings. 6. Four people can describe a building designed by Brancusi. 7. Four people can provide four different words to describe texture. 8. At least half the class can name five architecturally important buildings in their own capital city. 9. Five people can name five American architects and one building that they created. 10. Two people can explain why Antoni Gaudi was an important figure in the history of architecture.	

Subject examples

Biology: More than three people have broken their femur.

Economics: At least half of the class can explain the term *Complex interest*.

Geography: Most people have been to Asia.

History: More than three people can define and expain the term *Renaissance*.

ITC: All of the class is involved in some kind of social networking.

Maths: At least five people can explain how to calculate the area of a circle.

Music: Someone is not familiar with the theme of *Für Elise*.

PE: At least one learner has a famous sportsman's autograph.

Note
The idea for this activity is based on a game in Hadfield (1987).

○ Tips for cross-curricular cooperation between subject and language teachers

Before the lesson: The language teacher practises question forms with the learners.

During the lesson: The language teacher monitors the questions learners produce, noting any grammatical mistakes learners make.

After the lesson: The language teacher gives feedback on common mistakes made in formulating questions.

4.8 Ranking cards

Outline	Discuss and rank items related to a topic in order of importance.
Thinking skills	Ordering, comparing and contrasting
Language focus	Expressing ideas, persuading, agreeing and disagreeing, asking questions
Language skills	Speaking
Time	10 minutes
Level	B1 or above
Preparation	Prepare 10 to 15 cards about concepts or facts related to your chosen topic, one set per pair of learners. Each of the ideas or facts is written on a separate card. (See *Subject examples*.)

Procedure

1 Learners work in pairs. Each pair has a set of mixed-up cards in a pile in front of them.
2 Learners take the two top cards, decide which is the most important and put it on the right.
3 Learners then take a third card and compare it with the two cards they have on the table, asking the question *Which is more important?* They place it on the appropriate side (left, if less important and right if more important).
4 They continue until the pile of cards is used up, thus creating a row of cards with the most important idea on the right and the least important idea on the left.
5 As pairs finish, make groups of four learners. They compare their rankings and come to a consensus together to produce a new one.

Subject examples

Art, design and technology: materials

wood		plastic		glass fibre		metal

Question for learners: *Which of these materials is most suitable for making chairs and why?*

Music and drama: acting ability

voice projection		facial expression		body language		ability to sing

Question for learners: *Which is the most important aspect of acting and why? Rank these.*

Note

This activity works well for a revision lesson or at the end of a series of lessons on a topic; the learners need to know something about the topic before you start.

4.9 Role play: job interview

Outline	Learners are interviewed for a job in the role of a subject character.
Thinking skills	Creative thinking, evaluating
Language focus	Depends on topic
Language skills	Speaking
Time	50 minutes
Level	B1 and above
Preparation	Choose a character or object which plays an important role or has an important function in your subject and for which there is a fictional job vacancy (e.g. an historical character, an Olympic swimmer in PE). Write and make incomplete copies of the character's curriculum vitae and application letters for the job for learners to use as input. See Box 4.9 for an example.

Procedure

1 Introduce your learners to the role or function of the character you have chosen. Brainstorm together the most important qualities needed in order to carry out this person's job.

2 Explain that there is a vacancy for this job and that everyone in the class is going to apply. Brainstorm the procedures involved in a job application – the curriculum vitae (CV), the application letter and the interview.

3 Provide the learners with the incomplete sample CV and letter of application and complete these as a class. Alternatively, learners complete them individually or in pairs.

4 Discuss which questions an interview panel might ask the applicant. Write the questions on the board.

5 Divide the class into groups of four and ask them to prepare their answers for the interview.

6 Appoint a panel of three people to act as the interview panel. The interview panel interviews each group as if they are one candidate together.

7 As they listen, the class and/or the teacher decides who is the best candidate and why.

Subject examples

History: any historical character or role, e.g. a king, an explorer, a crusader, a knight, a military general, a renaissance artist

PE: an Olympic swimmer, athlete, trainer

Art, design and technology: an artist to paint the Sistine Chapel

Geography: the designer of an ideal continent / the most interesting mountain / the most fascinating volcano

ICT: the designer of a new school website

Box 4.9: Role play – job interview

Sample CV

Curriculum vitae

Name: Marcus Joannus
Adress: Behind temple
               Near Via Sacra
               Rome

Date of birth:
Place of birth:
Family status:

Type of gladiator ....

Training (where, by whom, for how long) ....

Experience and qualifications ....

Interests ....

Sample letter of application

Your address

Address of employer

Relevant historical date

    Dear M Crassus

    I am writing in response to your announcement in the market last week. I would be very pleased if you would consider me for a place in your renowned team of gladiators. As you can see from the enclosed curriculum vitae, I feel I would represent a valuable addition to your team. At the moment, your team …

    My experience and talents include …

    These would be a great asset in your team, as …

    In addition, my interests show …

    I look forward to hearing from you and hope very much you will invite me to demonstrate my skills in person to you.

    Yours sincerely

    Marcus Joannus

4.10 Rubric jigsaw for presentations

Outline	Learners assess each other using a rubric.
Thinking skills	Evaluating, justifying
Language focus	Giving opinions
Language skills	Speaking
Time	Variable
Level	B1 and above
Preparation	Use this peer assessment activity in a class where you are holding presentations. You will need one copy of the rubric you are going to use per learner (see Box 4.10b for an example). You will also need the rubric cut up into strips so that each learner has two assessment strips to assess the presentation in terms of two different criteria (see Box 4.10a strips).

Procedure

1 Divide the class into five groups. Explain that the learners are going to assess each other using a rubric.
2 Give each learner two different strips of assessment criteria from the rubric (e.g. for content and presentation, as in Box 4.10a) so that the criteria are spread around the group. Some learners will have the same criteria.
3 Learners give their presentations. Their classmates circle the appropriate box on their own assessment strips.
4 In their groups, the learners decide what scores to give the learners for each criterion on a complete rubric (see Box 4.10b).
5 Gather the class scores together on the board or a sheet of paper in a scoring rubric (see Box 4.10c).
6 Take the learners' scores into account when providing your marks.

Box 4.10a: Rubric jigsaw for presentations

Assessment Stips

Name(s) ....

Descriptors	Level	Excellent 4	Good 3	Average 2	Below average 1
1.	Content	Content completely accurate. Learner shows a deep understanding of the topic.	Content mostly accurate, mostly on topic. Learner shows a good understanding of the topic.	Some information accurate but some off topic. Learner shows some understanding of topic.	Learner shows no real understanding of topic. Some information irrelevant.

Name(s) ....

Descriptors	Level	Excellent 4	Good 3	Average 2	Below average 1
2.	Presentation skills and aids	Captured the attention of the audience. Great variety and use of visual aids. Clear, articulate and confident speech.	Interesting to watch. Used a variety of visual aids effectively. Spoke clearly and confidently most of the time.	Sometimes interesting. Some visual aids. Speech sometimes unclear. There is eye contact and facial expression.	Information hard to follow. Few visual aids. Speech often incomprehensible, audience frequently lost interest.

Box 4.10b: Rubric jigsaw for presentations

Example rubric: oral presentation

Name .... Class ....

Level Descriptors	Excellent 4	Good 3	Average 2	Below average 1
1. Content	Content completely accurate. Learner shows a deep understanding of topic.	Content mostly accurate, mostly on topic. Learner shows a good understanding of topic.	Some information accurate but some off topic. Learner shows some understanding of topic.	Learner shows no real understanding of topic. Some information not relevant.
2. Language (grammar)	Very few grammar mistakes. Sounds almost like a native speaker.	A few grammar mistakes, but they do not hinder presentation.	Grammar mistakes occasionally hinder presentation and make it unclear.	Grammar mistakes hinder communication and make presentation difficult to understand.
3. Presentation skills and aids	Captured the attention of the audience. Great variety and use of visual aids. Clear, articulate and confident speech.	Interesting to watch. Used a variety of visual aids effectively. Spoke clearly and confidently most of the time.	Sometimes interesting. Some visual aids. Speech sometimes unclear. There is eye contact and facial expression.	Information difficult to follow. Few visual aids. Speech often incomprehensible, and audience frequently lost interest.
4. Coherence and organisation	Thesis is clearly stated; examples relevant; information in a logical order; conclusion clear and transitions smooth.	Most information is in a logical order; thesis and conclusion present; some transitions choppy.	Concepts and ideas are loosely connected; lacks transitions; thesis and conclusion vague.	Presentation does not flow; no apparent logic to order of the information; no thesis and few conclusions and transitions.

Box 4.10b: Rubric jigsaw for presentations (cont.)

Descriptors \ Level	Excellent 4	Good 3	Average 2	Below average 1
5. Creativity	Very original presentation; content mostly original; uses the unexpected to catch audience's attention.	Some originality present; good variety of materials and method of presenting.	Presentation is one-sided and monotonous.	Presentation is repetitive; little or no originality.
6. Roles in group	All learners participate enthusiastically and equally; learners have clear roles that are performed effectively.	Most learners participate actively and share responsibility; roles not always clear or adhered to.	Half of learners participate actively and share responsibility; roles unclear.	One or two group members do most of the work; responsibility not shared and roles non-existent.

From *CLIL Activities* © Cambridge University Press 2012

PHOTOCOPIABLE

Box 4.10c: Rubric jigsaw for presentations

Scoring rubric oral presentation

Name ....   Class..................

Descriptors	Level	Excellent 4	Good 3	Average 2	Below average 1
1. Content	Group 1				
	Group 2				
	Group 3				
	Group 4				
	Group 5				
2. Language (grammar)	Group 1				
	Group 2				
	Group 3				
	Group 4				
	Group 5				
3. Presentation skills and aids	Group 1				
	Group 2				
	Group 3				
	Group 4				
	Group 5				
4. Coherence and organisation	Group 1				
	Group 2				
	Group 3				
	Group 4				
	Group 5				

Box 4.10c: Rubric jigsaw for presentations (cont.)

5. Creativity	Group 1			
	Group 2			
	Group 3			
	Group 4			
	Group 5			
6. Roles in group	Group 1			
	Group 2			
	Group 3			
	Group 4			
	Group 5			

Subject examples

This rubric can be used for all subjects.

4.11 Speak for an audience

Outline	Learners present to a (fictitious) audience. See Activity 5.12: *Real-life writing* for a similar idea for writing.
Thinking skills	Ordering, creative thinking, synthesis
Language focus	Various, depending on topic
Language skills	Speaking
Time	5–15 minutes per presentation; preparation time depends on level of learners
Level	B1 and above
Preparation	Design a task for your learners related to your subject where they give a presentation either for an audience (e.g. a team of investors, a government representative), or for a reason (to describe, argue, inform, explain, persuade). Find an example of an effective presentation related to your topic, for example on http://www.ted.com.

Procedure

1   Explain to learners that they are going to give a presentation. Watch your model presentation and discuss its good points with your class. Ask questions such as *Who is the audience? Why is this presentation successful? What effect does the presentation have on you? Why is the body language successful?*

2   In pairs, learners work on preparing their task, discussing aspects such as the following:
   * What the audience want to see and hear in the presentation – which information should be included?
   * The best order for the information – what is the best structure for the presentation?
   * The type of language they might use for this audience. For example, a presentation for participants in a reality TV show will use more informal language than a presentation for a government representative.
   * What type of body language helps?

3   Learners give their presentations to each other in small groups or to the class.

Variations

* If video facilities are available, learners can also make a short video of a presentation instead, and upload it for others to watch.
* You can list different possible audiences for the same presentation, and ask different groups to prepare for different audiences.

Note

It is important that learners learn to speak for different types of audiences, since that is what we do in real life. We often ask learners to give a presentation just for the teacher, but speaking for different audiences with a variety of aims can motivate learners to process subject topics more actively and help them to speak more effectively and be more creative.

Subject examples

Economics and business studies
Present a business plan to a panel of investors (see the TV programme *Dragon's Den*, for example).
Audience: a panel of investors
Reason: persuade

Geography:
Present a solution (e.g. letter) to a local environment problem.
Audience: a local government office
Reason: argue

Science: biology
Present a proposal for a new enclosure in a zoo.
Audience: the director of the zoo
Reason: describe (suggested changes)

Chemistry
Present an explanation of how to extract salt from sea water.
Audience: villagers in Indonesia
Reason: inform

Physics
Present an idea for how to make a generator on a desert island.
Audience: participants in a TV survival programme
Reason: explain

4.12 Speaking frames

Outline	Learners use language support during speaking activities.
Thinking skills	Remembering
Language focus	Any
Language skills	Speaking
Time	Depends on the activity
Level	A1/A2
Preparation	Choose a speaking activity for your learners. Imagine that your learners are carrying out the activity and make a note of the language you would expect them to use as they speak. Be as detailed as possible; brainstorm words, phrases and whole sentences. When you have as much language as you can think of, use the language to make a speaking frame similar to the example in Box 4.12 for PE. You will need one speaking frame per learner.

Procedure

1 Introduce the speaking activity to your learners. Learners suggest words and phrases they might use during the activity, in English or in their first language. Write the suggestions on the board, structuring the language in similar columns to the ones you have prepared.

2 Practise the pronunciation, word stress and intonation of the suggested words and phrases, paying attention to sounds which often cause difficulties for your learners.

3 Give the learners a copy of the speaking frame you have prepared. Check they understand the meaning of all the words and phrases as well as their pronunciation. Learners use the speaking frame to help them as they carry out the activity.

Subject examples

This approach can be used with any speaking activity.

Follow-up

Learners can produce their own speaking frames in preparation for a different speaking activity.

Variations

• Instead of providing a handout, you could also enlarge a number of copies and hang them around the classroom, or project the language onto a digital whiteboard. You could also use word clouds, for example with the online program at http://www.wordle.net.

• With more advanced learners, you could provide lists of words and phrases that you would like the learners to use, and ask them to listen to each other and give points each time they hear one of the words or phrases from the list.

> ### ◌ Teaching tip
>
> Speaking frames can be helpful for learners with limited language. However, once learners become more confident and have more language available to them, it is a good idea to reduce the use of speaking frames. In this way, learners will make use of their own language resources and become more independent users of language.

Box 4.12: Speaking frames

An example for a PE lesson on long jump

Your	run up	is	too slow
			unsteady
			too early
	take off		too late
			with the wrong foot
			too high
	position in the air		not high enough
			on one foot
			good
	landing		excellent
			fine
			perfect

4.13 Think, pair, share

Outline	Before learners are asked to say something in class, they are given time to think individually, discuss their ideas in pairs and then share their ideas with the class.
Thinking skills	Depends on the activity
Language focus	Any
Language skills	Speaking
Time	2–3 minutes
Level	A1 and above
Preparation	Prepare in advance some questions that you want your class to think about, related to the topic of your next lesson.

Procedure

1   Ask learners a question, e.g. *What is penicillin? Can you write down five words beginning with im-? What do you know about Salvador Dali?*
2   Tell them to write down their answer individually.
3   Ask them to discuss their answer with their neighbour.
4   Ask a number of learners at random to share their answer with the rest of the class.

Subject examples

This approach can be used with any speaking activity.

Art: Give three reasons why you like a painting.

Economics and business studies: Write down five words related to market research.

Geography: Give three reasons for deforestation.

History: What was Marie Antoinette's role in the French Revolution?

ICT: What is RAM?

Maths: Write down five words often used in equations.

Music and drama: How does this piece of music create tension?

PE: Suggest three ways of tackling someone in football.

Science: physics – What are atoms?

Note

It is important to allow CLIL learners time to search for the language they need to formulate an idea. This activity encourages that by giving them individual thinking time.

4.14 Vivid visuals

Outline	Learners create and explain an illustration or visualisation of their ideas.
Thinking skills	Creative thinking, synthesis
Language focus	Depends on topic
Language skills	Speaking
Time	20 minutes
Level	A1 and above
Preparation	Design a suitable task on your chosen topic for which learners can create an illustration. (See *Subject examples* for some ideas). Collect any sample illustrations that you can find to give your learners ideas, e.g. from coursebooks, postcards, the Internet.

Procedure

1   Introduce the topic you have chosen. Introduce the illustration you will ask your learners to produce. You could make use of examples learners have created in the past, or images in textbooks, on postcards or from the Internet to get the learners thinking creatively.

2   Learners work in pairs and brainstorm possible different types of illustrations (at least five). Give them guidelines for brainstorming: suspend judgement – consider all ideas which are mentioned; think freely – the crazier the better; build on the other person's ideas – take something up and add to it/change it; go for quantity first – think about quality later. Set a time limit (e.g. six minutes).

3   Ask learners to choose the idea they like the best and develop this into the final illustration. Allow them time to collect the materials they need.

4   Allow learners to work on the illustration (at home or in class) and set a deadline for when it should be finished.

5   Learners present their illustration to the class and explain how the illustration represents their ideas.

Subject examples

Art, design and technology: Make aboriginal art of an event in your own life. Explain the piece to an Aborigine.

ICT: Create an illustration to warn young children about what can happen when they place photographs on the Internet. Explain the illustration at a parents' evening.

Variation
It is also possible to use objects from your subject to play the game of pictionary.

Note
Visualisation allows learners to demonstrate their knowledge and insight without language. Adding a spoken explanation helps the learners to articulate their ideas and highlight any gaps between their understanding and their use of language.

5 Focus on writing

5.1 Advice column

Outline	Learners answer a letter to an advice column.
Thinking skills	Defining, reasoning, creative thinking, synthesis, evaluating
Language focus	Giving opinions, agreeing and disagreeing
Language skills	Writing
Time	30 minutes
Level	B1 or above
Preparation	Select a topic which is the cause of a disagreement between two friends. Adapt the example for physics (see Box 5.1b) to write a letter to a problem page which explains the disagreement about the subject. The subject of the letter could be a controversial issue in your subject, a common misconception or a counter-intuitive concept.

Procedure

1 Discuss the phenomenon of problem pages in magazines or newspapers, asking questions such as *What kinds of problems do people write in about? What kind of advice is usually given?*

2 Explain that learners are on the editorial team of a popular journal for your subject (e.g. *Great Geography*, *Phenomenal Physics*, *The Artful Magazine*) and that they have received a letter for the advice column. You want them to write a response for the readers.

3 Project the letter (see Box 5.1a) onto a digital whiteboard, or give learners copies. Learners brainstorm in pairs how they could write a letter to the couple and settle their argument.

4 Discuss the explanations as a class and summarise the main points that the learners want to make.

5 Learners write up their own letter for homework. With a lower-level class, you can provide a skeleton letter like the one in Box 5.1c to scaffold their response.

Box 5.1a: Advice column

Dear Dr [subject]

Please, please help me settle this argument I am having with my girlfriend. We were watching (a sport, a film, a TV programme) several weeks ago when [......]. Well, my girlfriend told me that [......]. I said she was wrong. If [.....], how could [.....]? Ever since then she has been making a big deal out of this and won't answer my phone calls. I love her, but I don't think we can get back together until we settle this argument. I've checked some [subject] books, but they weren't very clear. We agreed that I would write to you and let you settle the argument. But, Dr [Subject], don't just tell us the answer, you've got to explain it so we both understand because my girlfriend is really dogmatic. She said she wouldn't even trust [well-known subject expert] unless the explanation was really clear.

Sincerely,
[......]Blues

From *CLIL Activities* © Cambridge University Press 2012   PHOTOCOPIABLE

Box 5.1b: Advice column

Dear Dr Science,

Please, please help me settle this argument I am having with my girlfriend. We were watching a baseball game several weeks ago when this guy hit a high pop-up straight over the catcher's head. When it finally came down, the catcher caught it standing on home plate. Well, my girlfriend told me that when the ball stopped in midair just before it started back down, its velocity was zero, but its acceleration was not zero. I said she was wrong. If something isn't moving at all, how could it have any acceleration? Ever since then she has been making a big deal out of this and won't answer my phone calls. I love her, but I don't think we can get back together until we settle this argument. I've checked some physics books, but they weren't very clear. We agreed that I would write to you and let you settle the argument. But, Dr Science, don't just tell us the answer, you've got to explain it so we both understand because my girlfriend is really dogmatic! She said she wouldn't even trust Einstein unless he could explain himself clearly.

Sincerely,
Baseball Blues

Adapted from Bean, Drenk and Lee (1982)

From *CLIL Activities* © Cambridge University Press 2012   PHOTOCOPIABLE

Box 5.1c: Advice column

Sample skeleton letter for learners' response

Dear Baseball Blues

I hope I can settle your argument with your girlfriend. I can, of course, explain about the velocity and acceleration of the ball. Here goes. Velocity ....
....

Acceleration ....
....
....
....And the relationship between acceleration and velocity is
....
....
.... Finally, ...
....
....
....So you see, she's right! I hope you can make it
up with her.

Sincerely
Dr Science

From *CLIL Activities* © Cambridge University Press 2012   PHOTOCOPIABLE

Subject examples

Art, design and technology
Journal – *The Artful Magazine*
Controversial issue: A pile of bricks / an unmade bed is a work of art.

Economics and business studies
Journal – *Young Entrepreneurs*
Common misconception: A rise in VAT shifts the demand curve to the left.

Maths
Journal – *Mathematical Matters*
Common misconception: When you multiply two numbers together, the answer is always bigger than both the original numbers.

Tips for cross-curricular cooperation between subject and language teachers

Before the lesson: The language teacher helps the subject teacher write an accurate and clear problem page letter.
After the lesson: The subject teacher gives the language teacher the completed assignments; the language teacher picks out common errors and/or well-written examples and goes over them in their language lessons

5.2 Aliens

Outline	Learners brainstorm and organise ideas using sticky labels as preparation for writing.
Thinking skills	Remembering, ordering
Language focus	Linking words for ordering, describing
Language skills	Writing
Time	40 minutes
Level	A2 or above
Preparation	Decide on your topic in advance. You will need 10 sticky labels or cards per learner, 5–10 A3 posters and tape for sticking the posters up.

Procedure

1 Show learners a picture of an alien. Explain to your class that they are going to write a clear, short description of something related to your subject for this alien who is visiting earth for the very first time. They will also learn how to organise information into paragraphs.

2 Tell the learners the topic and hand out five sticky labels to each learner. On each label they write one piece of information about the topic.

3 When all learners have five points, they work in groups of four to organise their 20 pieces of information (see Box 5.2) into a maximum of five categories.

4 Write the categories the groups have made on the board and write each one on a poster on the wall.

5 Learners place each sticky label on a poster under the relevant category.

6 Each group now gets a poster and writes one paragraph on that topic. Remind learners that their description is for an alien and therefore needs to be very clear and complete. Encourage them to think about (i) words which link ideas, such as *because, so* and *however*, and (ii) 'organising' words, such as *firstly, secondly, thirdly, lastly/finally*.

7 If necessary, show the learners how to do this first, by writing one paragraph together as a model on the board.

8 When each group has finished, ask them to read their paragraph aloud to the other groups, who are the 'aliens'. They must imagine they are the aliens reading about this topic for the first time and should ask questions for clarification.

Box 5.2: Aliens

Piano

1. has keys
2. keys are arranged in a row on a keyboard
3. has 36 black keys
4. has 52 white keys
5. has a total of 88 keys
6. plays notes
7. has strings
8. has a sounding board
9. has two pedals
10. you sit on a stool in front of it
11. has a wooden case
12. keys hit strings to make a sound
13. each key hits a different string
14. left pedal makes sounds shorter
15. right pedal makes sounds longer
16. can play several notes together (in a chord)
17. you use fingers to press down keys
18. notes go from low to high, left to right
19. plays 7 octaves
20. can be upright or grand

Subject examples

Art, design and technology: a famous artist

Economics and business studies: wages

Geography: different types of climates

History: a health problem in a medieval village

ICT: web 2.0

Maths: the metric system

PE: a sport

Science: biology– butterflies; chemistry– liquids; physics – particles

Follow-up

Regroup the learners so that each new group is composed of learners who all wrote a different paragraph in step 6. The new groups now work together to write a complete webpage on the topic, aimed at learners who are two years younger than them.

Variations

Sticky labels can be used in this way for many writing topics.

 Tips for cross-curricular cooperation between subject and language teachers

After the lesson: The language teacher guides learners to link the paragraphs into a webpage for learners who are two years younger than they are.

5.3 Brainstorming for writing (1): posters

Outline	Brainstorming in class to generate ideas for writing.
Thinking skills	Remembering, ordering, classifying, thinking creatively
Language focus	Various, depending on the topic
Language skills	Writing (or speaking)
Time	20–25 minutes
Level	A2 and above
Preparation	Prepare a topic, key question or task for writing in advance. Decide how you will group the learners for the brainstorm. You will need a large piece of (poster) paper per group and one marker pen per learner.

Procedure

1 Learners sit around a table with a large piece of poster paper in the middle.
2 One learner writes the key question or topic in the middle of the sheet of paper.
3 Learners have two to three minutes to write all the responses they can think of, writing first individually and in silence. Encourage them to write everything that comes into their heads, and to write continually: this is important in brainstorming. They can cross out ideas later.
4 Learners discuss everything they have written and link their answers with arrows or lines.
5 Learners discuss how to organise the ideas they have generated and then write their piece together.

Subject examples

Geography: a letter to a mayor of a town discussing the impact of an event (music festival, the Olympics, parade) on the town

PE: a poster announcing an athletics competition between local schools

---

♀ Teaching tip

With brainstorming, it is important that you – and the learners – accept every idea that occurs, however silly it might seem. This produces fruitful ideas.

♀ Tips for cross-curricular cooperation between subject and language teachers

Before the lesson: The subject teacher informs the language teacher what the writing topic is. The language teacher can help learners look at similar text-types and examine the language that is used to organise the piece of writing. Teachers can also work together on assessment criteria for the piece of writing, discussing the question 'When is it a good piece of writing?' They can design a rubric to assess the piece of writing (see BOX 6.7c in Activity 6.7: *Jigsaw rubric - assessing speaking* for a sample rubric).

After the lesson: The language teacher can look at first drafts of the pieces of writing and give some feedback so that learners improve their writing themselves. The language teacher can give a mark for language use and organisation; the subject teacher for the ideas.

5.4 Brainstorming for writing (2): focused free writing

Outline	Learners write freely on a topic for a set time.
Thinking skills	Thinking creatively, ordering, classifying
Language focus	Various, depending on topic
Language skills	Writing
Time	30 minutes
Level	B1 and above
Preparation	Decide in advance what writing task you want to use for focused free writing. Make sure you think of an audience for your task (see BOX 5.12 inActivity 5.12: *Real-life writing*). You will need a timer or stopwatch. Each learner will need a large piece of paper (A3 or A2). (Free writing can also be done on the computer.)

Procedure

1 Before learners start writing, explain the reasons for free writing to them, i.e. to get them started, to generate lots of ideas, to help them become more fluent in writing rather than thinking at this stage about language mistakes, e.g. in spelling or grammar. If they can't think of anything to write, ask them to write 'I can't think of anything to write' over and over until new ideas are generated: any random thoughts or interesting words and phrases can be written down.

2 Explain the writing task and its audience to your learners; they write the task or title at the top of a large piece of paper.

3 Set a timer for 10 minutes and start the learners writing. As they write, encourage them to keep going. Shout 'stop!' when the 10 minutes are up.

4 Learners look over what they have written and choose and group ideas and phrases that they want to use in a final version of the writing task. They can also do this in pairs.

Subject examples

Art, design and technology: a letter from a famous artist to a member of their family

Economics and business studies: an email to a business partner about a new idea for marketing a product

Geography: a brochure about Nepal (or other country) as a tourist destination

History: my life as a slave on boat from Africa to another country

ICT: a webpage for a health information site for teenagers

Maths: an explanation of the results on a graph, referring to mean, median and average

Music and drama: three extra verses of a pop song which learners have studied

PE: a description of the most exciting game or match learners have ever seen

Science: a description of my life as a measles microbe or of my life as a battery

Note

Free writing can also be used as preparation for speaking or to activate ideas at the start of a topic (see also Chapter 1 of Part 3: *Activating*).

5.5 Class magazine

Outline	In groups, learners compile a complete magazine for younger peers about a current topic.
Thinking skills	Various, but can include ordering, comparing and contrasting, organising, creative thinking, evaluating
Language focus	Informing, describing
Language skills	Speaking and writing
Time	60 minutes or more
Level	B1 or above
Preparation	Find a suitable topic for a class magazine and think about possible articles which might appear in it (see *Subject examples*). You will need several lessons for learners to work in.

Procedure

1 Explain that the class is going to create a complete magazine for children two years younger than they are. The class will work in groups of three: there will be a group working as the 'editorial team' and the other groups will be the 'writing groups'.

2 Explain the roles of an editorial team and the writing groups using the information in Boxes 5.5a and 5.5b. The editorial team is responsible for organisation, magazine layout, editing of articles, writing the editorial at the start, maybe some ICT work. This group will coordinate the gathering of articles and the final layout of the magazine. The editors write only a short editorial, introducing the magazine. Learners can volunteer for this role or you can decide which learners would make a talented and responsible editorial team, i.e. a group that you think is good at organisation and planning and that will be able to cope with a complex task.

3 Brainstorm the contents of a magazine on the board. Your class might come up with items such as articles, crosswords, a problem page, reviews, puzzles, editorial or cartoons.

4 Decide which writing groups will create which parts of the magazine. Each group has to produce at least two different contributions to the magazine. If your learners are computer-literate, this work can be collected online in a virtual learning environment.

5 Agree on deadlines.

Subject examples

Economics and business studies: money made easy

ICT: the delights and dangers of the Internet

💡 **Tip for cross-curricular cooperation between subject and language teachers**

Before the lesson / during the lesson: The subject teacher introduces the subject content of the magazine in their lesson. The language teacher gives language input and support on the different types of texts which appear in newspapers, using examples from real life. Peer and teacher feedback on language is given using a rubric or correction code.

Box 5.5a: Class magazine

Sample handout: editorial team

The role of the editorial team is as follows:

- to keep track of what each group is doing and what topics they have chosen so that no subject appears twice.
- to collect all articles online. Agree on deadlines!
- to send articles back for improvement, if necessary.
- to design a front page and think of a title for the magazine.
- to determine the order and layout of the articles.
- to add a table of contents and page numbers.
- to write a short introductory editorial text for the first page of the magazine.
- to keep in contact with your teacher about progress.

From CLIL Activities © Cambridge University Press 2012   PHOTOCOPIABLE

Box 5.5b: Class magazine

Sample handout: writing groups

- Choose a topic and check with the editing team that no-one else has chosen it.
- Look up information about your topic. You can use sources such as the Internet, books and folders from your teacher.
- Decide on two different contributions and divide the tasks within your group.
- These contributions or articles can contain information about (topic), but bear in mind that there are other forms such as:
  - an interview
  - a day in the life of a …
  - a fact file: Did you know…?
  - a comparison
  - a cartoon
  - a problem page (letters and answers)
  - a comparison of the topic in different countries;
- Provide illustrations to go with the articles.
- Each article must include the name or names of the authors.
- Each article must be original text and not copied from the Internet or other sources.

From *CLIL Activities* © Cambridge University Press 2012   PHOTOCOPIABLE

5.6 Framing writing

Outline	Learners use writing frames as preparation for writing.
Thinking skills	Organising, ordering, reasoning, evaluating
Language focus	Various, depending on topic
Language skills	Writing
Time	40–60 minutes
Level	A2 and above
Preparation	One way of helping learners to structure and plan their writing is to work with writing frames, in combination with cognitive or graphic organisers (see Box 5.6a for examples of text-types). Prepare a writing frame for your learners in advance and make enough copies for everyone in the class. See the examples in Boxes 5.6b–g for ideas.

Procedure

1 Give each learner a copy of the writing frame.
2 Learners work in pairs to discuss how they will complete the writing frame.
3 Ask one pair to explain how they would complete the first section of the writing frame, using, perhaps, a digital whiteboard.
4 Discuss as a class any changes or improvements which could be made to the first section.
5 Learners work individually and complete the writing task, using their notes from steps 2 and 4 to help them.

Box 5.6a: Framing writing

Examples of text-types and graphic organisers (see Activity 2.4: *Graphic organisers* for illustrations)

text-type	purpose	writing frame
narrative	to retell events ordered in time	timeline
description or informative text	to describe characteristics	spider diagram
instruction	to tell someone how to do something	flowchart
explanation	to explain how or why something happens	flowchart
persuasion	to argue a case for one viewpoint	bullet points
discussion	to present arguments or information from different points of view	for and against grid

From *CLIL Activities* © Cambridge University Press 2012   PHOTOCOPIABLE

Box 5.6b: Framing writing

Music and drama: narrative – biography of a famous artist

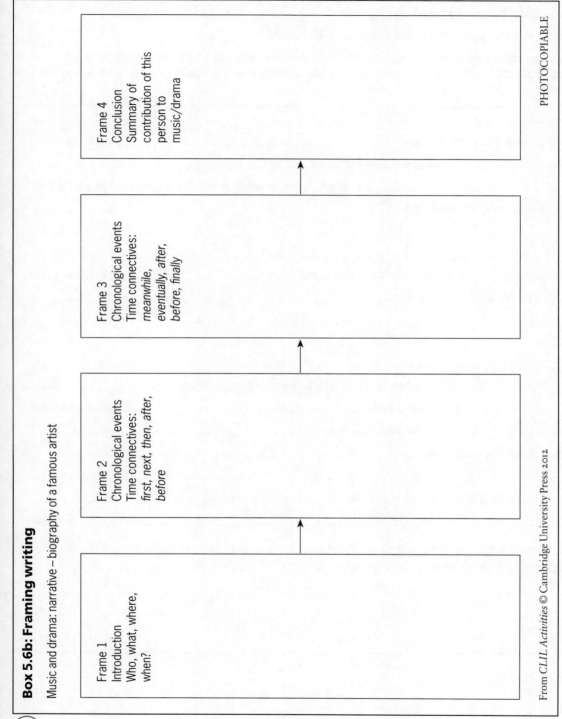

Frame 1
Introduction
Who, what, where, when?

Frame 2
Chronological events
Time connectives:
first, next, then, after, before

Frame 3
Chronological events
Time connectives:
meanwhile, eventually, after, before, finally

Frame 4
Conclusion
Summary of contribution of this person to music/drama

From *CLIL Activities* © Cambridge University Press 2012

Box 5.6c: Framing writing

Maths: report describing the results of a graph about traffic

Learners have made a graph (histogram) which illustrates how many cars of different colours they have counted on the road near their school. Their task is to comment in writing in pairs on the graph they have made.

Our names: 1 .... 2 ....

Title (write an interesting title here) ....

On........................... (date), we observed ....
.... Our graph shows the results of our observations, as follows. Our task
was (write here what you had to do) ....
....
....

Here are our results. Firstly, we counted a total number of ....cars. We noticed that (write
something about percentages here) ....
....
....
....

The results show the relative popularity of the colours. The most popular car colour is ....
............................We think this is because .... The least popular
car colour is..................... We think this is because ....
Other popular car colours are ....
....

The most interesting thing that we noticed about the colour of the cars was ....
.... because
....

What we found difficult about the activity was ....
....
....

Box 5.6d: Framing writing

PE: instruction – how to warm up for tennis

Title:

Equipment list:

General warm-up (whole body, e.g. run, skip, knee lift, sidestep, arm swing, skipping)

1. Start by …ing ….
2. ….
3.
4.

Illustrations

Tips: Remember to….

Stretching (6–8 second stretch of key muscles, repeated several times)

1. Now ….
2.
3.
4.

Illustrations

Tips: Remember to …

Specific warm up (practise movements used in this sport)

1. Now ….
2.
3.
4.

Illustrations

Tips: Remember to …

Useful language

Verbs: *lift, move, bend, twist, hold, lower, raise, turn*

Adverbs and prepositions: *straight, round, upwards, left, right, up, down, behind, in front of, next to*

Box 5.6e: Framing writing

Geography: explanation – effects of earthquakes

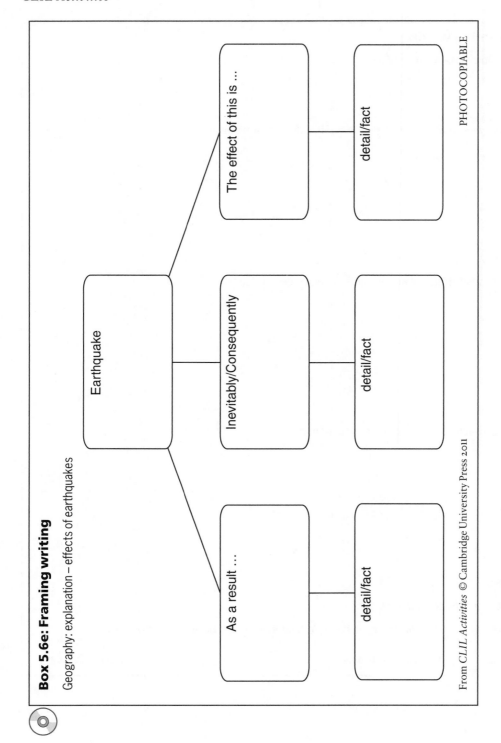

Box 5.6f: Framing writing

ICT: persuasion – review comparing two school websites

Learners take notes in a grid, preparing to write a review of two school websites.

Aspect of website	Website A	Website B	Comment	Useful language
Use of colour			Website x uses colour …	more, less
Design			The design of website A is …	whereas
Usability			Website A is easier to …	however
Appeal to audience (parents, pupils, teachers)			Website B will appeal to …	From the point of view of..
Graphics quality			The graphics used on website B are …	also, in addition
Information architecture			The information given in website A is …	nevertheless
Content (completeness of information)			The content included on website B is …	so
Text (spelling, grammar)			The text …	therefore
Other				

PHOTOCOPIABLE

Box 5.6g: Framing writing

History: discussion – Hitler's reasons for annexing Austria

1: What were the different reasons for Germany annexing Austria? Complete each box.

Personal reasons	Political reasons
Economic reasons	Cultural reasons

Hitler annexed Austria for a number of reasons. Write your reasons out in sentences.
Firstly, there were personal reasons. These were …

Next, there were political reasons. These were …

Then there were economic reasons. These were …

Lastly, there were cultural reasons. These were …

The most important of these reasons is …

I think this is because …

Subject examples

See Boxes 5.6b–g for examples illustrating each text-type.

5.7 I am a …

Outline	Learners narrate a strange journey in the first person.
Thinking skills	Organising, relating, reasoning, creative thinking, evaluating
Language focus	Present tenses, narrative
Language skills	Writing
Time	40–60 minutes
Level	B1 and above
Preparation	Choose a topic in your materials where a process occurs. This activity is suitable for use at the very end of a topic. Write an exciting introduction (see the biology example in Box 5.7).

Procedure

1 Learners write a story of a journey in the first person about a process in your subject. They imagine that they are part of an enormous system and that they are going on a journey through that system. In the report, learners describe what happens at every stage of their journey, for example which of their friends they encounter or lose at each stage. They should recount their journey as a narrative, starting at the beginning of the process and finishing at the end. Whether they survive or not, a report must be written for base headquarters. Create a handout for them like the one in Box 5.7 for biology about their journey.

2 Give your learners some input about how to structure their story: where the story takes place; what they can see, hear and taste; how their journey develops; what challenges the main character must face and overcome; how the character finally solves the problem.

Box 5.7: I am a …

Biology: the digestive system

Big Mac Under Attack

Imagine you are part of an enormous cheeseburger (yes vegetarians, you too!). Perhaps you are the bread roll, or the melted cheese, the pickles, the onions, the secret sauce, the lettuce or possibly even the beef. Whatever part you choose to be, you are the leader. It is your mission to lead the burger on a dangerous journey. A journey to the bottom of the world. A journey through the digestive system.

It is a journey involving many risks and not all of you will survive. All of you will come under attack and most of you will be destroyed along the way. Many of you will suffer a painful death and be broken down into many thousands of pieces, to be absorbed into the blood of the voracious monster: otherwise known as Homo sapien!

Whether you survive or not, a report must be written for base HQ. In the report you must describe what happens at every stage of your journey. Say which of your friends (food types / nutrients) is destroyed at each stage and who is responsible (yes, watch out for the vicious enzymes and evil acid!!). Tell it as a story, starting in the mouth and ending at the anus. At the end, only one of your friends is left over … let this 'person' take over the story after you have been destroyed.

From *CLIL Activities* © Cambridge University Press 2012   PHOTOCOPIABLE

Subject examples

Art, design and technology: the journey of a piece of cotton from a cotton plant to jeans or the journey of a piece of wood from a tree to a table
Economics and business studies: the journey of a product, from raw material to supermarket shelf (e.g. a coffee bean from the plantation to Starbucks)
Geography: the journey of a raw piece of cotton from a cotton plant to a T-shirt
History: the journey of an Egyptian artefact from its source to its burial in a mummy's tomb
ICT: the journey of a virus through various computers
Music and drama: the journey of a famous musical instrument
PE: the journey of a football/tennis player to stardom
Science: chemistry/physics: the journey/life of an electron

Tips for cross-curricular cooperation between subject and language teachers

Before the lesson: the language teacher reads a story about a process or a journey with the class and works on how a story is linked together with connectives. The class also works on what makes a story interesting and motivating to read, and talks about using language creatively – for example, adding adjectives and adverbs or writing different sentence lengths. The language teacher also talks about the importance of thinking about the audience when writing.

5.8 Instructions

Outline	Learners write instructions for their classmates and test them out.
Thinking skills	Reasoning, ordering
Language focus	Imperatives
Language skills	Writing
Time	45 minutes
Level	A2 or above
Preparation	Choose two different objects, models, drawings or processes from your current curriculum area which can be recreated from instructions, e.g. a papier-mâché mask and a wooden keyring (art, design and technology), models of two different chemical structures (chemistry), drawings of a plant cell and an animal cell (biology), two different experiments (science). Collect all the materials learners will need in order to carry out the instructions for the subject you have chosen. You will need to ensure that this activity can be done in a space where learners have access to all the equipment they need (e.g. art studio, science laboratory, gymnastics hall). Cover the objects or materials or put pictures of the objects into an envelope so that the learners cannot see them.

Procedure

1   Discuss with the class what is important when writing instructions, for example creating a list of equipment needed; using numbered steps; including only one instruction for each step; using the imperative (*saw the wood into pieces of 2 cm × 2 cm; pour 200 ml of acid carefully into the test tube; draw two parallel lines, 4 cm apart*); using illustrations to back up your instructions.
2   Divide the class into two groups, Group A and Group B, and give each group a different object or model or process to work with.
3   Subdivide the two groups into pairs; each pair writes instructions to make the object or model, or for the process. They can illustrate their instructions if they like.
4   Form groups of four consisting of one pair from Group A and another pair from Group B. One pair follows the instructions which the other pair has written, using the materials necessary to complete them. The pair that wrote the instruction watches.
5   When all the learners have finished, discuss as a class any problems they came across and what is important when they write instructions.

Subject examples

Economics and business studies: how to create a bar chart from statistics.

Geography: how to draw and label a diagram of a volcano.

History: how to mummify a pharaoh.

ICT: how to draw a room in a house using a 3D computer program.

Maths: how to solve a mathematical problem.

Music and drama: how to transfer music from one MP3 player to another/put a song on a mobile from an MP3 player; how to position all the props on stage set.

5.9 Lost in conversion

Outline	Learner A writes a text, Learner B completes a graphic organiser using that text, Learner C explains the graphic organiser to Learner A. Learner A compares the spoken version with the original written version.
Thinking skills	Remembering, evaluating
Language focus	Various, depending on topic
Language skills	Writing
Time	45–60 minutes
Level	A2 or above
Preparation	Design a writing task for your subject that can be represented in the form of a graphic organiser (see Activity 2.4: *Graphic organisers* for ideas). You will need lined paper, blank paper and pens.

Procedure

1 Put the class into groups of three learners: Learner A, Learner B and Learner C. Ask each learner to complete the writing assignment you have designed.
2 In their groups learners then exchange texts, so that Learner A has Learner B's text, Learner B has Learner C's text and Learner C has Learner A's text.
3 Each learner reads the text passed to them and visualises it in the form of a graphic organiser. When the graphic organisers are finished, learners pass these on again, returning the original text to its writer.
4 Learners then take it in turns to explain the graphic organiser passed to them to the learner who wrote the original text (e.g. Learner C explains Learner B's graphic organiser to Learner A, and so on).
5 Learners compare the graphic organisers with the original texts and identify any causes of misunderstanding in the cycle of communication.

Subject examples

Geography
Writing task: What are the similarities and differences between the north and south poles?
Text-type: magazine article for 10-year-olds
Graphic organiser: Venn diagram

History
Writing task: Describe the events leading to the French revolution.
Text-type: newspaper article to mark 200-year anniversary
Graphic organiser: timeline

Science
Writing task: Describe a food chain.
Text-type: web page for secondary school children
Graphic organiser: flowchart

Follow-up

For homework, ask learners either to improve and edit the text they wrote during the lesson or to create a similar text using a different subject.

5.10 Questions to paragraph

Outline	Learners write a paragraph by answering the teacher's written questions.
Thinking skills	Remembering, creating
Language focus	Various, depending on topic
Language skills	Writing
Time	30 minutes
Level	A1–A2
Preparation	Prepare a set of questions. Learners should be able to produce one paragraph of continuous writing by answering these questions. See Boxes 5.10a and 5.10b and *Subject examples* for ideas.

Procedure

1   Give your learners your set of questions, either on a handout or written on the board. Explain to them that you want them to answer the questions not in the form of a list but as a single continuous paragraph of writing.
2   Once learners have written their first draft, ask them to re-read the paragraph to see if the ideas fit together. Discuss linking words such as *and, but, however, firstly, secondly, lastly.*
3   Learners change their draft paragraph by adding descriptive or organising words to help link their ideas or make the text more interesting.

Subject examples

See Boxes 5.10a and 5.10b.

 Teaching tip

This works well with lower-level learners. By getting learners to write in this very structured way, they can feel a sense of achievement in their writing, even at lower levels.

Box 5.10a: Questions to paragraph

Maths

- What is a polygon?
- What are the names of four polygons?
- How many sides does a triangle have?
- How many sides does a quadrilateral have?
- How many sides does a pentagon have?
- How many sides does a hexagon have?
- What is the sum of the exterior angles of a polygon?
- What do the interior and exterior angles of each vertex on a polygon add up to?
- What is the interior angle of a polygon?
- Where do the interior and exterior angles of a polygon lie?

✂--

Paragraph

A polygon is any 2D shape with straight sides. The names of some polygons are triangle, quadrilateral, pentagon and hexagon. A triangle has three sides, a quadrilateral has four sides, a pentagon has five sides and a hexagon has six sides. The sum of the exterior angles of a polygon is 360°. However, the interior and exterior angles of each vertex on a polygon add up to 180°. The interior angle of a polygon is the angle within the vertex. The interior and exterior angles lie on a straight line.

(Based on: http://www.bbc.co.uk/schools/ks3bitesize/maths/shape_space/polygons/revise1.shtml)

From *CLIL Activities* © Cambridge University Press 2012　　　　　　　　　　PHOTOCOPIABLE

Box 5.10b: Questions to paragraph

Economics and business studies

- What is one of the most important aspects of a business plan?
- Where does the executive summary appear?
- What does an executive summary do?
- What does it include about the purpose of the business?
- What information does it include about the business?
- What does it include about the product or service and about company background?
- What does it include about the market and finance?

✂--

Paragraph

One of the most important aspects of a business plan is the executive summary, which appears at the start of your document. The executive summary gives the reader a quick overview of the business plan. It should include the statement of purpose, or the objectives of your business. It should also include information on the company background and the company's product or service as well as providing an overview of your strategy. Moreover, it discusses the market potential for your product or service and financial projections for at least three years.

From *CLIL Activities* © Cambridge University Press 2012　　　　　　　　　　PHOTOCOPIABLE

5.11 Recreate a text

Outline	Learners reconstruct a short text by listening and noting down key words.
Thinking skills	Remembering, reasoning
Language focus	Various, depending on topic
Language skills	Writing
Time	25 minutes
Level	A1 or above, depending on the text you select
Preparation	Select a short text of about 100 words linked to your current curriculum topic that you would like your learners to reproduce. This may come from a website, a textbook, a reference book or another source. You will need the following materials: one sheet of lined paper and a pen for each group of four learners; tape for sticking paper to walls; copies of the text you have chosen for each group of four learners.

Procedure

1 Introduce the topic of the text you have chosen. To focus learners on the topic, ask them briefly what they think the text will be about.
2 Ask learners to listen and note down key ideas and words as you read the text aloud.
3 Form groups of three or four and hand out a sheet of lined paper and a pen to each group.
4 Ask learners to work together using their notes and language skills to try to recreate the text as closely as possible. Set a time limit.
5 Hang the completed final versions of the text on the wall and ask learners to read all the texts, giving 1 point to the text they think is the most complete, by marking 1 point on the text.
6 Ask learners to return to their groups with their text. Hand out copies of the original text and ask them to compare their text with it. Discuss with the class which techniques helped them to work most effectively to write a good text.

Subject examples

Any text can be used for this activity.

Variations

• Learners work in groups of four. Learner number 1 from each table goes to the teacher's table to read a text for a maximum of one minute. They report back to the group and try to reconstruct the text. After two minutes, learner number 2 goes to the teacher's table, reads for one minute and then reports back to the group. The process continues until all four learners have read the original text.
• Supply pictures with the text so that learners can take notes below them (e.g. if the text describes the stages in the eruption of a volcano, provide illustrations of the stages).

5.12 Real-life writing

Outline	Learners write texts which have a realistic audience.
Thinking skills	Organising, ordering
Language focus	Various, depending on topic
Language skills	Writing
Time	20–25 minutes
Level	B1 or above
Preparation	In real life, we usually write texts for a particular 'audience' (a friend, the tax man, a newspaper), and we know what type of text we are trying to write (a magazine article, an email, etc.; see Box 5.12). We also have a reason to write. This is what we mean by 'realistic' writing. Design a task for your learners related to your subject where they write a realistic text. You will need to specify its audience (e.g. schoolchildren, readers of a website), the text-type (e.g. school magazine, website, poster, brochure) and its purpose (e.g. to describe, argue, persuade). See *Subject examples* for ideas for some tasks.

Procedure

1 Explain the task you have designed to your learners.

2 Remind them who the audience for their piece of writing is and discuss the type of language they might use. For example, a text for a webpage for teenagers will use more informal language than a serious review in a magazine.

3 Discuss the structure and features of the text-type with learners. For example, a magazine article discussing the advantages and disadvantages of genetic manipulation of plants will generally include an introduction, one or two paragraphs explaining the arguments for genetic manipulation, one or two paragraphs explaining the arguments against, and finally the conclusion, which includes the writer's opinion. Such a text will also include linking words (*firstly, secondly, but, nevertheless, finally*, etc.) and phrases which give opinions (*on the one hand, on the other hand, in my opinion, some scientists say*), and so spend some time talking about those.

Box 5.12: Real-life writing

Writing: text-types for CLIL

an essay	a blog	an analysis of an experiment
a lab report	an article	a website
a summary	a play script	a magazine
a poem	a manual	a poster
a travel brochure	an email	an extract of a journal
a letter	a questionnaire	a newspaper
a leaflet	a survey	
a (short) story	a biography	

Subject examples

Art, design and technology

You work for a museum and have been asked to write a text about a piece of art in an exhibition for an audio tour for primary school children.

- audience: children aged 10
- aim: to inform and motivate the children to look at the piece of art and understand it
- text-type: text for audio tour

History

You are a soldier (German or British) in the trenches in 1917 during the First World War. Write a letter home to your family or wife about your experiences.

- audience: family
- aim: to describe experiences
- text-type: letter

Music and drama

Write a review of a new music video in the rubric 'Music: Whaddya think?' for the MTV website.

- audience: website visitors (young people)
- aim: to inform and persuade
- text-type: review on a website

Note

Encouraging writing helps learners to structure their ideas about a subject and to experiment creatively with language. It is important that learners learn to write different kinds of texts, since that is what we do in real life. We often ask learners to write (an essay or a description) just for the teacher, but learning to write for different audiences, with a variety of aims and text-types can motivate them to process subject topics more actively and write more effectively as well as helping them to be more creative.

 Tips for cross-curricular cooperation between subject and language teachers

Before the lesson: The language teacher can discuss the importance of thinking of the audience when writing, of having an aim when you write – to describe, or persuade or instruct, for example. He or she can use models of the type of text that the subject teacher is going to use and discuss how formal or informal the writing is. He or she can also discuss the features and structure of the text and what type of language is used in that text-type (e.g. the language of persuasion for a persuasive text, imperatives for instructions).

After the lesson: The language teacher gives feedback on the final products that the learners have created.

5.13 Storyboard

Outline	Learners create an illustrated text in the form of a storyboard.
Thinking skills	Remembering, creative thinking, synthesising
Language focus	Describing cause and effect; describing a process
Language skills	Writing
Time	50 minutes
Level	A2 and above
Preparation	Select a subject topic which describes an event, process, story or journey in the form of a narrative. Each pair of learners will need A3 or larger paper, pencils, crayons and felt tip pens.

Procedure

1 Write the topic you have chosen for the storyboard on the board (e.g. the digestive system, a symphony). Explain to the learners that they are going to create a storyboard on the topic.
2 Learners brainstorm ideas for their storyboard (pictures and language) in pairs.
3 They organise the points into key events or stages. How many frames (pictures) will they need in order to be able to represent these ideas in the form of a storyboard?
4 Each pair draws their storyboard on an A3 sheet of paper.

Subject examples

Art, design and technology: key events in the life of an artist

Economics and business studies: the development of a successful brand

Geography: natural disasters (volcanoes, tsunamis, earthquakes, tornadoes)

History: key events leading to a revolution (Industrial/ Russian/ French)

ICT: the development and effect of a computer virus

Maths: the properties of quadrilaterals

Music and drama: the key events in the scene of a play/opera

PE: causes and types of sports injuries

Science: chemistry – the effect of heating and cooling on states of matter;

Note
A storyboard is a series of sketches or photographs showing the sequence of shots planned for a film; it is a way of telling a story in pictures and words. Working on a storyboard can help learners to select, organise and express subject concepts. Encouraging learners to illustrate their ideas can also motivate visual learners and reluctant writers to engage with a subject. It is important for CLIL learners to show their understanding in visual as well as linguistic ways.

5.14 Visuals

Outline	Learners write a text which describes an illustration or picture.
Thinking skills	Defining, comparing and contrasting, reasoning, evaluating
Language focus	Present tense, describing words (adjectives and/or adverbs), prepositions (*behind*, *in front of*, *next to*)
Language skills	Writing
Time	25 minutes
Level	A2 or above, depending on the complexity of the illustration
Preparation	Select a number of fairly complex illustrations – for example pieces of art, drawings, pictures of objects, graphs – which learners can describe to each other in writing. For each pair of learners, you will need copies of two different pictures or illustrations related to your current topic or theme and tape for sticking up work on the wall.

Procedure

1 Divide the class into two groups. Give each group a picture (A or B) and tell them not to show it to the other group.
2 Hand out the pictures, A to half of the class and B to the other half.
3 Learners work in pairs to write a detailed description of their picture. Explain that the description must be as clear as possible to ensure that any person reading it will be able to recreate/draw the picture.
4 Remind learners of prepositions of place and how to use them – i.e. words like *next to*, *below*, *above*, *in the bottom/top right-/left-hand corner*, *under*, *underneath*.
5 Learners write their descriptions. (This step can be done for homework.)
6 Collect the written descriptions and the illustrations. Give each pair a written description from a pair in the other group. Each learner then tries to draw the picture using the written description.
7 When learners have finished, display the written descriptions, the original illustration and their second drawings on the classroom walls.
8 Discuss misunderstandings with the class: what didn't they understand clearly enough to be able to draw accurately?

💡 Tips for cross-curricular cooperation between subject and language teachers

Before the lesson: The language teacher can do a similar task in the language lesson. He or she describes a picture to the whole class, while they draw, practising describing words and prepositions (*next to*, *beside*, *under*, *above*, *beneath*, *underneath*). He or she then revises prepositions with the learners. The teacher can also work with the class to brainstorm specific adjectives to describe the picture.

Subject examples
Art, design and technology: a work of modern art
Economics and business studies: a graph
Geography: a series of diagrams describing a process
History: a piece of art related to the period learners are studying
ICT: a flowchart
Maths: a graph
PE: a series of pictures describing an exercise
Science: a diagram

6 Assessment, review and feedback

6.1 Assessment questions

Outline	Learners design a content and language checklist with the teacher to check through a piece of work before submitting it.
Thinking skills	Analysing, evaluating
Language focus	Question forms, present tense
Language skills	Writing or speaking
Time	30–40 minutes
Level	B1 or above
Preparation	Design a realistic speaking or writing task (see Box 6.1a for ideas).

Procedure

1 Introduce your task. Include an imaginary audience who might read, listen to or watch the learners' final product or performance (see Box 6.1a).
2 Tell your learners they are going to design a self-assessment checklist, in the form of yes/no prompt questions, for the assignment. Give them some examples of questions, one on content and one on language use (see Box 6.1c).
3 In pairs, learners write four more questions for the checklist (two on content and two on language use).
4 Collect all the suggested questions on the board and delete any repetitions.
5 Discuss the questions and ask learners to make a final version of the checklist. Make copies.
6 Learners complete the checklist and hand it in with their final product.

Box 6.1a: Assessment questions

Examples of realistic products:

Spoken product	Visual product (with spoken or written explanation, justification or report)	Written product
• an individual, pair or group presentation • a debate • an elevator pitch • a description of a picture • instructions • an explanation of a problem • a role play • a radio show • a podcast • a television show • a vodcast • a speech • an interview • a (short) film • a scene from a play	• a drawing • a graph • a silent film • a sculpture • a model (e.g. a hovercraft, a molecule) • a painting • a freeze frame • an emblem • an illustration for a book or CD cover • a map • a game • a picture • a technical design • a diagram • an experiment • a storyboard • a physical exercise • a poster • an animation	• an essay • a lab report • a summary • a poem • a travel brochure • a letter • a leaflet • a short story • an analysis of an experiment • a musical composition such as a song or a rap • a play script • a manual • instructions • an email • a questionnaire • a survey • a biography • a website • a magazine • a poster • a diary • a journal (extract) • a newspaper • a blog • an article • a cartoon • a wiki

Box 6.1b: Assessment questions

Examples of yes/no questions related to all subjects for inspiration: self-assessment

Content

1. Is your message clear to the audience? (Does it persuade/argue/complain/narrate effectively?)
2. Does your work give a detailed explanation of …?
3. Does your work cover all of the points required by the teacher?
4. Does your work suggest …?
5. Are your arguments convincing?
6. Do you give appropriate evidence to support your main points?
7. Have you involved the audience by asking questions? Are the questions relevant?
8. Are you able to answer questions about the topic from your audience?
9. Is it clear that all the members of the group participated equally?
10. Does your work make an effective visual impact on the reader?

Language

11. Is the presentation or layout clear?
12. Have you used an appropriate style for your audience?
13. Is the language accurate (spelling, grammar, vocabulary, linking words)?

From *CLIL Activities* © Cambridge University Press 2012   PHOTOCOPIABLE

Box 6.1c: Assessment questions

Examples of prompt questions for learners working at A2 level:

Content

1. Is the information on our poster correct?
2. Can you read our poster from 1 metre away?
3. Do the pictures help people understand the text?
4. Is our poster colourful?
5. Has everyone written on the poster?

Language

6. Are there about 50 words on our poster?
7. Did we use the right words?
8. Is our spelling right?

From *CLIL Activities* © Cambridge University Press 2012   PHOTOCOPIABLE

Box 6.1d: Assessment questions

Geography: redevelopment of the rainforest

Your role

You and your group are representatives of the Kayapo Indians, the Government or the World Wildlife Fund (WWF). You are going to make suggestions to landowners of the rainforest about how the rainforest should be redeveloped. Choose who you want to be.

Your task

1. Produce a poster which will explain how you think the rainforest should be developed and which will persuade the landowners that this is what they should do. Remember that you have been asked to present the viewpoint of a particular group. In your poster you need to include:
   a) an explanation of why the natural forest environment is under threat
   b) possible alternative solutions
   c) detail about the method which you are suggesting and why this would be the best solution
   d) pictures and written information.
2. Make a group presentation explaining your ideas. Every member of your group is expected to contribute to this presentation. After you have given your presentation, other pupils will have the opportunity to ask questions. You will be expected to provide answers to these questions.

Content and group work checklist

1. Does the poster make an effective visual impact on the reader?
2. What viewpoint does it take? Is the message clear?
3. Does it give a detailed explanation of why the forest environment is under threat?
4. Does it offer a range of solutions?
5. Do you provide appropriate evidence to persuade the audience that your solution is a good one? Is your argument convincing?
6. Is the presentation clear? Do all members of the group participate?
7. What sort of questions do you ask and how well do you answer the questions asked of your group?

Language checklist

8. Is the written information on the poster accurately spelt?
9. Is the written information grammatically correct?
10. Is the speaker's pronunciation accurate (individual sounds, word stress)?
11. Does the speaker use sentence stress, rhythm and intonation to maintain the interest of the audience?
12. Does the poster presentation use the language of geography (specialised terms) appropriately?

Box 6.1e: Assessment questions

PE: cartwheel

Your task

Design an assessment sheet for learners performing a cartwheel.

Content checklist

1. Does the assessment sheet include assessment of balance, poise, placement, alignment and control?
2. Can anyone use the assessment sheet to give a fair grade for a cartwheel?
3. Does the assessment sheet make it clear what the characteristics of a good cartwheel are?

Language checklist

4. Is the correct terminology used to describe characteristics of a good cartwheel?
5. Is the assessment sheet clearly laid out?
6. Is the language grammatically accurate?
7. Is the spelling on the assessment sheet correct?

- -

Sample assessment sheet for PE

THE CARTWHEEL

1. Does your weight move from feet to hands to feet (hand, hand, foot, foot)?
2. Are your arms and legs straight and stretched?
3. When you do the cartwheel, do you keep your arms at '10 o'clock' and '2 o'clock'?
4. Are your legs at about '20 minutes to the hour' and '20 minutes after the hour' – like spokes in a wheel?
5. Do you do the cartwheel in a line on the floor?
6. Are you in control of your body during the cartwheel?

This checklist could also be used by learners observing each other.

From *CLIL Activities* © Cambridge University Press 2012   PHOTOCOPIABLE

Subject examples

See Boxes 6.1d and 6.1e.

Variations
- Learners make a poster of assessment criteria. Put learners into groups of three or four and tell them they are going to work on assessment criteria for a piece of work. Learners work together to think of different ways of completing the following sentence: *The ideal (name of piece of work) …* One learner notes down ideas for a group poster. Remind them to think about content and language. For example, *The ideal laboratory report …* (physics) or *The ideal collage …* (art).
- The groups create a poster which includes a minimum of five and a maximum of eight aspects of their ideal piece of work.
- Learners hang their posters around the room, look at each other's posters to get some more ideas about the assessment criteria and improve their own posters.
- Discuss the assessment criteria with the class. Take the posters in and use them to create assessment criteria for your piece of work. Make a handout for your learners of the criteria and use them to mark their work.

♀ Tip for cross-curricular cooperation between subject and language teachers

Before the lesson: The language teacher can help the subject teacher think of questions for the language checklist and can remind learners about how questions are formed.

6.2 Complete a rubric

Outline	Create a rubric in class with learners for assessing longer pieces of spoken or written work or projects.
Thinking skills	Evaluating, reasoning
Language focus	Depends on rubric content
Language skill	Writing or speaking
Time	30 minutes
Level	B1 and above
Preparation	You will need a copy of a spoken or written task or project for your learners and one empty rubric per learner (see Box 6.2b).

Procedure

1 Explain to the learners what a rubric is and show them an example (see Box 6.7c, p. 253).

2 Brainstorm assessment criteria for the task or project with your class, asking them to think about questions such as: When is the task done well? How do you know? Give examples of subject criteria (accurate information), language criteria (use of linking words) and task-specific criteria (posters are visually appealing). Note the criteria on the board and organise them into the categories *subject*, *language*, *task-specific*. See Box 6.2a for an example of brainstormed criteria for a speaking project in history.

3 Give out copies of the empty rubric. Together, select five of the assessment criteria, which learners write in the left-hand column.

4 Explain how to write specific and positive descriptors for each of the criteria. Start with column 4, *the best achievement*, and work backwards. They should write what IS true as far as possible, rather than what is not. A useful technique for writing descriptors is to use these phrases while writing each category: *4. yes; 3. yes, but; 2. no, but; 1. no.*

5 Learners work in pairs to complete one row of the rubric. Ensure you spread the work around the class.

6 Combine learners so you have people who have completed different rows together. Learners combine their ideas to make a first draft of the complete rubric. Alternatively, edit the learners' ideas yourself.

7 Create a final version for the class.

Subject examples

The rubric can be used for any subject.

Variations

- Use a digital whiteboard or data projector to adapt an existing rubric from the Web, e.g. rubistar or teachnology.
- Give learners a half-completed rubric to complete to save time and to help them to think of ideas.

> ## ○ Tip for cross-curricular cooperation between subject and language teachers
>
> Before the lesson: The language teacher helps the subject teacher to think about specific language aims to be assessed in the assignment.

Box 6.2a: Complete a rubric

Brainstormed criteria for a speaking project in history: a PowerPoint® presentation to a German commandant justifying the use of gas in the First World War:

Example subject criteria	*Example language (speaking) criteria*	*Example task-specific (presentation) criteria*
Clear introduction about gas	Pronunciation	Attention-grabbing start
Correct information (dates, events)	Intonation	Enthusiasm
Complete information on how gas was used and by whom	Word stress	Visual support points
Reasons why the use of gas can be justified	Correct grammar	Props (real objects)
Reasons why its use cannot be justified	Variety of grammar forms	Eye contact
Clear conclusion about gas	Variety of vocabulary	Body language
…	History vocabulary	Audience involvement
…	Variety of linking words	Amount of text on PowerPoint slides – not too much or too little
	Fluency	…
	Use of language which persuades well	
	…	

Box 6.2b: Complete a rubric

Empty rubric

Task:..................

Class:..................   Date:..................

Criteria	Descriptors			
	4	3	2	1
	This column describes an excellent piece of work (*Yes!*)	This column describes a good piece of work (*Yes, but ...*)	This column describes a piece of work that is not really up to standard (*No, but ...*)	This column describes a piece of work which is definitely not up to standard (*No!*)

6.3 Correction code

Outline	Learners receive feedback on their work (language) with a correction code.
Thinking skills	Analysing
Language focus	Any
Language skills	Writing
Time	20–30 minutes
Level	A2 and above
Preparation	Prepare a handout like the one in Box 6.3a for each learner explaining your correction code.

Procedure

1 Give each learner a copy of your correction code.
2 Help your learners to understand the correction code by writing some examples of mistakes and the relevant code on the board. Ask them to improve the sentences. Alternatively, ask learners to complete a task like the one in Box 6.3b for history, using the codes and correcting the mistakes.
3 Project an example of a learner's written work on a digital whiteboard /data projector. Use the correction code to edit the text. Avoid providing the correct answer; simply identify the type of mistake.
4 Hand back the writing task you have marked using your correction code. Learners try to correct their own mistakes. Answer any questions they have.

Box 6.3a: Correction code

Example of correction code

Code	Meaning	Example
☺	Well-written section: apt and clear	The French Revolution started in 1789.
V	Vocabulary: find a different word for this	The revelation started in 1789.
T	Correct the tense	The revolution has started in 1789.
WO	Change the word order	The revolution in 1789 started.
WP	wrong phrase	The revolution of France.
Sp	Try spelling this again	The revalation started in 1789.
P	Correct the punctuation	The Revolution started in 1789
S	Style is a problem	The revolution kicked off in 1789.
^	Put in the missing word	The revolution started 1789.
X	There is an extra word	The revolution started in the 1789.
?	Meaning is unclear	The revolution which started was 1789.
/	Split word or sentence up	The Frenchrevoluation started in 1789.

From *CLIL Activities* © Cambridge University Press 2012   PHOTOCOPIABLE

Box 6.3b: Correction code

Correction task for history: The French Revolution

Common mistakes	Code	Correct sentence
The revelation started in 1789.	V	The revolution started in 1789.
The revolution has started in 1789.		
The revolution in 1789 started.		
The revalution started in 1789.		
The Revolution started in 1789.		
The revolution started in the 1789.		
The revolution which started was 1789.		
The revolution started 1789.		
The revolution kicked off in 1789.		

From *CLIL Activities* © Cambridge University Press 2012   PHOTOCOPIABLE

Box 6.3c: Correction code

History: First World War

Learners have written a letter from a soldier in the trenches to his family at home.

_ Mom, dad and lovely sister,   ^, P

I can't hide it anymore, it is too hard to be here without telling you. I am really sorry, but I

lied. I am not at a boarding school, but I am at the army. I know you wouldn't accept it,   V, T

that's why I didn't told you anything. The teacher at school (Mister Webber) said that we   T, S

needed to serve our country by going into the army and that we would be honred a lot if the   ☺, Sp

war would be over. I signed _ for the army with a lot of my friends, and now I need to serve   T, ^

the army till the war is over. I really want to go home, but I can't anymore. With my friends   /

I'm now fighting against the Germans in the trenches. It is horrible, killing someone is much   P, ☺

harder than I expected and I've seen one of my friends getting killed. I dream now every   WO

night about that moment.

From *CLIL Activities* © Cambridge University Press 2012   PHOTCOPIABLE

Subject examples
See Box 6.3c.

Note
The most effective code is one which is designed and then used by all the teachers in the school together, so that learners become used to using the same symbols.

Variations
*   Use the correction code for peer correction or self-correction.
*   Learners can also create their own personalised correction codes for their own common mistakes.

 Tip for cross-curricular cooperation between subject and language teachers

Before the lesson: The language teacher can introduce the correction code in a language class and use it in writing assignments before subject teachers implement it in their lessons.

6.4 Correction cards

Outline	Learners play a card game correcting typical mistakes.
Thinking skills	Identifying
Language focus	Any, agreeing and disagreeing (when discussing the cards)
Language skills	Speaking
Time	10–30 minutes, depending on the number and difficulty of your materials
Level	A2 or above
Preparation	Create sets of about 20 correction cards of either language or content mistakes (see Boxes 6.4a and 6.4c), enough for one set per group of learners. To make it more difficult, include some correct sentences in your set of cards.

Procedure

1   Learners sit in groups of three or four around a table. Give each group a set of correction cards and ask them to make a pile of cards in the middle of the table. Explain that the mistakes are all content mistakes (*Water boils at 105 degrees*) or language mistakes (*Water boil at 100 degrees*) but that some of the sentences are correct.
2   Learners turn over a card in turn, read the sentence aloud and decide as a group if it is correct or not.
3   If the sentence is correct, they keep the card. If the sentence is not correct, the learners discuss what is wrong with it and how it should be corrected.
4   The group with the most correct cards is the winner.

Note

Over a number of years, it is possible to collect a large resource bank of typical mistakes for each subject. These can also be used by the English teacher to make learners aware of the kinds of mistakes they need to look for when checking their work.

 Tip for cross-curricular cooperation between subject and language teachers

Before the lesson: The subject teacher collects sentences including errors and gives them to the language teacher. The card game is played in the language lesson or a subject lesson.

Box 6.4a: Correction cards

Language mistake cards
Art, design and technology; economics and business studies; geography; history; ICT; maths; PE; science

Art I was at the exhibition together with a friend.	History His mother she was the head of volunteers.	Science She's good in measuring.
Maths I've been working on equations on school.	Geography I didn't knew about erosion.	Drama Is it possible that I get some tea?
Economics We're with the four of us in the marketing team.	Science On our school that's impossible.	Drama What do you like of this school?
Business studies They produce this for about four years.	Economics I do my shoppings on Saturdays.	Music He's playing it enthusiastic.
Geography The volcano is erupting for four weeks.	Physical education The children are to the gym.	Maths You can't give maths in English.
Physical education I want to learn them to play football.	Art The man in the photograph like to drink beer.	Drama Two times we went to the theatre.
ICT I'm not used to talk English.	Music It will be dramatically!	History I am at this school for half a year.
Economics He don't have free time.	Art, design and technology That is my idee, too.	Business studies He don't sell shoes.
Maths There are problems with the results since three years.	Geography No sms-ing in class!	History That's much more better.
Drama I've got that movie two years ago on DVD.	History The kids were sitting every day in the room.	Geography Some will be talking very well English.
ICT They will make the project on the computer.	Economics He has not a job.	Geography It's the worst city of the country.
Music The children on this school are very nice.	Maths I don't know nothing about that.	Drama He's watching always to the English programmes.

Box 6.4b: Correction cards
Key to language mistakes

I was at the exhibition together with a friend.	I was at the exhibition with a friend.
His mother she was the head of volunteers.	His mother was the head of volunteers.
She's good in measuring.	She's good at measuring.
I've been working on equations on school	I've been working on equations at school.
I didn't knew about erosion.	I didn't know about erosion.
Is it possible that I get some tea?	Could I have some tea?
We're with the four of us in the marketing team.	There are four of us in the marketing team.
On our school that's impossible.	At our school that's impossible.
What do you like of this school?	What do you like about this school?
They produce this for about four years.	They have been producing this for about four years.
I do my shoppings on Saturdays.	I do my shopping on Saturdays.
He's playing it enthusiastic.	He's playing it enthusiastically.
The volcano is erupting for four weeks.	The volcano has been erupting for four weeks.
The children are to the gym.	The children have gone to the gym.
You can't give maths in English.	You can't teach maths in English.
I want to learn them to play football.	I want to teach them to play football.
The man in the photograph like to drink beer	The man in the photograph likes drinking beer.
Two times we went to the theatre.	We went to the theatre twice.
I'm not used to talk English.	I'm not used to talking English.
It will be dramatically!	It will be dramatic!
I am at this school for half a year.	I have been at this school for half a year.
He don't have free time.	He doesn't have any free time.
That is my idee, too.	That's what I think, too.
He don't sell shoes.	He doesn't sell shoes.
There are problems with the results since three years.	There have been problems with the results for three years.
No sms-ing in class!	No texting in class!
That's much more better.	That's much better.
I've got that movie two years ago on DVD.	I got that movie two years ago on DVD.
The kids were sitting every day in the room.	The kids sat in the room every day.
Some will be talking very well English.	Some will speak very good English.
They will make the project on the computer.	They will do the project on the computer.
He has not a job.	He doesn't have a job.
It's the worst city of the country.	It's the worst city in the country.
The children on this school are very nice.	The children at this school are very nice.
I don't know nothing about that	I don't know anything about that.
He's watching always to the English programmes.	He's always watching English programmes.

Box 6.4c: Correction cards

Content mistake cards

Art, design and technology The particles in gouache are smaller than in watercolours. Gouache dissolves in water.	Economics and business studies A business plan is written for a general audience.	Geography The last ice age began about 100,000 and ended about 70,000 years ago.
History The Black Plague travelled about 10 miles a day. It killed 10 million people in Europe.	ICT HTML stands for HighText Markup Logo.	Maths The volume of a cylindrical canister with radius 7 cm and height 12 cm is 1845, 70 cm³.
Music and drama A semibreve is half the length of a minim and twice the length of a breve. It is sometimes written on the stave as hollow, sometimes as black.	PE Anaerobic work is important for marathon runners in order to build up endurance to a maximum.	Science In a neutral solution, red litmus paper stays red and blue litmus paper turns red.

From *CLIL Activities* © Cambridge University Press 2012   PHOTOCOPIABLE

Box 6.4d: Correction cards

Key to content mistakes

Art, design and technology The particles in gouache are larger than water colours. Gouache dissolves in water.	Economics and business studies A business plan is written for a specific audience.	Geography The last ice age began about 70,000 and ended about 15,000 years ago.
History The Black Plague travelled about 2 miles a day. It killed 25 million people in Europe.	ICT HTML stands for HyperText Markup Language.	Maths The volume of a cylindrical canister with radius 7 cm and height 12 cm is 1847,50 cm³.
Music and drama A semibreve is twice the length of a minim and half the length of a breve. It is always written on the stave as hollow.	PE Aerobic work is important for marathon runners in order to build up endurance to a maximum.	Science In a neutral solution, red and blue litmus paper stays red and blue.

From *CLIL Activities* © Cambridge University Press 2012   PHOTOCOPIABLE

6.5 First person revision

Outline	Learners revise concepts.
Thinking skills	Comparing and contrasting, remembering, identifying
Language focus	Giving and asking for opinions; subject vocabulary
Language skills	Listening and speaking
Time	15 minutes
Level	A1 or above
Preparation	Write 7–10 words or concepts (more advanced learners can cope with up to 20) that are important for your learners to revise or remember on sets of cards, one set of cards per group or pair. Create about 10 statements in the first person, to which the words or concepts on the cards are answers; each word should correspond to at least one statement and preferably to more of them. An example for maths is: *My sides are all the same length.* Possible concepts on cards are: *equilateral triangle, rhombus, square.* The sentences should begin with *I* or *My* (history: *I am an important person in the Renaissance*; geography: *I am very cold*). See Box 6.5 and *Subject examples* for some ideas.

Procedure

1 Put learners into pairs or groups of three. Give each group a set of cards and ensure that everyone can see all the cards.

2 Explain that when you read out a sentence (or question), they should find one or more answers to your question in their set. Read out your first sentence. The groups hold up the card(s) which they think correspond(s) to the sentence.

3 Continue until you have read out all your sentences, one by one.

Box 6.5: First person revision

Science: biology – the digestive system

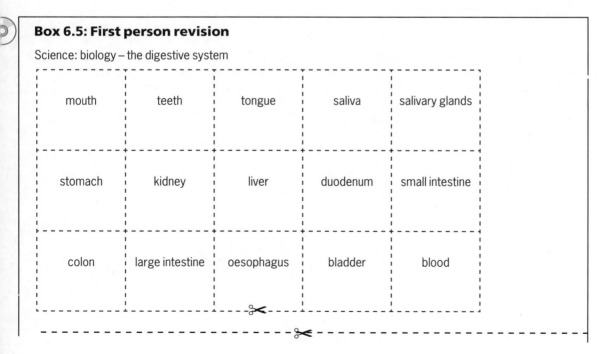

mouth	teeth	tongue	saliva	salivary glands
stomach	kidney	liver	duodenum	small intestine
colon	large intestine	oesophagus	bladder	blood

Statements:

1. I clear the blood of toxins.
2. I help food travel from the mouth to the stomach.
3. We chew the food and help it to go into the throat.
4. I start to digest the food.
5. I clear the blood of salt, hormones and water.
6. I produce urine.
7. I accept partially digested food.
8. I kill germs in food with acid.
9. I am the first part of the intestines.
10. When I am full, the body needs to urinate.
11. I digest food.
12. I am a chemical in the mouth.
13. Food arrives in me just after leaving the stomach.
14. I collect urine.
15. I absorb intestinal fluids.
16. I keep the food in me for a couple of hours.
17. I am about 25 centimetres long.
18. I am the first stop for food.
19. I carry nutrients away from the intestine.
20. I am about 1.5 metres long.

--✂--

Key: 1. liver; 2. oesophagus; 3. teeth, tongue; 4. saliva, salivary glands; 5. kidney; 6. bladder; 7. duodenum; 8. stomach; 9. small intestine; 10. bladder; 11. stomach, saliva; 12. saliva; 13. colon, large intestine; 14. bladder; 15. colon; 16. stomach; 17. oesophagus; 18. mouth; 19. blood; 20. large intestine.

From *CLIL Activities* © Cambridge University Press 2012

Subject examples

Maths: two-dimensional shapes

Words: rhombus, square, parallelogram, rectangle, isosceles triangle, equilateral triangle, right-angled triangle

---

Statements:

1. I have axes of symmetry. (key: rhombus, square, rectangle, isosceles triangle, equilateral triangle)
2. I have point symmetry. (key: rhombus, square, parallelogram, rectangle)
3. I am a parallelogram. (key: rhombus, square, parallelogram, rectangle)
4. I am a rhombus. (key: rhombus, square)
5. My diagonals are perpendicular to each other. (key: rhombus, square)
6. All my sides have the same length. (key: rhombus, square)
7. I have two pairs of opposite sides that are parallel. (key: rhombus, square, parallelogram, rectangle)
8. I am a geometrical triangle. (key: isosceles triangle, right-angled triangle)
9. I have rotational symmetry. (key: rhombus, square, parallelogram, rectangle, equilateral triangle)

Variation

You can also do this activity in the form of a competition between the groups, giving points for wholly correct or partly correct answers.

Follow-up

Once learners are used to this activity, they can create statements for each other.

💡 **Tips for cross-curricular cooperation between subject and language teachers**

Before the lesson: The language teacher reminds learners about the use of the first person (*I am/have/live*) and the use of the possessives *my* and *mine*.

During the lesson: The language teacher listens out for the use of the first person and *my* and *mine*.

6.6 Group self-evaluation

Outline	Learners complete a self-evaluation sheet during a project, experiment or longer piece of work.
Thinking skills	Evaluating, giving opinions
Language focus	Giving opinions, evaluating
Language skills	Writing
Time	20 minutes
Level	B1 and above
Preparation	Prepare one self-evaluation sheet (see Box 6.6) – one per learner per lesson, so that they keep a record of the process and their progress as a group.

Procedure
1 Explain that each learner needs to keep their own individual record of how group work goes during each project lesson.
2 Give each learner a copy of a self-evaluation sheet to complete each time and tell them to keep it in their file. You can use the handouts to coach the learners as they go along, too.

Box 6.6: Self-evaluation sheet

CLIL GROUP WORK SELF-EVALUATION SHEET

Name ....Date ....

Names of other members of your group ....

....

Project title ....

	Content	Language	Other
1. Who worked the hardest in your group on content and language or other aspects of this task in this lesson, or did you all contribute equally? If so, what did each group member do?			
2. What did you personally do well in this lesson, regarding content and language or other aspects of the task? What did the group do well in this lesson?			
3. Say what aspects of the task you personally didn't do well and would like to improve on next lesson.			
4. Say what aspects of the task the group didn't do well and would like to improve on next lesson.			
5. How have you divided the tasks between you to prepare for next lesson? Say who is doing what.			
6. Are you on schedule with your plan? Explain where you are with your planning.			
7. Make an estimate of the time you personally spent on the project outside the lesson (between this and the previous lesson).	_____ minutes	_____ minutes	_____ minutes

From *CLIL Activities* © Cambridge University Press 2012   PHOTOCOPIABLE

6.7 Jigsaw rubric: assessing speaking

Outline	Learners put together a rubric.
Thinking skills	Classifying, ordering
Language focus	Present tenses, descriptive language
Language skills	Reading and speaking
Time	20 minutes
Level	B1 and above
Preparation	Prepare a rubric for assessing speaking (e.g. an individual group or individual presentation, a song, a poem, a role play). A rubric consists of a number of assessment criteria to be rated and a number of descriptors (usually four), outlining the different stages of development of work. You can also use an online rubric generating site, such as Rubistar (http://rubistar.4teachers.org/). Prepare a rubric replacing some of the information with numbered gaps like the one in Box 6.7a. Make cards of the information from the gaps and give each card a letter to identify it.

Procedure

1 Introduce your rubric for assessing oral work. Explain what a rubric is and show them an example (see Box 6.7c) (not the one you are going to use).
2 Learners work in pairs. Give the learners a copy of your gapped rubric and a set of cards (the missing descriptors). Learners match the descriptors on cards to the gaps.
3 Check their answers with the key. Give them copies of the complete rubric to use while preparing their oral presentation.

Variations

* To differentiate, ask more skilled learners to complete the gaps in their own words, i.e. to work without the sets of cards.
* Vary the number of gaps you use in your rubrics depending on the level of your learners: use rubrics with more gaps when teaching more skilled learners and ones with fewer gaps with less skilled learners.
* For a good group, give the learners a completely empty rubric and a set of descriptor cards to complete the rubric. Limit the total number of descriptors to no more than 20 to avoid overwhelming learners.

Follow-up

Use the rubric for peer assessment during oral presentations. Divide the class into five groups. Give each group one category to score using the rubric.

Box 6.7a: Jigsaw rubric – assessing speaking

Sample partial gapped oral presentation rubric (for all subjects)

Category	4	3	2	1
Content	Shows a full understanding of the topic.	Shows a good understanding of the topic.	1	Understands a bit of the topic.
Comprehension	2	3	Able to answer a few questions posed by classmates about the topic.	Unable to answer questions posed by classmates about the topic.
Vocabulary	Uses vocabulary that is appropriate for the audience and related to the subject. Extends audience vocabulary by defining words that might be new to most of the audience.	Uses vocabulary that is appropriate for the audience. Includes one or two words that might be new to most of the audience, but does not define them.	4	Uses simple words that everyone understands or over-complicated specialised words that no-one can follow.
Speaks clearly	Speaks clearly and distinctly all (95–100%) the time, and does not mispronounce any words.	5	Speaks clearly and distinctly most (85–94%) of the time. Mispronounces more than five words.	Often mumbles or cannot be understood and/or mispronounces words.
Enthusiasm	6	Facial expressions and body language sometimes generate a strong interest and enthusiasm about the topic in others.	Facial expressions and body language are used to try to generate enthusiasm, but seem somewhat faked.	Very little use of facial expressions or body language. Did not generate much interest in topic being presented.

This rubric was developed using Rubistar, an online rubric generator. http://rubistar.4teachers.org/

Box 6.7b: Jigsaw rubric – assessing speaking

Sample cards to put into the gaps (Key: 1B, 2E, 3A, 4C, 5F, 6D)

A Able to answer most questions posed by classmates about the topic.	B. Shows a good understanding of parts of the topic.	C Uses vocabulary that is appropriate for the audience. Does not include any vocabulary that might be new to the audience.
D Facial expressions and body language generate a strong interest and enthusiasm about the topic in others.	E Able to answer all or almost all questions posed by classmates about the topic.	F Speaks clearly and distinctly all (95–100%) the time; mispronounces fewer than five words.

From *CLIL Activities* © Cambridge University Press 2012   PHOTOCOPIABLE

Box 6.7c: Jigsaw rubric – assessing speaking

Complete rubric oral presentation

CATEGORY	4	3	2	1
Content	Shows a full understanding of the topic.	Shows a good understanding of the topic.	Shows a good understanding of parts of the topic.	Understands a bit of the topic.
Comprehension	Able to answer all or almost all questions posed by classmates about the topic.	Able to answer most questions posed by classmates about the topic.	Able to answer a few questions posed by classmates about the topic.	Unable to answer questions posed by classmates about the topic.
Vocabulary	Uses vocabulary that is appropriate for the audience and related to the subject. Extends audience vocabulary by defining words that might be new to most of the audience.	Uses vocabulary that is appropriate for the audience. Includes one or two words that might be new to most of the audience, but does not define them.	Uses vocabulary that is appropriate for the audience. Does not include any vocabulary that might be new to the audience.	Uses simple words that everyone understands or over-complicated specialised words which no-one can follow.
Speaks clearly	Speaks clearly and distinctly all (95%–100%) the time, and does not mispronounce any words.	Speaks clearly and distinctly all (95–100%) the time; mispronounces fewer than five words.	Speaks clearly and distinctly most (85–94%) of the time. Mispronounces more than five words.	Often mumbles or cannot be understood AND/OR mispronounces words.
Enthusiasm	Facial expressions and body language generate a strong interest and enthusiasm about the topic in others.	Facial expressions and body language sometimes generate a strong interest and enthusiasm about the topic in others.	Facial expressions and body language are used to try to generate enthusiasm, but seem somewhat faked.	Very little use of facial expressions or body language. Did not generate much interest in topic being presented.

6.8 Language feedback

Outline	Give feedback to learners on their successful language use as well as their mistakes.
Thinking skills	Analysing
Language focus	Accuracy and appropriacy
Language skills	Speaking
Time	5–10 minutes, depending on number of language points
Level	Any
Preparation	Photocopy the table in Box 6.8.

Procedure

1 As learners carry out a speaking task in groups or pairs, listen to their spoken language and use the table in Box 6.8 to note the names of learners who speak. For each learner, note an example of good use (☺) of language, e.g. vocabulary, grammar, pronunciation, and a language mistake (M), e.g. vocabulary, grammar, pronunciation.
2 At the end of the speaking task, ask learners to correct the language mistakes you noted.
3 Photocopy the table including corrections and give it to the learners or the language teacher.

Box 6.8: Language feedback

Name	☺	M	Correction

From *CLIL Activities* © Cambridge University Press 2012   PHOTOCOPIABLE

Subject examples

You can use the language feedback table in Box 6.8 for any subject.

Variation
Learners complete similar tables for each other during group work.

6.9 Multiple intelligences: exploring

Outline	Learners discover their own 'intelligences'.
Thinking skills	Evaluating
Language focus	Present tenses, adverbs of frequency
Language skills	Reading and speaking
Time	45–50 minutes
Level	B1 or above
Preparation	Make a handout on multiple intelligences for your learners using the *Key idea: multiple intelligences in a nutshell* (see Part 1, pp. 13–14) reproduced in Box 6.9a and any other materials that you have. Have enough copies of this information and the Multiples intelligences (MI) questionnaire (Box 6.9b) and 'MI pizza' (Box 6.9c) for each learner.

Procedure

1 Introduce the theory of multiple intelligences (MI) to your class, using Box 6.9a and any other information gathered. Explain that we all learn in different ways, and develop a range of different intelligences that are helpful in different situations. Discuss the ideas with your class, using discussion questions such as:
   - Which intelligences do you think you are strong in?
   - In what ways is your best friend/brother/sister/parent intelligent?
   - Which famous people possess one strong intelligence?
2 Give each learner a copy of the MI questionnaire to complete (Box 6.9b). They answer each question with a score of 0 to 4.
3 Learners add up their scores, complete the key and then complete an 'MI pizza' for themselves (see Box 6.9c) to visualise their scores.
4 Learners tell you their top three intelligences and write these on a poster for everyone to see.
5 You can use the results of the MI test to create groups according to similar or different intelligences.

Subject examples

This activity is suitable for all subjects as well as for a lesson with a class teacher or mentor.

Note

Multiple intelligence (MI) theory is important for CLIL, since when teachers are aware of MI theory, they can provide input and tasks which appeal to different 'intelligences' and which help learners to take in input, show understanding and produce output in other than linguistic ways.

> 💡 **Tips for cross-curricular cooperation between subject and language teachers**
>
> Before the lesson: The language teacher can do work on the position of adverbs of frequency (*always, sometimes, never*, etc.) in sentences and how to ask *How often ...?* questions, e.g. *How often do you play tennis? I never play tennis.*
>
> After the lesson: The language teacher holds a discussion about multiple intelligence theory. The teacher puts learners of similar intelligence together and asks them to discuss their profiles and where in their lives they recognise their 'intelligences'.

Box 6.9a: Multiple intelligences – exploring

Multiple intelligences in a nutshell

Linguistic-verbal: You like working with words, reading and writing.

Logical-mathematical: You like concepts, think logically and like puzzles and problems.

Bodily-physical: You enjoy sports and games. You like to move around and learn by doing. You use body language to communicate.

Visual-spatial: You think in images or pictures, learn by seeing and by using charts or diagrams.

Musical: You enjoy learning and/or making music. You have a sense of rhythm and melody.

Naturalistic: You enjoy the natural world, animals and are interested in the environment.

Interpersonal-social. You like working in groups, and learn well if you study or discuss things with other people.

Intrapersonal: You understand your own feelings and thoughts. You like to daydream and fantasise and to work alone. You like to know why you are doing something.

From *CLIL Activities* © Cambridge University Press 2012   PHOTOCOPIABLE

Box 6.9b: Multiple intelligences – exploring

Multiple intelligences questionnaire

You are going to discover your own 'intelligences' by completing a questionnaire and a pie graph (pizza).

Instructions

Score each of the 40 statements below like this:

4	always true for me
3	often true for me
2	sometimes true for me
1	very occasionally true for me
0	never true for me

MULTIPLE INTELLIGENCES QUESTIONNAIRE

1. English, social studies and history are easier for me at school than maths and science.   1. ____
2. I am aware of the weather.   2. ____
3. Friends come to me for advice.   3. ____
4. I am good at chess, draughts and other strategy games.   4. ____
5. I see words in my head.   5. ____
6. I can imagine how something might look from above, like a bird would.   6. ____
7. I can tell when a music note is out of tune.   7. ____
8. I sometimes walk down the street with a tune playing in my head.   8. ____
9. I consider myself a leader (or others think I am a leader).   9. ____
10. I would rather spend my evenings at a lively party than having a quiet talk to someone.   10. ____
11. I enjoy word games like Scrabble, anagrams, crosswords and tongue twisters.   11. ____
12. I like analysing, calculating and measuring things.   12. ____
13. I find it difficult to sit still for long periods of time: I need to move around.   13. ____
14. I use a camera or video recorder.   14. ____
15. I love animals and think about working with them.   15. ____
16. I have a good sense of direction.   16. ____
17. I enjoy biology lessons and learning about the natural world.   17. ____
18. I have a very close friend.   18. ____
19. I like learning about my own personality.   19. ____
20. I keep a personal diary where I write down my thoughts.   20. ____
21. I like working with my hands, e.g. model-building, sewing, weaving, carving or woodwork.   21. ____
22. I make tapping sounds or sing little melodies when I work or study.   22. ____
23. I am interested in 'green' issues related to the environment.   23. ____

24. I have music on in the background when I study.   24. ____

25. I need to DO things with a new skill rather than simply reading about it or seeing a video that describes it.   25. ____

26. I often see pictures when I close my eyes and I often have vivid dreams at night.   26. ____

27. I prefer looking at reading material with pictures.   27. ____

28. I regularly spend time alone to think about important life questions.   28. ____

29. I see myself as a loner (or others see me as a loner).   29. ____

30. I sometimes have good ideas when doing physical activities.   30. ____

31. I like planning, e.g. my school work or a party.   31. ____

32. I am interested in how (mechanical) things work, e.g. a clock, a computer or a CD player.   32. ____

33. I would describe myself as physically well-coordinated.   33. ____

34. I like watching nature programmes on television.   34. ____

35. I would prefer to spend a weekend at a busy place with lots of people and action than alone in a house in the woods.   35. ____

36. I've written something that I am proud of or that others enjoyed reading.   36. ____

37. If I hear a song or piece of music once or twice, I can sing it accurately.   37. ____

38. Maths and/or science are some of my favourite subjects at school.   38. ____

39. When I drive down a road, I pay more attention to words written on signs than to the scenery.   39. ____

40. When I've got a problem, I look for someone to share it with rather than try to work it out on my own.   40. ____

Box 6.9c: Exploring intelligences

Scoring

Multiple intelligences questionnaire: insert your scores for each MI question in the grid below and add them up.

	A	B	C	D	E	F	G	H
	1	4	13	6	7	2	3	18 .....
	5	12	21	14	8	15	9	19 .....
	11	31	25	16	22	17	10	20 .....
	36	32	30	26	24	23	35	28 .....
	39	38	33	27	37	34	40	29 .....
Total scores								

Write your scores in the key below to discover your own intelligences.

KEY

A.	Linguistic (Ling)	_____
B.	Logical-mathematical (LM)	_____
C.	Bodily-physical (BP)	_____
D.	Visual-spatial (VS)	_____
E.	Musical (Mus)	_____
F.	Naturalistic (Nat)	_____
G.	Interpersonal (Inter)	_____
H.	Intrapersonal (Intra)	_____

We are all a mixture of intelligences. You now have scores which make up a profile of your own (stronger and weaker) eight intelligences. On the left, is an MI 'pizza' – a pie graph – made by a third-year learner, completed according to her scores. Fill in the right-hand pizza, showing how your scores are divided.

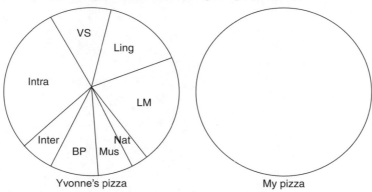

Yvonne's pizza   My pizza

Adapted from an activity in Mulder and Tanner (1998) and used later in Dale, L., van der Es, W. and Tanner, R. (2010).

6.10 Multiple intelligences: assessment

Outline	Offer learners an assessment that suits their type of multiple intelligence.
Thinking skills	Depends on the type of assessment
Language focus	Any
Language skill	Any
Time	Depends on the type of assessment
Level	All
Preparation	Create a choice of assessment tasks appealing to different intelligences. For example, to show what learners understand about light in physics: write a paragraph, draw a diagram, act out a role play or make a chart or table (see Box 6.10).

Procedure

In the table in Box 6.10 you can find examples of types of assessment tasks and the different types of intelligence they appeal to.

Variations

1. Use the table in Box 6.10 to plan with your subject team how you will use a range of assessments throughout the school year.
2. Ask the learners to think of assessment tasks using the table in Box 6.10.
3. Let learners choose which assessment task they would like to do.

Box 6.10: Multiple intelligences – assessment

Intelligence used→ Example assessment↓	Interpersonal	Intrapersonal	Visual-spatial	Bodily-physical	Logical-mathematical	Verbal-linguistic	Musical	Naturalistic
Interview	✓				✓	✓		
Role play	✓			✓		✓		
Class magazine	✓	✓	✓	✓	✓	✓		
Classroom debate	✓			✓		✓		
Diary		✓				✓		
SWOT analysis		✓			✓	✓		
Self-evaluation		✓				✓		
Group collage	✓		✓	✓	✓	✓		
Diagram					✓			
Graphic novel	✓		✓	✓		✓		
Map			✓		✓			✓
Freeze frame	✓		✓	✓				
3D model			✓		✓			
Logic game					✓			
Newspaper article		✓				✓		
Open question in test						✓		
Spoken presentation	✓					✓		
PowerPoint presentation	✓		✓		✓	✓	✓	
A rap or song		✓		✓		✓	✓	
A soundtrack to accompany a video	✓		✓		✓	✓	✓	
Fieldwork			✓	✓		✓		✓
Observation task		✓	✓		✓	✓		

From *CLIL Activities* © Cambridge University Press 2012   PHOTOCOPIABLE

6.11 Rewrite together

Outline	Learners work together to rewrite a short text written by a peer.
Thinking skills	Evaluating, comparing and contrasting
Language focus	Various, depending on the sample writing task
Language skills	Writing
Time	20 minutes
Level	A2 or above
Preparation	Learners send or hand in a short writing task (150–250 words) to you in advance. Select a weak example of the same writing task and make it anonymous. The example could be taken from another class or a previous year or, in advance, you can ask a learner from your current class for permission to use his or her work anonymously. Organise to project the original piece or write it out on a poster or the board. Make one photocopy of the completed writing task per pair in your class.

Procedure

1 Project or show the learners the first paragraph of the writing task. Explain that you are going to rewrite a version of the task they sent you to produce a well-written and appropriate piece of subject writing.

2 Remind learners what the writing task was that you set them, who the audience was, what the aim was and what type of text they needed to write.

3 Learners say what they like about the first sentence and suggest improvements. Change the sentence, using their suggestions, and comment on how this improves the text. Do this with a few sentences.

4 Hand out the piece of writing you have photocopied and ask the learners to improve it in pairs.

5 After about 15 minutes, work with the whole class on rewriting and perfecting the projected text. Think aloud about the text with the learners as you go along to keep the class engaged and focused. Ask questions to elicit improvements, such as, *Which other word might be used here? Is this a clear sentence? How might it be clearer?* (See Box 6.11a for an example.)

6 When you and the class are satisfied with the final text, make photocopies for all the learners. If you are not working with a smartboard or computer, you (or a learner) will need to type it out and make copies.

7 Give the learners another text or their own text and ask them to rewrite it in pairs.

 Teaching tip

If you are using this technique for the first time, try rewriting the paragraph yourself first. Consult a colleague English teacher or subject teacher for help: your aim is to produce a piece of model writing.

Subject examples

See Box 6.11a and Box 6.11b (Variation 1).

Box 6.11a: Rewrite together

Example of original learner text (biology task: write a report about a fictitious food chain on Mars for an information booklet for biologists visiting the planet for the first time)

This story goes about the food chain on Mars. At that planet live some strange animals and plants.

The envril is a really small animal, it's a bacteria it lives on groters, groters are bleu plants who live in dark spots, that dark sport live also the renter, a small animal who eats the whole day plants it's a real herbivore, but he has to watch out for other animals, for instance the menester, this animal hunts at night he eats everything it's a omnivore, the ventral is a kind of a meet eating plant he eats only meat it's a reducer, the the dangaroust of all is the arbier, it lives in the craters but it hunts all day, it a carnivore he only eat meat it's a consumer you better not met him.

This was animals that are a little part of Mars' food chain.

✂ -

Version rewritten with the class

This report is about the food chain on Mars. Some strange animals and plants live on this distant planet.

The envril is a very small animal. It is a bacteria and lives on groters. Groters are blue plants which live in dark places. Renters also live in similar dark places. A renter is a small animal which grazes on plants all day: it's a herbivore. However, the renter has to beware of other animals, for instance the menester, an omnivore which hunts at night and eats everything. The ventral is a carnivorous plant which is a reducer. Watch out, though, for the most dangerous animal: the carnivorous arbier! It lives in craters and hunts all day. Arbiers are consumers, and other animals avoid them at all costs! This report describes a small part of the food chain on Mars.

Improvements:

1. Use of written (*very*) rather than spoken (*really*) language
2. Use of formal academic words (*report, describes*) rather than everyday words (*story, is about*)
3. Use of linking words (*and, however, which, though*)
4. Avoidance of repetition by use of reference words and linking words (*it, which*)

From *CLIL Activities* © Cambridge University Press 2012   PHOTOCOPIABLE

Variation 1

Give learners two versions of the same piece of writing (one strong and one weak) and ask them to compare them. (See Box 6.11b for an example for history.) Then give them another text to rewrite themselves.

Box 6.11b:

The task: Write a story about how Phillip – on a journey by sea to Virginia – was saved by Timothy and how they came across the Cay Island group.

Learner text A

This story is about a small, white boy called Phillip which took place during the Second World War. When Germans became a threat to the island of Curacao. His mother became worried and decide to flee the island and return to Virigina in the U.S.A. His father need to stay on Curacao for his work and could not join them. The father was worried because the Germans had U–Boats patrolling in the coast. Mr Enright want his wife to fly back to the U.S.A., however she refused because of her fear for flying. In the end they went by a boat. On the second day of the journey the boat was torpedoed. Phillip woke up on a raft with a big, old Negro man called Timothy. He asked for his mother but Timothy didn't answer. Many problems happened to them including Phillip turning blind. Then Timothy saw land .It was a Cay. Timothy knew that they had a problem because they didn't have enough resources for the trip to Jamaica, so they thought they would be safer on the Cay.

 -

Learner text B

Phillip and Timothy's journey ended at Devil's mouth which is located at 15°N and 80°W. Phillip started his journey in Willemstad which is about 10°N and 69°W. He left Willemstad with his mother. Somewhere near Panama the ship was sunk and Phillip and his mother were seperated. At a certain point Phillip was pulled out of the water by Timothy. Toghether they ended up on an island called the Cay. It is located on a series of islands called the Devil's Mouth. In reality they are not located in an Atlas so I put them near Panama. Below I will plot their journey.

Variation 2

Provide learners with a list of questions to direct learners' thinking. See Box 6.11c.

Box 6.11c: Rewrite together

Questions about content

1   What do you like about Text A?

2   What is the best phrase or sentence in Text A? Why?

3   What do you like about Text B?

4   What is the best sentence in Text B? Why?

5   Which text is better, according to you, and why?

6   In both texts, more information is needed for the reader to understand who Phillip is. Add two sentences to one of the texts where you give some background information to help explain.

7   In Text A, Timothy didn't answer. Add something to the text to explain why not.

8   In Text B, it's unclear where Willemstad is. Add some information to the text to make that clearer.

9   Text B doesn't have an introductory sentence. Add a good one.

Questions about language

10 Are all the words with capital letters right? Should some other words have capital letters too?

11 Underline all the present and past tenses in both texts. Correct the ones which are used incorrectly.

12 Find two spelling mistakes in Text B and correct them.

13 In Text A, the following isn't a complete sentence. 'When Germans became a threat to the island of Curacao.' Can you either link it to another sentence or make a complete sentence?

From *CLIL Activities* © Cambridge University Press 2012   PHOTOCOPIABLE

Variation 3

Use screen capture software to record the changes as you make them, and upload the video to a virtual learning environment (VLE) for learners to watch again. An example of screen capture software can be seen at: http://www.techsmith.com/jing/.

Variation 4

The English teacher can do this activity in an English class using written work done in content lessons.

💡 **Tips for cross-curricular cooperation between subject and language teachers**

Before the lesson: The language teacher can work with the subject teacher on selecting the pieces of writing to be used. This should include typical problems experienced by several learners. The language teacher can also help by pointing out which errors occur in the learners' pieces of work and suggesting improvements for the model paragraph.

After the lesson: The subject teacher gives the language teacher the rewritten paragraphs for language analysis.

6.12 Revision circles

Outline	Learners sit or stand in two circles and answer revision questions.
Thinking skills	Recalling, reasoning
Language focus	Various, depending on topic
Language skills	Speaking
Time	15–30 minutes
Level	Any
Preparation	Tell learners in advance that they are going to have a test and need to revise for it. Prepare your test questions.

Procedure

1   Explain to your learners that they will revise together and then take the test individually.
2   Learners stand or sit in two parallel circles (e.g. 10 in the inner circle and 10 in the outer circle), facing each other. If you have an odd number of learners, ask two of them to work together as a pair.

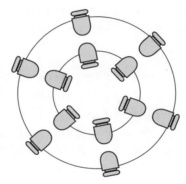

3   Reveal your first question on the topic – on the board or in a PowerPoint® presentation.
4   Learners discuss their answer(s) with the person opposite them. Remind them to speak in English, since the test will be in English.
5   Then say: *Outer circle move one person/two people to the left,* so that learners are then facing a new partner.
6   Show them your second question and ask them to discuss it with their new partner.
7   Call out: *Inner circle move two people to the left,* and show your third question. Continue rotating the circles alternately so that each question is discussed with a different partner.
8   After all the questions have been asked and discussed, give the learners the questions in writing and allow them to write down their answers.
9   Grade as a test.

Subject examples

Science: biology

Photosynthesis

1. What is the location of the light stage of photosynthesis?
2. Light energy is absorbed by chlorophyll and is used to:
   (a) regenerate ATP and reduce carbon dioxide
   (b) aplit water and regenerate ATP
   (c) oxidise glucose and split water
   (d) split water and fix carbon dioxide
3. What is the hydrogen acceptor in photosynthesis?
4. What is the carbon dioxide acceptor in the Calvin cycle?
5. Where does the carbon fixation stage of photosynthesis occur?
6. The carbon fixation stage of photosynthesis requires:
   (a) ATP, $NADPH_2$ and CO_2
   (b) ATP, NAD and hydrogen
   (c) ATP, hydrogen and oxygen
   (d) ATP, $NADPH_2$ and oxygen

Adapted from http://www.bbc.co.uk/apps/ifl/scotland/education/bitesize/higher/biology/cell_biology/quizengine ?quiz=photosynthesis.

Note

The circle arrangement makes it easy to swap partners. If space is an issue, of course, it is possible to keep a more traditional classroom seating arrangement.

Variations

This doesn't necessarily have to be a revision activity. For example, you could also use it for activating learners before they start working on a topic.

6.13 Stickers

Outline	Learners play a guessing game related to central concepts in a topic.
Thinking skills	Reasoning, understanding
Language focus	Vocabulary
Language skills	Reading, listening and speaking
Time	15 minutes
Level	A2 and above
Preparation	This is a revision activity. Choose one page of information about a topic that you want learners to revise. You will need one sticky label (6 × 3 cm) per learner.

Procedure

1   Learners read the page of information quickly.
2   Give out one sticky label per learner. They choose and write one idea (e.g. hormone – biology; revolution – history) or part of speech (e.g. noun) on their sticker. Collect the stickers and check there is no repetition.
3   Stick one label on to each learner's back, without telling them what it is.
4   Remind learners how to ask questions in the first person (with *I*).
5   Learners circulate around the classroom with the information, asking each other yes/no questions in the first person (*Am I an A? Am I related to B? Am I found in C?*) to try to discover what their own label reads. For each question they ask, they write an X on their classmate's label.
6   Once they have guessed who or what they are, they move the sticker from their back to their front, but keep on answering other learners' questions.

Subject examples
This activity can be used with any topic.

Note

This fun activity can help a class with low initial interest engage with your topic and is useful for revising difficult concepts which learners need to know.

6.14 Visual assessments

Outline	Assess learners' progress using a visual product.
Thinking skills	Creative thinking
Language focus	Any
Language skills	Reading, listening
Time	30–40 minutes
Level	A1 and above
Preparation	Decide on an aspect of your subject that you want to assess. Choose a visual product for learners to demonstrate their knowledge and understanding. This could be a drawing, graph, silent film, sculpture, model (e.g. hovercraft, molecule), painting, freeze frame, emblem, illustration for a book or CD cover, map, game, picture, technical design, diagram, experiment, storyboard, physical exercise, poster, animation. (See *Subject examples* for some ideas.) Create an imaginary but realistic audience for the product. Find or make an example of a possible product as a model. Prepare assessment criteria or provide a rubric (see Activities 6.2: *Complete a rubric* and 6.7: *Jigsaw rubric: assessing speaking*).

Procedure

1 Introduce the visual assessment task to your learners and provide your assessment criteria or rubric.
2 Show learners an example or model of a completed product.
3 Brainstorm with learners how they will approach making the visual product: where can they find the information they need to include in the product? Where can they find tips on producing a good visual product?
4 Help learners with any language they will need for their visual.
5 Once the assessments have been made, display them in an art exhibition. Divide the class in half: half of the learners stand by their assessment, the other half circulates. Learners ask and answer questions about their visual assessments. Swap roles.

Subject examples

(Some of these examples are illustrated with real learner work.)

Art, design and technology: Create a modern-day Aboriginal painting, explaining an event in your own life, accompanied by your artistic statement.

Artistic statement 1 (accompanying the aboriginal art painting on page 00)

This painting is about a group of Aboriginals. This group is divided in women and men. The children of both groups want to play with each other. But the parents believe that if the children don't see each other, they will become stronger.

There is only one way which the children can try to see each other: a river with snakes. Everyday the children try to cross the river. Once it was done without being attacked by snakes.

Artistic statement 2

This painting is about my younger years. The time that I fell off my bicycle (and hurt myself). Some parts don't really fit in the painting I made. But that's because it would be a very empty painting if I didn't put all the other stuff in.

Economics and business studies: Read a company's annual report and choose or create an image to illustrate the front cover of the report. Explain your choice to the managing director of the company.

Geography: Illustrate the changes that take place in a small village when tourists start to visit. Explain your illustration to the town council.

History: Draw two pictures showing the differences between life in a town in 1350 and 1600 (see Part 1, page 9).

Maths: Draw instructions for how to calculate the surface area of a shape. Explain the instructions to the class.

Music and drama: Choose or draw an illustration for the front cover of a CD or film poster and explain your choice to the marketing manager.

PE: Draw instructions for a sport. Explain them to a beginner.

Science: biology – Create a poem poster for an animal. Chemistry – Create a model of a carbon molecule. Physics – Create a poster of an electrical circuit.

ᛒ Tips for cross-curricular cooperation between subject and art teachers

Before the lesson: The art, design and technology teacher can help the subject teacher think of visual products learners can make, and which tools they will need.

During the lesson: The art, design and technology teacher helps learners think of ways of improving their visual products.

After the lesson: The subject teacher gives the art, design and technology teacher the completed visual products; the art, design and technology teacher gives feedback on the learners' use of appropriate techniques. Subject examples

References and further reading

Bilingualism and bilingual learners

Baker, C. (2006) *Foundations of Bilingual Education and Bilingualism*, 4th edition, Clevedon: Multilingual Matters.

Cummins, J. (2000) *Language Power and Pedagogy: Bilingual Children in the Crossfire*, Clevedon: Multilingual Matters.

Cummins, J. (2005) 'Teaching for cross-language transfer in dual language education: possibilities and pitfalls', paper presented at the TESOL Symposium on Dual Language Education, Istanbul Turkey, September 2005. Available at: http://www.achievementseminars.com/seminar_series_2005_2006/readings/tesol.turkey.pdf (accessed 12 January 2011).

CLIL

Coyle, D. (2006) 'Content and Language Integrated Learning: motivating learners and teachers', *Scottish Languages Review* 13, 1–18. Available at: http://www.strath.ac.uk/media/faculties/hass/scilt/slr/issues/13/SLR13_Coyle.pdf (accessed 15 January 2011).

Coyle, D., Hood, P. and Marsh, D. (2010) *CLIL*, Cambridge: Cambridge University Press.

Dalton-Puffer, C. (2007) *Discourse in Content and Language Integrated Learning (CLIL) Classrooms*, New York and Amsterdam: Benjamins.

Dale, L., van der Es, W. and Tanner, R. (2010) *CLIL Skills*. Published under Creative Commons Attribution-NonCommercial-ShareAlike 2.5 Generic (CC BY-NC-SA 2.5) license, Leiden: Leiden University Press.

Echevarria, J., Vogt, M. and Short, D.J. (2004) *Making Content Comprehensible for English Learners: The SIOP Model*, Boston: Allyn and Bacon.

Eurydice Report (2006) *Content and Language Integrated Learning (CLIL) at School in Europe*, Eurydice European Unit, Brussels.

Mehisto, P., Marsh, D. and Frigols, M.J. (2008) *Uncovering CLIL*, Oxford: Macmillan.

Language learning and teaching

Chamot, A.U. and O'Malley, J.M. (1994) *The CALLA Handbook: Implementing the Cognitive Academic Language Learning Approach*, New York: Addison Wesley.

Collier, V.P. (1995) 'Acquiring a second language for school', *Directions in Language Education* 1/4, pp. 1–12.

Council of Europe, Common European Framework of References for Languages (CEFR) (2009) Available at: http://www.coe.int/t/dg4/linguistic/CADRE_EN.asp (accessed 12 January 2011).

Gibbons, P. (2002) *Scaffolding Language, Scaffolding Learning*, Portsmouth: Heinemann.

Goldstein, B. (2008) *Working with Images*, Cambridge: Cambridge University Press.

Hadfield, J. (1987) *Advanced Communication Games*, Nashville: Nelson. Out of print.

Harmer, J. (2004) *How to Teach Writing*, Harlow: Pearson Education.

Harmer, J. and Thornbury, S. (2002) *How to Teach Vocabulary*, Harlow: Pearson Education.

Lightbown, P. M. and Spada, N. (2006) *How Languages Are Learned*, 3rd edition, Oxford: Oxford University Press.

Lyster, R. and Ranta, L. (1997) 'Corrective feedback and learner uptake: negotiation of form in communicative classrooms', *Studies in Second Language Acquisition*, 19, 37–66.

Lyster, R. (2007) *Learning and Teaching Languages through Content: A Counterbalanced Approach*, Amsterdam: Benjamins.

Thornbury, S. (2005) How to Teach Speaking. Pearson Education.

Williams, M. & Burden, R. L. (1997) *Psychology for Language Teachers: A Social Constructivist Approach*, New York: Cambridge University Press.

Theories of learning and teaching

Assessment Reform Group (2002) Assessment for Learning: 10 Principles. Available at: http://www.assessment-reform-group.org/CIE3.PDF (accessed 12 January 2011).

Dodge, B. (2009) Webquest. http://webquest.org/index.php (accessed 12 January 2011).

Dawes, L. and Wegerif, R. (1998) *Encouraging Exploratory Talk: Practical Suggestions*. Available at: http://primary.naace.co.uk/curriculum/english/exploratory.htm (accessed 12 January 2011). First published in MAPE Focus on Literacy pack, Autumn .

Mercer, N. (2000) *Words and Minds*, Abingdon: Routledge.

Mulder, J. and Tanner, R. (1998) *Engels in het Studiehuis Bronnenboek* [Sourcebook for English for Secondary Schools], Zutphen: W. J. Thieme (out of print).

Vygotsky, L. (1978) *Mind in Society: The Development of Higher Psychological Processes*, London: Harvard University Press.

Wood, J., Bruner, D. J. and Ross, G. (1976) 'The role of tutoring in problem solving', *Journal of Child Psychology and Psychiatry*, 17/2, 89–100.

Wragg, E. C. and Brown, G. (2001) *Questioning in the Primary School*, Abingdon: Routledge Falmer.

Wegerif, R. (2002) *Literature Review in Thinking Skills, Technology and Learning*. Future Lab Series, no. 2. Available at: http://www2.futurelab.org.uk/resources/documents/lit_reviews/Thinking_Skills_Review.pdf (accessed 19 February 2009).

Thinking skills

Anderson, L. W., Krathwohl, D. R., Airasian, P. W., Cruikshank, K. A., Mayer, R. E., Pintrich, P. R., Raths, J. and Wittrock, M. C. (eds.). (2001) *A Taxonomy for Learning, Teaching, and Assessing: A Revision of Bloom's Taxonomy of Educational Objectives*, New York: Addison Wesley Longman.

Leat, D. (2001) *Thinking Through Geography*, Cambridge: Chris Kington Publishing.

Fisher, P. (2002) *Thinking Through History*, Cambridge: Chris Kington Publishing.

Subject-specific language

Bean, J. C., Drenk, D. and Lee, F. D. (1982) 'Microtheme strategies for developing cognitive skills', in C. W. Griffin (ed.), *Teaching Writing in All Disciplines*, New Directions for Teaching and Learning, no. 12. San Francisco: Jossey-Bass. Available at: http://www.thinkingwriting.qmul.ac.uk/documents/shortwritingexercise.pdf (accessed 12 January 2011).

Christie, F. and Derewianka, B. (2008) *School Discourse: Learning to Write across the Years of Schooling*, London: Continuum.

Coffin, C. (2006) 'Mapping subject-specific literacies', *Naldic Quarterly* (Online), Spring 2006, Available at: http://www.naldic.org.uk/docs/members/documents/NQ3.3.4.pdf (accessed 12 January 2011).

Department for Education and Skills (DfES) (2002a) *Access and Engagement in History: Teaching Pupils for Whom English is an Additional Language*, DfES. 0656–2002, Norwich: HMSO.

Department for Education and Skills (DfES) (2002b) *Literacy in Art and Design: For School-Based Use or Self-Study*, DfES. 0054–2002, Norwich: HMSO.

Department for Education and Skills (DfES) (2004a) *Pedagogy and Practice: Teaching and Learning in Secondary Schools –Unit 14: Developing Writing*, DfES. 0443–2004, Norwich: HMSO.

Department for education and skills (2004b) Pedagogy and practice: teaching and learning in secondary schools - Unit 7, DfES. 0430–2004, Norwich: HMSO.

Kersaint, G., Thompson, D. R. and Petkova, M. (2009) *Teaching Mathematics to English Language Learners*, New York: Routledge.

Rose, D (2008) 'Writing as linguistic mastery: the development of genre-based literacy pedagogy', in D.Myhill, D.Beard, M.Nystrand and J.Riley (eds.), *Handbook of Writing Development*, London: Sage, pp. 151–66.

Schleppegrell, M. J. and Achugar, M. (2003) 'Learning language and learning history: a functional approach', *TESOL Journal*, 21/2, 21–7.

Schleppegrell, M. J. (2007) 'The linguistic challenges of mathematics teaching and learning: a research review', *Reading & Writing Quarterly*, 23, 139–59.

Wellington, J. and Osborne, J. (2009) *Language and Literacy in Science Education*, Maidenhead: Open University Press.

Lesson plans, handouts

http://www.bbc.co.uk/skillswise
BBC Skillswise has many useful, clearly written handouts which you can easily adapt for your lessons.

Dictionaries

Oxford Student's Dictionary for Learners Using English to Study Other Subjects (2007), Oxford: Oxford University Press.
Cambridge School Dictionary (2008), Cambridge: Cambridge University Press.

Appendix:
The Common European Framework of Reference for Languages (CEFR)

		A1	A2	B1	B2	C1	C2
UNDER-STANDING	Listening	I can recognise familiar words and very basic phrases concerning myself, my family and immediate concrete surroundings when people speak slowly and clearly.	I can understand phrases and the highest frequency vocabulary related to areas of most immediate personal relevance (e.g. very basic personal and family information, shopping, local area, employment). I can catch the main point in short, clear, simple messages and announcements.	I can understand the main points of clear standard speech on familiar matters regularly encountered in work, school, leisure, etc. I can understand the main point of many radio or TV programmes on current affairs or topics of personal or professional interest when the delivery is relatively slow and clear.	I can understand extended speech and lectures and follow even complex lines of argument provided the topic is reasonably familiar. I can understand most TV news and current affairs programmes. I can understand the majority of films in standard dialect.	I can understand extended speech even when it is not clearly structured and when relationships are only implied and not signalled explicitly. I can understand television programmes and films without too much effort.	I have no difficulty in understanding any kind of spoken language, whether live or broadcast, even when delivered at fast native speed, provided I have some time to get familiar with the accent.

Reading					
I can understand familiar names, words and very simple sentences, for example on notices and posters or in catalogues.	I can read very short, simple texts. I can find specific, predictable information in simple everyday material such as advertisements, prospectuses, menus and timetables and I can understand short simple personal letters.	I can understand texts that consist mainly of high frequency everyday or job-related language. I can understand the description of events, feelings and wishes in personal letters.	I can read articles and reports concerned with contemporary problems in which the writers adopt particular attitudes or viewpoints. I can understand contemporary literary prose.	I can understand long and complex factual and literary texts, appreciating distinctions of style. I can understand specialised articles and longer technical instructions, even when they do not relate to my field.	I can read with ease virtually all forms of the written language, including abstract, structurally or linguistically complex texts such as manuals, specialised articles and literary works.

Appendix (cont.)

		A1	A2	B1	B2	C1	C2
SPEAKING	Spoken Interaction	I can interact in a simple way provided the other person is prepared to repeat or rephrase things at a slower rate of speech and help me formulate what I'm trying to say. I can ask and answer simple questions in areas of immediate need or on very familiar topics.	I can communicate in simple and routine tasks requiring a simple and direct exchange of information on familiar topics and activities. I can handle very short social exchanges, even though I can't usually understand enough to keep the conversation going myself.	I can deal with most situations likely to arise whilst travelling in an area where the language is spoken. I can enter unprepared into conversation on topics that are familiar, of personal interest or pertinent to everyday life (e.g. family, hobbies, work, travel and current events).	I can interact with a degree of fluency and spontaneity that makes regular interaction with native speakers quite possible. I can take an active part in discussion in familiar contexts, accounting for and sustaining my views.	I can express myself fluently and spontaneously without much obvious searching for expressions. I can use language flexibly and effectively for social and professional purposes. I can formulate ideas and opinions with precision and relate my contribution skilfully to those of other speakers.	I can take part effortlessly in any conversation or discussion and have a good familiarity with idiomatic expressions and colloquialisms. I can express myself fluently and convey finer shades of meaning precisely. If I do have a problem I can backtrack and restructure around the difficulty so smoothly that other people are hardly aware of it.

Appendix

Spoken Production						
	I can use simple phrases and sentences to describe where I live and people I know.	I can use a series of phrases and sentences to describe in simple terms my family and other people, living conditions, my educational background and my present or most recent job.	I can connect phrases in a simple way in order to describe experiences and events, my dreams, hopes and ambitions. I can briefly give reasons and explanations for opinions and plans. I can narrate a story or relate the plot of a book or film and describe my reactions.	I can present clear, detailed descriptions on a wide range of subjects related to my field of interest. I can explain a viewpoint on a topical issue giving the advantages and disadvantages of various options.	I can present clear, detailed descriptions of complex subjects integrating sub-themes, developing particular points and rounding off with an appropriate conclusion.	I can present a clear, smoothly-flowing description or argument in a style appropriate to the context and with an effective logical structure which helps the recipient to notice and remember significant points.

Appendix (cont.)

		A1	A2	B1	B2	C1	C2
WRITING	Writing	I can write a short, simple postcard, for example sending holiday greetings. I can fill in forms with personal details, for example entering my name, nationality and address on a hotel registration form.	I can write short, simple notes and messages relating to matters in areas of immediate needs. I can write a very simple personal letter, for example thanking someone for something.	I can write simple connected text on topics which are familiar or of personal interest. I can write personal letters describing experiences and impressions.	I can write clear, detailed text on a wide range of subjects related to my interests. I can write an essay or report, passing on information or giving reasons in support of or against a particular point of view. I can write letters highlighting the personal significance of events and experiences.	I can express myself in clear, well-structured text, expressing points of view at some length. I can write about complex subjects in a letter, an essay or a report, underlining what I consider to be the salient issues. I can select style appropriate to the reader in mind.	I can write clear, smoothly-flowing text in an appropriate style. I can write complex letters, reports or articles which present a case with an effective logical structure which helps the recipient to notice and remember significant points. I can write summaries and reviews of professional or literary works.

Index